C000108960

30127 06217593 5

Depictions and Images of War in Edwardian
Newspapers, 1899–1914

Depictions and Images of War in Edwardian Newspapers, 1899–1914

Glenn R. Wilkinson

© Glenn R. Wilkinson 2003

All rights reserved. No reproduction, copy or transmission of this publication may be made without written permission.

No paragraph of this publication may be reproduced, copied or transmitted save with written permission or in accordance with the provisions of the Copyright, Designs and Patents Act 1988, or under the terms of any licence permitting limited copying issued by the Copyright Licensing Agency, 90 Tottenham Court Road, London W1T 4LP.

Any person who does any unauthorised act in relation to this publication may be liable to criminal prosecution and civil claims for damages.

The author has asserted his right to be identified as the author of this work in accordance with the Copyright, Designs and Patents Act 1988.

First published 2003 by
PALGRAVE MACMILLAN
Houndmills, Basingstoke, Hampshire RG21 6XS and
175 Fifth Avenue, New York, N. Y. 10010
Companies and representatives throughout the world

PALGRAVE MACMILLAN is the global academic imprint of the Palgrave Macmillan division of St. Martin's Press, LLC and of Palgrave Macmillan Ltd. Macmillan® is a registered trademark in the United States, United Kingdom and other countries. Palgrave is a registered trademark in the European Union and other countries.
ISBN 0–333–71743–0

This book is printed on paper suitable for recycling and made from fully managed and sustained forest sources.

A catalogue record for this book is available from the British Library.

Library of Congress Cataloging-in-Publication Data
Wilkinson, Glenn R., 1963–
    Depictions and images of war in Edwardian newspapers, 1899–1914 / Glenn R. Wilkinson.
        p. cm.
    Includes bibliographical references and index.
    ISBN 0–333–71743–0 (cloth)
    1. War–Press coverage–Great Britain–History–20th century. I. Title.

PN5124.W36 W55 2002
070.4'4935502–dc21

                                                                    2002072625

10 9 8 7 6 5 4 3 2 1
12 11 10 09 08 07 06 05 04 03

Suffolk County Council
Libraries & Heritage

CYPHER GROUP 21·5·03

This book is dedicated to
Evelyn Mae Wilkinson (1933–1997),
whose love of history influenced me enormously,
and who taught me about the importance and influence of history.
I cherish her stories still.

Contents

List of Plates

Preface

The origins of the First World War have traditionally been seen in the light of diplomatic and economic rivalries, the scramble for colonies, alliances, arms races, and the popular belief in a short, easy victory. However, the attitudes and perceptions of those who freely and enthusiastically volunteered in large numbers have received very little attention. Studies in Edwardian 'militarism', the creation of new military organizations such as the Territorial Army, the influences of public schools and youth groups have been made, but while these traditional approaches are important, they do not tell the whole story. The images of *actual* warfare as reported and consumed in the pages of the expanding and increasingly commercial press must also be examined. The goal of this study is to augment these efforts and expand our understanding of the origins of the war in 1914 by examining the vicarious experiences of war conveyed in the press.

Edwardian newspapers are used to determine attitudes because of their close relationship with their readers. Being commercial organs they had to reflect and respond to not only reader taste, but also the way that their audiences saw their world. The newspapers themselves contained a wide variety of sources that display these images, and a large sample of newspaper titles indicates the depth to which these perceptions were present in Edwardian society. In this work, the coverage of six wars, three in the British Empire and three involving foreign powers, will act as case studies to determine the breadth of imagery across a wide variety of conflicts.

The ways that readers perceived warfare reveals much about their attitudes to war and indicates the type of experiences they were expecting in 1914. War was essentially seen as a positive event, both for nations and individuals, and images of sport, games, hunting, theatre and spectacle created a distance between reader and war, and denied its essential 'reality'. However, these positive aspects of warfare were not countered by the negative consequences of death and wounding on the battlefield.

These images were present well before 1914, but the Edwardian period represented a particular point in time where media, culture and technology interacted in ways that were unique. In addition to this, the period suffered from the new and debilitating influence of modernism, where the rock of meaning and purpose was eroded away by the sea of fear and anxieties particular to the late-nineteenth and early-twentieth centuries. In this context, these images took on a new resonance that should be studied in depth, as war became a solution to these social, cultural and intellectual problems. The following pages will outline this convergence to help explain an enthusiasm for war that is usually taken for granted. For the sake of clarity, this study will avoid the use of fashionable jargon and trendy concepts, as they tend to obscure meaning.

The focus here will be on the depictions of *actual* warfare on the ground and not at sea. Given the lack of naval warfare (the most notable exceptions being episodes in the Russo- Japanese War), this is virtually a necessity. Similarly, discussions of images concerning the organization, recruitment, training and activities of martial institutions such as the Territorial Army must be sought elsewhere. A variety of newspapers, not just a few major London dailies, will form the core of the material to be examined here. However, given the vast number of local and regional papers, there will be some who are disappointed that specific papers are not utilized more. It is hoped that this volume encourages further investigations into these rich sources.

This study was born in the shadow of the Gulf War. The popular representations of that war were fascinating. The war was presented and consumed as a 'video game', where 'smart' bombs dropped on toy trucks or buildings, with little 'collateral' damage. Regardless of our personal view of the war's legitimacy, it is clear that people appeared not to be horribly maimed or die in this war. The war's reality was not discussed or presented in the mainstream media, except in a very few cases such as Kenneth Jarecke's black and white photograph of a charred Iraqi soldier in a burnt-out tank in the 3 March 1991 issue of the *Observer*. This photograph sparked much debate and consternation about whether we really need to know what war looks like to know it is horrible.

Yet the media coverage indicates that we know very little about what *real* wars, initiated and fought in our name, are like. This situation is quite a dangerous one, for if we are not aware of the reality of war, we are more likely to acquiesce and support the use of violence in the future without thought, debate or consciousness. Wars, whether they be full-scale efforts or high-tech bombing of a Third World country, must be fought with the cold and naked realization of their nature. Then and only then will we be able to make rational and serious decisions about whether we should resort to arms in a given situation, rather than use war as a political gambit to distract attention from embarrassing presidential affairs, to influence re-election to Downing Street, to maintain high profits for stockholders in the oil industry, or to defend access to fish stocks. We must therefore look at the ways in which we imagine warfare.

There are many ways that we do this. Hard news accounts in various media are the first that come to mind, but there are also others. Films such as *Saving Private Ryan* purport to be 'realistic', and given the context of war films in the twentieth century, perhaps they are more realistic. But audiences go to films such as *Private Ryan* to be *entertained*, watching from the safety of their plush seats and eating popcorn. These are vicarious experiences, and although we might know intellectually that war is hell, we know emotionally that it is also fascinating. In this way it is important to recognize that we are no different from our Edwardian ancestors. It is the entertainment value of the depiction of war at an emotional level which is important and which needs to be examined and evaluated.

The next time we 'howl' for war and send troops into battle, be it a 'war against terrorism' or a new 'crusade against Islam', we would be doing well if we considered the way that we vicariously experience war and whether we are making conscious and informed decisions. In doing so, we will use violence only as a last resort and will search earnestly for alternative solutions whenever possible. We might also save many lives.

Glenn R. Wilkinson
Bellagio, Italy
September 2001

Acknowledgements

The acknowledgement of the many people who have supported, aided and abetted and generally helped in the writing of this book is in many ways a difficult task. I can never find enough ways to thank all the people who helped in the production of this work. However, John Gooch and Stephen Constantine deserve high praise indeed for giving their time and encouragement, as do Bridget Taylor and the staff of the Institute of Historical Research, University of London. I must acknowledge my debt to scholars, colleagues and friends who have read many drafts of my work and given suggestions, support and comfort over the years. They include: Harry Berger, Robert Bickers, Kelly Boyd, Laurel Brake, Stuart Carroll, Peter Catterall, Barbara Craig, Kent Fedorowich, Beth Fitch, Michael Harris, Stephen Heathorn, Nicholas Hiley, Brian Keaney, Andrew Lewis, John M. MacKenzie, Peter Marshall, Rohan McWilliam, Dan Page, Doug Peers, Paul Phibbs, Carolee Pollock, Andrew Porter, Glenn Richardson, Ruth Richardson, Jennifer Ridden, Jane Samson, Claire Schen, Mike Silvestri, Greg Smith, Howard Spencer, Keith Surridge, Sinharaja Tammita Delgoda, Justine Taylor, Tim Travers, Tim Wales, Chris Waters; my colleagues and partners in crime in both the History Department and the Faculty of Communication and Culture at the University of Calgary; the staff and faculty of the History Department at the University of Lancaster; the staff at the British Library; the Imperial, Media, Military and Post-Graduate Seminars at the IHR; and the London House Reading Group. Portions of Chapter 3 are reprinted by kind permission of Sage Publications Ltd from the *Journal of Contemporary History*, vol. 33, no. 1, January 1998. I must also thank Caroline Johns for editing the typescript and Laurel Halladay for proof editing and indexing.

I must acknowledge a special debt to the Rockefeller Foundation for a fellowship to the Bellagio Study and Conference Center in Bellagio, Italy, for giving me the time, space and good fellowship to complete this work. In particular, my thanks go to Gianna Celli, Susan Garfield and the staff of the Foundation in both New York and Bellagio.

Mostly, however, I should like to acknowledge my enormous debt to my family (in Britain, Australia and Canada), in particular to Ursula and Marilyn, Lynn and Bill, Ken, and to Evelyn, whose spirit is always with us.

1
Introduction: 'They Had Been Taught to Howl'

In his 'Reflections on the First World War', the distinguished military historian Michael Howard suggests that those examining the origins of the war would do well to consider what he calls its 'real' causes. He recommends that they 'look beyond' diplomatic documents, great-power rivalries, invasion scares and naval arms races, and study the works of military thinkers, pre-war editorials, speeches at prize awards and contemporary military literature. In doing so, historians would learn 'far more about the causes of the First World War than in a lifetime of reading diplomatic documents'.[1] Howard states that though 'the elder statesmen did their feckless best to prevent war...the youth of the rival countries were howling impatiently at their doors for immediate war'. It is this 'howling', along with the way that youth 'had been taught to howl', that must be examined.[2]

The value of this kind of study is that it will contribute substantially to our understanding of the origins of the First World War. It would have been difficult, if not impossible, to wage war without the active support, or at least the acquiescence, of the civilian population who either became soldiers themselves or encouraged others to volunteer. *Attitudes* make war possible, as even dictatorships need to be sure of popular support, and it is no different for the origin of the war in 1914.[3] An important way to discern the attitudes of those who supported war is through a study of the way that *actual* warfare was imagined in the years leading up to the outbreak of the war. Howard's suggestion that pre-war editorials should be examined points to a deeper study of war reporting and representations of wars fought before 1914. This involves more than merely looking at the views of individual newspapers, or the methods of owners and editors who condemned or condoned particular wars seeking to 'manipulate' readers for political gain. Instead, this study will

1

examine the imagery employed in the press to convey the idea of warfare to readers, representing their 'reality' of war and the way that they vicariously experienced it.

We have a clear picture of the pattern and structure of recruitment and of the 'surge of enlistments' in 1914. By the end of August, this rush had reached a peak of 300,000 men, and by the end of that year totalled a million. This was an astonishing mass voluntary movement, one of the most significant of modern times, where 'all classes shared patriotic fervour' in the early stages of the war. For example miners, who, as well-paid workers with little threat of unemployment and by far the largest pre-war union[4] joined up willingly and enthusiastically. By mid-1915, 230,000 miners had enlisted, almost a quarter of the mining workforce, with the highest rates in areas where Edwardian industrial militancy was most acute. For some, the 'compatibility of class-consciousness and patriotism could have no better illustration'.[5]

Yet, this notion of 'patriotism' as motivation is incomplete. The diplomatic and economic rivalries, including the Anglo-German naval rivalry, the range of diplomatic and domestic crises, and the system of slowly building alliances, are all important background for an understanding of patriotic fervour. However, the role of public school education, youth movements, the militarist leagues, and the influences of Social Darwinism are also necessary considerations.[6] More specifically, the role of the press, such as the 'great dailies', like the *Daily Mail* and the *Daily Express*, reported what they believed their readers wanted to see in the papers. The *Daily Mail*, in particular, has been singled out as having been anti-German, concerned with invasion and spy scares, and anxious for Britain to not fall behind the Germans in naval matters. All of these sensational topics were described as 'scaremongering'.[7] Even the socialist press of editors such as Robert Blatchford of the *Clarion*, and Henry Meyers Hyndman of *Justice*, revealed that the mass of working-class readers were uninterested in 'Angellism', the doctrine of pacifism propagated by Norman Angell.[8]

It is important for historians to 'turn their energies towards penetrating the obscurities that surround the popular response to war', even though 'public opinion' is a difficult and elusive concept to gauge. It has been suggested that it is not sufficient simply to examine the scholarly works of J. R. Seeley or the popular poetry of Rudyard Kipling, both arch-imperialists. But it is also not enough to read only serious newspapers or influential books; we also need to examine the 'banal and more pervasive influences' of the popular press, music-hall songs, school textbooks and children's books and comics.[9]

In many ways, both popular and elite attitudes were dependent upon available knowledge. Readers of the 'serious' and the popular press read about military matters with fascination, tending to be jingoistic and anti-German, all contributory causes to the origin of the war. It is not a question of whether the information and analyses available to readers constituted a reflection or stimulation of particular ideologies. Rather, the pervasiveness of modes of expression is evidence of their currency in the country, giving an indication of the degree to which perceptions were held in British society.[10] The pervasiveness of ideas can be extended beyond the concerns of jingoism and anti-German sentiment, to the examination of written and visual images of war in order to establish how the Edwardians perceived warfare before 1914. The ubiquity of particular images of war in the press establishes its 'currency in society', and constitutes the vicarious experiences of warfare possessed by those who volunteered and those who supported them.

Perceptions of war can be determined by examining many different types of publications. For example, assessments can be made of the importance of serious war literature written by military experts. These show the 'degree to which British society was conditioned to accept military activity as necessary or desirable'. Books and periodical articles published by both serving and retired officers, clergymen, and academics, show that though war might have been unexpected in 1914, it was not unconsidered.[11] In addition to specialist military publications, more popular forms can be studied to show how the British looked upon war in 1914 and how those ideas reached the 'public mind'. Most work has concentrated on the way that upper and middle-class opinions developed, suggesting that attitudes were set 'very largely' by members of these classes and that these ideas were conveyed and willingly accepted 'much lower down the social scale'.[12]

Popular newspapers and cheap books or 'part works', usually both published by the same firms 'popularized notions of war on a lower intellectual level', particularly those concerning the work of writers of boys' adventure stories and of war correspondents.[13] The career and work of G. A. Henty can be used to demonstrate this mechanism for conveying ideas of war, but this is too brief and too narrow. To suggest that images of warfare can be so tidily summarized by the career of one person is rather simplistic. In addition, though emphasizing the significance of war correspondence, many works do not examine the actual reports themselves, and some do not cite newspapers at all.[14]

This unwillingness to examine the dispatches as they appeared in the newspapers seems to be prevalent among those who examine the role of the war correspondent in more detail. One of the first histories of war correspondents, F. Lauriston Bullard's *Famous War Correspondents* published in September 1914, was a celebration of the men and the profession. It acted as a thinly veiled appeal to allow reporters to be sent to the Western Front.[15] Other, more recent, works involving war correspondents are usually popular treatments that are general in scope, attempting to examine a long time period and the personal biographies of several correspondents, but similarly do not undertake a detailed examination of the original writings printed in newspapers.[16]

The image of war and the war correspondent 'image-makers' must be put into the larger context of other representations of warfare. This work must encompass not only the written impressions of the correspondents, but also the visual depictions in the illustrated press and the battle paintings of studio artists.[17] However, to understand the origins of the First World War, this analysis must extend beyond the Victorian and include the Edwardian period right up to the outbreak of war. In addition, middle and upper class papers should not be the only targets of research, nor should the personalities of the image-makers themselves. The result of these latter tendencies is too often that the images originate from the personal, post-battle monographs rather than the text of newspaper reports written at the time. This use of material has prompted John MacKenzie, influential historian of propaganda and empire, to observe that 'the book-length accounts of the war correspondents have been more studied than their newspaper despatches', highlighting the importance of this research.[18] What correspondents actually wrote at the time of battle and was read immediately following a report's dispatch not only offers a means of comparison with the later book-length accounts, but also enables an examination of a multi-layered source representing clearly defined audiences.

In addition to the written reports of war correspondents, visual imagery of war is also important in that it reveals a great deal about vicarious experiences of warfare. However, limiting examinations to the battle paintings displayed at the Royal Academy, for example, would not be representative of British society as a whole. The wealth of visual imagery in the Edwardian period should not be forgotten, as 'in the years 1901–14 the proportion of battle pictures was higher than it had been at anytime in the nineteenth-century'.[19]

But, visual imagery must be examined with caution. For example, images in battle paintings can be problematic. Condemnations of late-Victorian and Edwardian paintings of the period as racist and nationalist are harsh and not all examples are necessarily convincing. The analysis of visual imagery is difficult, but in a study of G. D. Giles's paintings, 'An Incident in the Battle of Tamai' and 'The Battle of Tamai', seems to overstretch its argument. While British superiority was indeed conveyed in both paintings, aspects of leadership, bravery and organization can also be seen among the Sudanese, particularly in 'The Battle of Tamai'. Both paintings appear in essence to be complementary, rather than contradictory to Kipling's poem 'Fuzzy-Wuzzy', where a Dervish is described as 'a pore benighted 'eathen, but a first class fightin' man'. The inability to explain the apparent contradiction adds weight to the suggestion that both paintings and poem were positive, or at least respectful, descriptions of the Sudanese enemy, making British victory that much more significant.[20]

However, the examination of war imagery must also take into account the wealth of illustrations in the Edwardian press, a medium much more sensitive to popular imaginations than elite art. Examining war imagery in newspapers helps develop a clearer and more detailed picture of attitudes of war in British society, particularly in the illustrated press, such as the *Graphic* and the *Illustrated London News*. While it is important to see the imagery from the illustrated press as more than simply 'propaganda', which is a problematic concept, it can demonstrate that visual images are particularly useful in determining how the British saw themselves, rather than just in the accurate portrayal of events. However, the analyses must use a wider selection of illustrated newspapers, as the *Graphic* and the *Illustrated London News* spoke to a similar audience, and to see them as conduits of 'popular art' stretches the definition of the term somewhat.[21]

Any study of images of war must make reference to Paul Fussell's *The Great War and Modern Memory*. The greatest testament to the importance of Fussell's work is that it continues to been criticized, both fairly and unfairly, several decades after the book was first published.[22] The importance of Fussell's book is that it combines a literary analysis with a discussion of the First World War, showing that the way the war was 'remembered' had a great cultural significance and can be used to determine a cultural mindset regarding war. Some aspects of Fussell's thesis can be contested, such as his stern belief in the Great War as a sharp watershed and a complete break from the pre-war period. However, his use of language can be applied as a model for interpretations of how war was perceived before 1914 to act as a means of contextualizing the early and enthusiastic recruitment.

Perceptions of war in 1914 must be put into the cultural context of the late-Victorian to Edwardian period, one that was fraught with anxieties and crises. Significant crises centred on politics, economics, philosophy, religion, sex, homosexuality, the Empire, and women's rights. More importantly, contemporary discussions and fears concerned the poor physique of British army recruits and the impact this had on anxieties regarding racial degeneration and invasion, especially after the Boer War.[23] It is within this cultural context, rather than a purely military one, that the origins of the First World War need to be understood. In this way, it is possible to 'capture the spirit of an age' and to examine the tensions of the pre-war era.[24]

Another important context of the period centres on the degree that Britain was 'militaristic' before the war. In the past, there have been works that have linked militarism and imperialism, suggesting that they rarely exist independently, and, more importantly, that militarism flourishes more readily in times of peace than during wartime.[25] More directly, some work has been done regarding the question of militarism in Britain before 1914, suggesting that though its degree and scope differed from 'Prussianism', it was nevertheless a 'popular cause', albeit a 'peculiarly British one'. There was a 'tremendous upsurge of interest in things military in Edwardian Britain', mostly as a result of the Boer War, seen as the 'disaster narrowly averted', and the concomitant fear of national, racial degeneration.[26]

Similarly, the public schools, the influence of youth movements, and the context of juvenile literature have been examined to address the diffusion of militarism in Britain. Over the course of the nineteenth century, the public schools changed from institutions of scholarship to ones concerned with the formation of character, and fostered a relationship with the concept of a 'nation in arms'.[27] While the public school ethos influenced those who attended them and became officers in the First World War, they also influenced those who did not attend them and who became future foot soldiers. This group felt its influence through mechanisms of dissemination such as youth groups and boys' literature.[28]

While it is clear that there was indeed a widespread interest in things military, the way that *actual* warfare was perceived is unclear. An analysis of the press of the period will foster just such an examination and reveal a great deal about not only aspects of 'militarism', but also whether the negative consequences of warfare were presented in ways that countered the more positive perceptions associated with the conduct of war.

Newspapers changed a great deal over the course of the nineteenth century, not only in the increasing number of titles, but also in form, content and purpose. The abolition of the so-called 'Taxes on Knowledge', a campaign led by Richard Cobden and John Bright, facilitated the enormous expansion of a cheap press. While the origins of the 'popular' press can be traced to the working-class Sunday newspapers of the 1840s, such as the *News of the World* and *Lloyd's Weekly News*, the repeal of the Advertisement Duty in 1853, the end of the stamp tax in 1855, and the removal of the tax on paper combined to create an environment in which the cheap, popular daily press could flourish.[29]

The last two decades of the nineteenth century saw the parallel developments of a decline of political influence and control over the press, and the rise of what came to be known as the 'New Journalism', a more commercial, reader-oriented press. This shift corresponded with the decline of radical papers, when newspapers became less organs of instruction and more sources of amusement. The press had previously been the conduit through which political leaders conveyed their ideas to the nation, but by the 1880s this relationship had been reversed. In addition, it had become more difficult to sustain a party political paper, as the costs and the commercialization of newspapers increased.[30]

With the changing purpose of newspapers came a change in layout and the development of more selective reading. The visual plane of the newspapers developed as editors and owners of the press changed from being printers using newspapers as subsidiary businesses to entrepreneurs, like George Newnes, Arthur Pearson and Alfred Harmsworth, who were much more innovative and reader-sensitive. During this period, layout changed from large monolithic blocks of small, uninterrupted print, unbroken by cross headings or illustrations, to more broken columns with headlines. Formerly, readers were expected to read the whole of the newspaper and thus be moved by argument and persuasion. With the 'New Journalism', however, readers became their own editors as they chose the stories they wished to read from a myriad of headlines and attractively laid-out stories.[31] The addition of photographs, published in newspapers with the perfection of the half-tone process in the 1880s, increased the visual aspect of 'reading' a newspaper and thus the selection of material based upon reader interest. Photographs became common in daily papers with the 1904 launch of the *Daily Mirror*, the first daily paper to have no line illustrations but use photographs exclusively.

One of the main reasons for this change was that the new proprietors had discovered a new type of reader in the self-improving lower-middle classes, both female and male. Harmsworth's *Daily Mail*, founded in 1896, was the most popular example of the 'New Journalism', a term that was initially pejorative, indicative for some of the decline of

intelligent newspapers.[32] The *Mail* was enormously successful, averaging 750,000 readers per day during the Edwardian era, and achieving
a sustainable circulation of over one million by 1910.[33] Yet, though
circulation figures are unreliable, they are enough to indicate that the
number of daily newspapers increased substantially in the period,
having doubled from 1896 to 1906, and doubled again from 1906 to
1914. This degree of press expansion made the Edwardians better
informed and better entertained than any previous generation.[34]

These developments show that the press of the late-nineteenth
century is a worthy source in its own right. The press was indeed unique
in the late-nineteenth and early-twentieth centuries since, though its
political influence declined, there were still few alternative conduits of
information. Pamphleteering had 'gone out of fashion', as illustrated by
the inability of the pro-Boers to convince the public of their cause. In
addition, public and parliamentary speeches were no longer regularly
quoted verbatim at length, and increasing secularization meant that
the power of the pulpit as a political force diminished. Other alternative
media had not yet developed a political significance, for although the
cinema had been well established by 1914, it had a principally working-
class audience and was concerned about entertainment to a greater
degree than the 'New Journalism'.[35]

Its having little competition from other media, it is important to chart
the relationship between the perceived political influence of the press
with its actual declining political importance. However, newspapers are
an important and valuable source for historians for more than their
ability or inability to deliberately influence public opinion or to conduct
propaganda. They contain within their pages a large number of sources
of imagery that can be examined to reveal the way that the Edwardians
saw their world. The newspapers must be used not simply for what was
written in leading articles and news reports regarding particular political
issues. The way that other, more general topics of wider interest, such as
warfare, were discussed, whether for or against, and the imagery mar-
shalled to convey ideas, can be used to identify the perceptions of
readers.

But a newspaper also contains more than the editorial and main news
stories. Feature articles are a major source of imagery, as 'experts' employ
images to convey their knowledge or opinions. Reader feedback can be
gauged through the letters columns, though these must be assessed with
care. Letters published by an individual newspaper were usually selected
to make particular points, but the importance of readers' letters is not
simply whether or not they agreed with a paper's position on an issue,

but that they reveal the images that readers used to convey their ideas, indicating that the same language was employed. Similarly, drawings, illustrations and photographs can be examined to determine the visual image or impression of warfare held by readers. Cartoons can also be examined and are of even more importance, for they depend upon a more active participation of readers. Cartoons are what Marshall McLuhan calls a 'cool medium', with little visual detail and dependent upon the audience to understand and 'fill in' the absent data.[36]

Advertisements are also important, as they combine both visual and written elements, and represent a medium that, by its very nature, had to be sensitive to its audience. Advertisers used images that would appeal to readers and created positive associations between image and product. At the very least, advertisers would have been wary of utilizing images readers disliked or those with which they failed to identify. Through an analysis of these images, those characteristics or images that readers esteemed, or were believed by advertisers to do so, can be traced. For the social and cultural historian, advertising acts not only as a reflection of society, but 'holds the key' to an understanding of the evolution of urban society towards the end of the nineteenth century.[37] Advertisements depict recognizable and socially acceptable scenarios and, as they are expensive, must be brief and strike a responsive chord immediately amongst readers.[38]

In many ways, advertisements, particularly those in newspapers, are composed of images frozen in time and therefore have an increased reliance on stereotyping. To be successful, this stereotyping must link the product with a positive cultural image, thus transferring a positive symbol onto the commodity and increasing the likelihood that consumers will find it appealing and buy it.[39] Historians can therefore examine advertisements to find these links and discover the meanings of the advertising symbols within a context that is exact and date specific.

Advertising in the periodical press has been traced back to the seventeenth century, but the repeal of the Stamp Act in 1855 acted as the first impetus for modern advertising, although initially firms were reluctant to resort to it. Newspaper owners in the mid-Victorian period tended to be printers rather than journalists, ensuring that advertisements were more written than visual, confined to the monotonous constraints of columns and word repetitions. These conventions remained in place until the mid-1870s when new attitudes to typeface and more frequent use of block illustrations became standard. These changes, linked with the rise of the cheap popular press, contributed to a growing industry upon which Britain spent £10 million a year by 1914.[40]

The end of the nineteenth century saw a change in advertising from 'the girl' as the symbol of the age selling hats, clothes, health foods and bicycles, to that of the British soldier. Since the image of 'The Soldier' sold everything from paint to cigarettes, the image of the soldier became more positive from the 1890s.[41] By the very nature of advertising, these images must have been positive ones or they would not have found a role in selling commodities. The South African War influenced a move whereby products were given a 'patriotic glow' by association with images of the war, thus capitalizing on popular sentiment and increasing sales. For the first time on a large scale, both famous and ordinary soldiers were used to sell products. There was by this time 'value in the testimonial of a humble warrior'.[42]

These component parts of the newspaper can be used to determine the 'world view' of Edwardians. In this way, newspapers as a source are much more valuable than collections of personal letters, diaries or private papers that tend to reflect elite or idiosyncratic opinion. Newspapers are a regular, serialized source that can be traced over relatively lengthy periods with few gaps or interruptions between the creation of one piece of information and another. For this reason, they are readily datable, making them different from other forms of ephemera, such as posters or cigarette cards. Unlike letters or diaries, newspapers do not have an eye to posterity, because they are created for and consumed by a contemporary audience, with a lifespan no longer than the publication (or consumption) of the next issue. In this way, they have to address and be of relevance to their audience immediately, as they cannot be 'discovered' long after their publication, as can great works of literature. The immediacy and ephemeral nature of newspapers helps determine those modes of expression and types of imagery that are time and class specific.[43]

There are, though, problems in using newspapers as a source that must be addressed. The most obvious is the idea that it is difficult to know which parts of the newspaper were read and which were skipped. Individuals might purchase a particular paper in order to read specific sections, such as the sport or classified advertisements, to make a political statement or simply out of habit. However, examining a general phenomenon such as war, and using a wide variety of newspapers over a long period of time, solves this difficulty. If images of war continued to be presented in similar ways over time and through differing kinds of newspapers, then it has to be the case that those images had a strong currency. Further, if those images were present in diverse forms of publications, the general nature of images and the 'imagining' of war throughout society can be determined.

It is this 'imagining' that is most important. Historians can argue about the 'reality' of a situation or belief, such as 'real' soldiers being pariahs before the First World War. But the *image* of soldiers conveyed in newspapers gives us a much better and more immediate idea of how people felt about them at the time. Since most people outside of garrison towns had a vicarious experience of soldiers and soldiering, the way that they *imagined* them is crucial in understanding their perceptions. A systematic search of primary documents produced in the context of the times carries far more weight than historians pontificating back through decades of distance and relying on mostly secondary documents. We need to understand the Edwardians on their own terms. For them, the ubiquitous 'romantic fantasy about brave, noble warriors' generated by Imperial and foreign wars was central in their conception of 'The Soldier', while what modern revisionist historians now see as the 'reality' of real soldiers was far less important.[44]

Warfare, and the images it generated, was of enormous economic importance for newspapers because news of war was felt by editors to increase sales dramatically. Ralph Blumenfeld, editor of the *Daily Express*, believed that newspapers did not make wars, but that 'it would be more true to say that wars made newspapers', as people were anxious for war news.[45] His own paper, established in 1900, was itself able to take advantage of interest in the news from South Africa. Kennedy Jones, an associate of Alfred Harmsworth at the *Daily Mail*, wrote that: 'war not only creates a supply of news but a demand for it . . . a paper has only to be able to put on its placard "A Great Battle" for its sales to mount up.'[46] Furthermore, newspapers, as commercial business operations, would not have indulged in the expensive practice of gathering war news if it was not seen as profitable, either in making money or by not losing readers to rival newspapers. These costs have been outlined by Frederick Arthur McKenzie, war correspondent for the *Daily Mail* in Manchuria during the Russo-Japanese War, as including £100–150 per month for a war correspondent's salary, with miscellaneous expenses averaging a further £100, and up to £1000 in a 'special' week for telegraph fees.[47]

News organizations were satisfied with the sort of war coverage that they were receiving from their correspondents. Francis Younghusband, the diplomatic leader of the expedition to Tibet and a seasoned Asiatic explorer, felt that the correspondents 'invent or rather report any absurd rumour', and that Henry Newman, the Reuters correspondent with the British forces, was 'not a bad fellow personally, but he does write the most appalling balderdash'.[48] However, Reuters wrote in their annual report for 1904, 'we are being well served by our correspondent with the Tibet Expedition', whose accounts were 'much appreciated by our newspaper subscribers'.[49] Newman's 'balderdash', while dismissed by Younghusband, was in fact quite welcomed by the newspapers, as many of them published his Reuters reports.

An additional problem with using newspapers as a source is the extent to which censorship, both official and self-imposed, was a factor in war correspondence. Military historians have addressed the issue of official censorship, indicating that it originated in the Edwardian period.[50] But an analysis of press censorship must begin in 1879 with the expedition to Afghanistan led by Major-General Roberts, when he complained to the War Office about reporters from Kabul.[51] Far more important than the issue of official censorship is the fact that war correspondents censored themselves. They identified with the soldiers with whom they lived, worked, slept, and occasionally fought alongside. They also tended to come from similar backgrounds as the officers, not unusually having military experience themselves. More importantly, war correspondents, particularly in the more remote reaches of the world, were often heavily dependent upon the military authorities for access to telegraphs and transportation. Bullard asserted that war correspondents would rarely betray a trust fairly committed to them if the importance of its secrecy was also explained. Bennet Burleigh, one of Bullard's 'famous war correspondents', denounced a correspondent 'who would betray the host with whom he remains as an honoured guest'.[52]

However, while it is necessary to be aware of the problems of censorship, a study that examines the appearance of war images present in the press that were consumed by readers is not handicapped by the issue of censorship. It is the images found in the pages of the press that can reveal attitudes and perceptions of warfare, rather than the ones left out. Neither editors nor military officials can impose images of war on such a large scale as to be effective without the willing consent of readers in a commercial press. Such consent runs counter to the suggestion of 'manipulation' or 'propaganda'.

A further problem in examining aspects of the press is the sheer bulk of the source. It is difficult to access the information in newspapers as there are very few indexed serials, and those that exist tend to be unhelpful. However, in looking at images of war it is possible to select a number of case studies to facilitate a detailed analysis. Specific wars and battles are easily dated and it is possible to read sample newspapers before and after those dates to ascertain the ways that military activity was reported. The case studies in the present work consist of both British Imperial conflicts and foreign wars not directly involving British troops. Each one of these samples in turn includes a range of engagements to represent victories and defeats, sieges and open-field battles, and retreats and advances, in order to determine whether images of war were consistent.

Of the many British Imperial wars of the Edwardian period, this study focuses on the South African War (1899–1902), the four expeditions to Somaliland (1901–1904), and the Tibet Expedition (1903–1904) representing a difficult and costly victory, an outright defeat and a relatively easy and complete victory. Foreign wars that did not involve British forces for the same period include the Russo-Japanese War (1904–1905), the Turco-Italian War (1911–1912), and the Balkan Wars (1912 and 1913). Each of these expeditions and wars contains a variety of engagements that can be analysed and assessed for a range of war imagery. In addition, the newspaper issues published between the reports of individual battles and other engagements are also examined in order to discover those elements of newspapers that were less dependent on timing of specific battles, such as letters, reviews, feature articles, advertisements, and cartoons.

The newspaper titles in which these images were presented must also represent a wide variety of differing types of newspapers. It is not enough to limit a study of newspaper images of war to the upmarket 'quality' press, even if assumptions can be made about the trickle-down of imagery to other groups in society. The quality press does not have a monopoly on cultural expression, and it is no more 'legitimate' or important than the tabloids of the New Journalism. The popular press of the new self-improving, lower middle-classes is also included in this analysis, as are working-class Sunday papers, the provincial press, illustrated papers and satirical journals. These samples are, in turn, representative of diverse political ideologies, publication frequency, geographic location and cover price.

In studying the images of war in newspapers, certain themes present themselves. It is this thematic approach, rather than a chronological one, that lends itself as the most suitable avenue of analysis, raising several key aspects of the military and warfare. These include the depiction of the soldier-warrior, the presentation of the use of force, images of war as sport or games and as theatre or spectacle, and the representation of the negative consequences of war such as death and wounding. Two themes of distance and denial emerge, particularly in the latter chapters. Readers were emotionally and intellectually distanced from the horrors of war, just as they were physically distant. The dead and the wounded were essentially removed from the conscious understanding of those who vicariously experienced warfare through the newspapers. This denial and distancing, combined with the positive images of warfare and the soldier, greatly contributed to the origin of the First World War. Anyone trying to understand how this war or any war (past, present or future) began and built up such tremendous momentum, must take into account the picture of war accepted by those who later participated in and supported it.

2
'Uncouth, Unkempt Barbarians':
The Depiction of Belligerents

Introduction: 'the favourable and acceptable face of the soldier'

When William Robertson, later to become a Field Marshal, informed his mother in 1877 that he intended to join the army, her famous reply was: 'I would rather Bury you than see you in a red coat.' For her, the army was 'such a Low Life' and 'a refuge for all Idle people'.[1] This was, according to Robertson's biographer, a prevalent attitude in the 1860s and 70s where 'no one' took the Queen's Shilling unless they had to.[2] Furthermore, while admitting that patriotism, fear of invasion, and ideas of social recreation combined to influence a 'small proportion' of men to join the Territorial Force, some historians have concluded that 'attitudes towards military service had not radically changed in Edwardian Britain'. For them, part-time soldiering, as well as the military itself, had 'a distinctly limited appeal', because 'the vast majority of the populace were not interested in military service'.[3] It is with this reluctance as background that 'one of the most remarkable mass movements of modern time'; the voluntary enlistment of 2,500,000 men between August 1914 and December 1915, must be explained.[4]

One way of understanding the reaction to the declaration of war in 1914 and the desire of civilians, who were previously reluctant to become soldiers, to volunteer for active service, is to examine the image of the soldier/warrior presented in pre-1914 newspapers. Such an examination will give a strong indication as to the basis of the eagerness to join up and for non-combatants to lend their support and encouragement. It will also provide an indication of the degree to which these perceptions were positive ones regarding officers and other ranks, as well as foreign and colonial troops. In addition, the portrayal of the

Imperial enemy and its conduct on the battlefield affords further insight into the martial traits valued by the Edwardians.

John MacKenzie has outlined many of the significant factors that brought about a change of perspective regarding the military in Britain. He explains that during the early part of the nineteenth century, soldiers were employed to quell civil unrest, billeted with an unwilling civil population, and poorly treated by their officers. The end of the century, however, saw 'the favourable and acceptable face of the soldier everywhere', as the soldier became a popular hero. This change had much to do with the creation of a civilian police force, the recognition of the brutal and unhealthy conditions of military service, and the institutional reforms brought about by Edward Cardwell in the 1870s. Wellington's 'scum of the earth' had indeed become 'saints' after the Indian Rebellion (1857–58),[5] a perspective that continued in the later colonial campaigns, and fostered a general change of attitude from that held by Mrs Robertson.[6]

However, the image of 'The Soldier' in Britain must be seen in a wider context, one which includes the contemporary concerns for National Efficiency and the fears of racial degeneration. The concept of 'National Efficiency' was one which encompassed virtually all shades of opinion and attracted widespread support, cutting across class and party. The movement was related to the relative decline of Britain as a great power, the loss of confidence in liberalism and laissez-faire socio-economics, and the search for alternative 'efficient' forms of government.[7] These concerns were given further impetus by the shocking defeats of the Boer War and the concomitant recruitment problems relating to the poor physical health of volunteers. This was the crisis which revealed the latent feelings of doubt and insecurity, leading to what has been termed the 'Edwardian cult of "National Efficiency"'. In addition, there were growing fears of imperial decline in the Edwardian period, with perceived similarities to the end of the Roman Empire, resulting in the publications of such books as *The Decline and Fall of the British Empire*, after Gibbon's famous book, attributed to Elliott E. Mill dated about 1905 but set as a Japanese school text in 2005. This particular work, while poor satire, sold well and influenced people such as the founder of the Boy Scouts, Baden-Powell, who included references and comparisons to the Roman Imperial decline in his handbook, *Scouting for Boys*.[8]

In a similar manner, the Boer War also acted as a catalyst for concerns about physical degeneration, resulting in the creation of the Inter-Departmental Committee on Physical Deterioration, the report of which was published in 1904. While the report attempted to allay fears of racial degeneration, its effect was the opposite, as the very existence of such a report confirmed concerns and acted as official recognition, and supported ideas of deterioration by using the 'language of degeneration'.[9] These fears of physical decay were seen not simply in a social context, but as a military problem, in an era of growing antagonism and rivalry with Germany, a nation held to be a paragon of national efficiency and racial strength. For many, this military problem was seen as having a military solution in, for example, the creation of paramilitary organizations such as Baden-Powell's Boy Scouts and the call for universal military training.[10]

Recent scholarship of the attitudes towards the military have stressed that Edwardian Britain was not a militaristic society akin to that which existed on the Continent. British society was conditioned to believe that military activity was necessary and desirable, but that 'militarism', or what Michael Howard calls the 'proto-fascism' of figures such as Colonel F. N. Maude, was present only in 'very mild solution'.[11] Others concur, believing that a 'wide and pervasive range of military or militaristic modes of thinking' existed in Britain, but that they manifested themselves not as the obvious expressions of militarism seen in Germany, but in the form of military pressure groups such as the National Service League.[12]

The image of the soldier found in newspapers offers a further way in which these 'militaristic modes of thinking' can be viewed. A positive representation of belligerents would indicate an extension of the 'favourable and acceptable face' of the soldier. Furthermore, such a representation would illustrate those qualities which were of value in British society for their ability to counter fears of physical and racial decay. These images of belligerents can be divided into two groups, the first relating to the display and representation of 'civilization' through the fostering of justice and order, conduct on the battlefield, and military organization. The second group of images concerns the possession of martial virtues and how approbation was afforded to those who were seen to display them. The importance of these images was demonstrated in the way that readers were encouraged and believed to identify with them through illustrations and advertisements.

'A remarkable leap from barbarism': representations of civilization

J. R. Seeley, in his influential book *The Expansion of England*, proposed the idea that the English, through their Empire, held 'the position not merely of a ruling but of an educating and civilizing race'. This position applied not only to India but to the whole Empire, particularly after the abolition of the slave trade.[13] This idea of civilization occurred also in the military sphere, as C. E. Callwell indicated in *Small Wars: Their Principles and Practice*. Here, Callwell equated the suppressing armies with 'the forces of civilization', while the enemy were 'foes who have opposed the forces of civilization'.[14] Other commentators specifically referred to the civilizing role of the British military during the pre-1914 period. The Right Reverend James Edward Welldon, formerly Lord Bishop of Calcutta (1898–1901), felt that the British army during the Tibet Expedition created 'an open road for civilization and Christianity in the last great Pagan Country in the world'.[15]

Most of the Edwardian press reflected this idea of the military representing civilizing influences and 'opening' dark, barbarous sections of the globe to modern civilization. The *Daily Express*, for example, stated that the presence of British troops in Lhasa at the end of the Tibet Expedition was the first time that the city had been occupied 'by the soldiers of a civilized Power', and that 'this has brought Tibet into contact with modern civilization. In spite of themselves, the Tibetans have been lifted from the Dark Ages.'[16] The very presence of soldiers from a 'civilized' Power was enough to raise the Tibetans from their barbaric state and to show the beauty of civilization, despite the ability of the military to force compliance through armed force and the threat of destruction, the underlying purpose of armies.

However, the civilizing role of the military depended upon the accoutrements of civilization the British took with them, such as what Lord Milner saw as 'the primary blessings of order and justice'.[17] The main justification for the British expeditions to Somaliland was to act as the protectors of the defenceless tribes in the interior. It was felt that the British authorities 'could not permit the establishment of a rule of despotic proselytising and the terrorising of unarmed tribes'.[18] In addition to armed force, the military also brought the physical trappings of justice. This point was highlighted in two drawings by Melton Prior in the *Illustrated London News*, subheaded 'British Justice at Bohotle'. In the same issue that brought news of Plunkett's disastrous defeat, the way in which the British administered justice in the field – 'even in the minute particulars' – was demonstrated. The first drawing showed 'a properly convened court' run by officers in uniform, with tables, chairs and court reporters within the confines of a protective zariba (a defensive square made from thorn bushes) under the Union Jack flying from a flagpole. It is a picture of justice and order cradled in the protective powers of the imperial army. The second picture showed the results of British justice; compensation paid to the relatives of the young boy who was shot accidently. Thus not only was justice seen to be done by an ordered and proper court, it *was* done in the awarding of compensation.[19]

If the British military represented the forces of civilization, law and order, it followed that those who struggled against it were irrational. The most obvious and direct reference to the irrationality of an imperial enemy occurred in Somaliland, where the leader of organized resistance to British rule, Mohammed Abdulla Ibn Hassan, was described as the 'Mad Mullah'. The root of his 'madness' lay not simply in his religious 'fanaticism', for his influence and power was initially tolerated by the British even to the extent of allowing him to exercise the use of Islamic law to settle disputes in the interior. His 'madness' was not an issue until he challenged British rule in the area and sought to rid Somaliland of infidel influences completely.[20] *Justice*, one of the few newspapers to criticize the Expeditions, recognized this tendency to see the mullah's madness in terms of opposition to the 'civilizing' influence of the British. Seeing the objective of the Expeditions as 'robbery and plunder', *Justice* described the mullah as the 'Somali patriot who ventured to defend his country against the marauding bands of British mercenaries sent to steal it – and who, since he is opposed to the undeniable blessings of British brigandage, must perforce be regarded, in the face of things, as mad . . .'.[21]

Yet as resistance to the British grew and became more successful, the perspective in the press altered. This change can be traced in such diverse newspapers as the *Daily Mail*, a 'jingo' paper which supported the Expeditions, and the *Daily News*, a liberal paper which was rather more critical. Both newspapers referred to the mullah as 'mad' throughout the build-up and course of the First and Second Expeditions. However, after the defeat at Erigo on 6 October 1902,[22] the papers dropped references to the mullah's 'madness'. The *Daily Mail*, for example, referred to the Somali leader by his full name for the first time on 20 October 1902 as the first news of Erigo arrived in London, referring to him as 'Haji Muhammad Abdullah' in a leading article, rather than the 'Mad Mullah'. While a further article in the same issue did describe him that way, it was the last time such a reference appeared. For the remainder of the Second Expedition and throughout the Third and Fourth, the Somali leader was simply called 'the Mullah'. Indeed, following a further defeat at Gumburu on 17 April 1903, the *Mail* felt that the mullah had demonstrated that he was not 'mad' through his military competence. The paper stated that 'his military tactics are admitted by those who have come in contact with them to be eminently astute, while as an organizer he has proved his ability by establishing his rule over vast tracts of country'.[23] Similarly, the *Daily News* frequently described the Somali leader as the 'Mad Mullah' until the defeat at Erigo, when it felt that 'the "Mad Mullah"... seems to be showing increasing signs of sanity', and that, 'for a mad man, the Mullah planned his tactics skilfully... he is no fool, this Mad Mullah'.[24] Military skill and success in fighting the British suggested that he was not simply 'mad' to oppose their civilizing role, but that he was to be granted a higher level of respect, for it required careful planning and skill to defeat such a powerful and civilized force.

Thus it was the British military which represented civilization, progress and justice in the remote regions of the Empire, while the imperial enemy demonstrated their 'uncivilized' nature in opposing the representative of civilization until proven otherwise. Yet the image of these belligerents depended on more than just their relation to the British military. They evoked images of civilization which were their own and which depended on their adoption and display of military practice understood as familiar by the British. There were two main areas where the imperial enemy's level of civilization was determined. One was the degree to which belligerents recognized and followed rules of 'civilized' warfare and the second was the level of martial development and organization they had attained.

For the British press, the Boers were the most civilized of the imperial enemies of the period. They were a white, Christian and 'European' enemy, and the war itself was viewed as a 'white man's war'. The image of the Boers was contradictory and unclear, primarily because they were neither modern European fighters nor were they 'savages' who acknowledged no rules of war, and though they were of European stock, they were tainted through generations of contact with Africa. The *Illustrated London News* saw them as a small but valiant people who had created by force of arms a military oligarchy, full of pride and ideas of their own self worth. The paper hinted at their cowardly, uncivilized nature, reminding its readers of the defeat at Majuba in 1881 where the Boers treacherously hid behind rocks and fired on an inferior number of British troops.[25] However, even their status as 'European' was not enough to make the Boers fully equal to the British. In describing the Boer as the 'Dutchmen of South Africa' the *Daily Mail* expressed confidence on the eve of war that the 'Anglo-Saxon' would ultimately win. The expansion of the British Empire and the concomitant contraction of the Dutch Empire proved that 'brain for brain, body for body, the

English-speaking people are much more than a match for the Dutch-
man, despite the superior trickery and cunning of the men of the Low
Countries'.[26] This derision of the Dutch Empire was not simply pre-war
propaganda or puffing, but a part of a larger concern for imperial
decline. The Dutch were seen to have lost their Empire because of their
decaying and degenerating culture and their declining civilized status.[27]

It was this tendency to resort to 'trickery and cunning' which was seen
to abrogate the Boer claim to civilization. The Boer 'trick' of showing a
white flag of truce and then firing on British troops as they moved from
cover was roundly condemned. It was felt that while the Boers were
'ordinarily held to be a civilized enemy', the misuse of the white flag
'would seem somewhat seriously to discount their claim to such consideration'. *Punch* emphasized this perspective in a cartoon entitled 'The
Sullied White Flag', published in December 1899. Here, a Boer was
confronted by John Bull, who hinted that the British troops might
become ruthless if the Boers continue to abuse the flag of truce. The
Boer was portrayed as dark, scruffy and shifty; an uncivilized, almost
evil-looking character, while John Bull was immaculately dressed, stern
and noble-looking; the essence of a civilized yeoman.[28]

The image of the Boers in the press was not uniformly hostile, as they
were seen to display gentlemanly and chivalrous modes of behaviour.
De Wet was described as possessing a 'quiet, kindly manner' and the
'bearing of a gentleman' as he issued orders to prevent excesses against
the British wounded. *Lloyd's* similarly extended this perspective to the
Boer's treatment of prisoners of war, describing it as 'humane and chivalrous'.[29] For newspaper readers, acts of chivalry such as these showed
how 'gentlemen' were supposed to live and die,[30] so their presence in
the Imperial opponent highlighted the perception of an honourable
enemy.

This contradictory picture, where the Boers simultaneously flouted
the rules of civilized warfare and behaved like perfect gentlemen, was
recognized by the press and explained in several ways. The *Daily News*
justified the Boers' use of trickery as a part of the native warfare with
which they were familiar, a cunning and necessary element of fighting
the natives. The *Daily Mail*, however, went further by stating that there
were different *types* of Boers. The first kind was a rough type of Boer,
dirty and scruffy, with no British blood. The paper's correspondent
described this type as a 'scoundrel', who 'wore stiff, bristling hair all
around his face, whose features were those of primitive man'. Others,
however, possessed British blood and 'hold their heads up, display
bright eyes and frank faces, and say bluntly that they have not believed

in the war or have taken part in it except under compulsion'. To compare the two types of Boer was like 'comparing cultivation with Barbarism, a Londoner with a cave-dweller'.[31] One type of Boer was depicted as like the British, 'civilized' because of their perceived acceptable modes of behaviour in a military sense and the other, not related to the British, as barbarous because of their military tactics. Their deportment on the battlefield, along with racial pedigree, determined their degree of civilization.

To the Edwardian press, the Tibetans represented an enemy which was only half-civilized, but one which possessed a recognizable if inferior culture.[32] The Tibetans, like the Boers, displayed uncivilized behaviour through what the British perceived as 'treacherous' activities. Their attempts at ambushing the mission such as that on the Tuna Plain, were seen as simple and crude. But, as *The Times* warned, 'even the most childish piece of treachery occasionally achieves its object if circumstances combine to favour it'.[33] However, unlike the Boers, it was not expected that the Tibetans would follow 'civilized' rules of warfare and there was therefore no need for explanation when they were disregarded. Owing to their conduct on the battlefield, the Tibetans were unquestionably a less civilized enemy.

The newspaper perception of the Japanese army was not simply the support of a new ally, but was similar to that of Callwell's view of the British army as a force of civilizing progress. The Japanese army was on the side of justice, and it was also seen to have brought law and order to areas within its sphere of operations such as Korea. On 30 January 1904 the *Penny Illustrated Paper* published a full page drawing entitled 'Japanese Troops Quelling Disturbances Caused by Riotous Koreans', which showed Japanese troops as stern and calm aiming their rifles at a crowd of Koreans with sticks and rocks. It is not simply the Japanese who brought order and thus 'civilization' to Korea, but specifically the Japanese army. There was no question as to why the Koreans were resisting or whether they saw themselves as struggling for their independence.[34]

Examples of the Japanese transgressing the rules of war were explained, played down or ignored. Instances of Japanese looting shops at Liaoyang were said to be due to lack of proper food 'which probably excuses the apparently outrageous looting which went on', and were given little attention or prominence. Similarly, a photograph illustrating the use of Chinese temples to house Japanese wounded and Russian prisoners of war received no comment or complaints that they were violating Buddhist shrines. Instead, attention was drawn to the gentlemanly conduct of the Japanese and their kindness to Russian prisoners. As one paper indicated, 'nowhere can the least sign be detected of that cruelty...deemed inseparable from Oriental warfare' emphasizing that they had left barbarism far behind and stood forth as 'champion[s] of civilization'.[35]

However, while *The Times* saw the Japanese as forces of civilizing progress, the Russians were seen as 'forces of mechanical repression'.[36] An example of the contrast between the image of two combatants occurred in the *Daily Express*, where on the front page the paper headlined a section on the war 'Cossack Brutality', while the first leader was headed 'Japanese Humanity'. The paper went so far as to suggest that 'mercy and mildness have never been characteristic of Russian methods of warfare', and to remind the Russians that they could not play fast and loose with the laws of civilized warfare.[37]

Similar images occurred in descriptions of belligerents in the Turco-Italian War where, despite the recognized 'civilized' status of the Italians as fellow Europeans, the British press attacked the Italians with varying intensity, soon after the invasion of Tripoli. It was a delicate situation as the British had supported the Italians in their move towards unification under Garibaldi and Italy had been one of the few countries to defend British activity in South Africa. *Lloyd's* recognized that 'almost without exception, the Press of Europe condemn the action of Italy', yet in the early stages, it was perceived in Britain as a war 'between civilized peoples'.[38] The massacre of the Arabs in the Oasis around Tripoli, however, changed the perception of the Italians in the British press. The first instance of serious fighting began on 23 October 1911 in a coordinated attack by Turks and Arabs, and resulted in the near annihilation of a regiment of Bersaglieri, the elite of the Italian army. What followed was four days of summary executions and random shootings of most of the Arabs in the Oasis. The Italians claimed that the result was a legitimate suppression of an Arab 'revolt' in the occupied Oasis, but for the British newspapers, the action was described as an unnecessary massacre. *The Times*, while attempting to explain the Italian reaction, described the event as 'indiscriminate slaughter'. Italian soldiers roamed the Oasis out of control 'shooting indiscriminately all whom they met without trial, without appeal' where 'innocent and guilty were wiped out', including women and children.[39]

This action raised serious doubts about the Italian army representing the forces of civilization. The *Daily Mail* described the 'Oasis massacre' as an 'indiscriminate and ruthless slaughter which has tarnished the arms of a civilized nation'. Others described the 'ruthless methods' of the Italians in 'clearing' the Oasis as an action where 'no mercy was shown . . . every Arab that was encountered was at once put to death'. Indeed, it was 'an episode which will leave an imperishable stain upon Italian arms', with the only redeeming feature being the stoic contempt of death displayed by the Arabs.[40]

Thus Italy, as a European nation, was expected to have soldiers who acted as representatives of civilization, but their actions during the Oasis massacre raised serious questions about the army's civilizing role. In addition, the Italian army was not universally seen as a harbinger of justice and order. The initial image of the Italians holding properly convened courts, where witnesses testified to the military officials conducting the trial and where sentence was duly carried out, changed after the Oasis massacre. The trial of an Arab who worked in the German embassy, accused of the murder of an Italian officer, was publicized extensively by the press from the moment the trial began to his ultimate execution. Yet photographs taken later of the results of the massacre belied this image of order and justice. Indeed, Francis McCullagh, the anti-Italian war correspondent for the *Westminster Gazette* and the *Daily News*, wrote that the Italian occupation of Tripoli marked an end to the peace and harmony which reigned under Turkish administration. There were no massacres or inhuman acts against Christians, and Ottoman rule was characterized by mercy, forethought and restraint.[41]

One of the most striking images of the relation between the military discipline of the Italian soldiers and their degree of civilization was presented in an *Illustrated London News* photograph entitled 'Roman Remains as Modern Italian Defences in Tripoli'. Here, the Italian soldiers lounged among Roman ruins with helmets askew, untidy uniforms, smoking 'long rat-tailed cigars', and not acting alert or sharp while on duty. The caption referred to the discipline of the army of occupation as 'very slack', pointing out their general disposition and battered helmets as proof.[42] The Italians, while basking in the reflected glory of the Roman Empire, lacked the discipline and the temperament to be a truly strong civilizing force like the British Empire or their own Roman ancestors. The Italians in this photograph represented the fears of Imperial decline prevalent in Britain and acted as a warning, rather like Mill's satire of Gibbon's work, suggesting that civilizations which lose their military skills will lose their empires.

This photograph can be contrasted with an illustration which juxtaposed British officers, their Somali enemy, Sikh soldiers and the local levy. This drawing, entitled 'The Defeat of the Mad Mullah in Somaliland: Interrogating Prisoners at the Base Camp at Burao', showed a British officer, a clear figure of authority and civilization who stood smoking, with his weight on one foot, interrogating a Somali who cowered on his knees before the officer. The Somali, with wild eyes, wore the vestiges which corresponded to his level of civilization, such as animal skins and bangles, just as the uniformed British officer wore his. On the left was a local Somali levy standing loosely at attention with native clothing and rudimentary webbing, but without the wild eyes or bangles of the Mullah's follower. On the right stood a turbaned Sikh in full uniform, correct and erect with a sword. The condition which made these soldiers different was their exposure to and assimilation of military discipline. This is made clearer as one goes up the scale of military development from the Somali to the levy, the Sikh and ultimately the British officer. Those cultures which had adopted or were in the process of adopting British/European modes of military organization, discipline and stature, were more 'civilized' than those who had not.[43] This drawing also indicates the close relationship between martial discipline and high levels of 'civilization', necessary to maintain Imperial dominance, and acted as the way in which readers wished to see their soldiers and themselves in relation to those under their influence.

The awareness of the relationship between martial development and the level of civilization was prevalent in the representation of levels of military organization. The image of the 'mob' or the 'crowd' had a special resonance in the late nineteenth century in that it represented the scene of degeneration and regression, a move away from order and civilization towards 'a world of dangerous instincts and primitive memories'.[44] This sentiment was made clear in Gustav Le Bon's famous work, *The Crowd (Psychologie des foules)*, first published in 1895, which outlined the psychology of the crowd and linked it to the rise of the irrational urbanization and sublimation of the rational individual. The crowd, it was felt, could come alive and spark violence, disorder, and anarchy.[45] Newspaper depictions of the Imperial enemy reveal this perspective, but also indicate that with military success, dependent as it was upon high levels of organization and martial development, the image of the enemy changed. This can be seen in the images relating to the Boers. In a secret report compiled by the Intelligence Division of the War Office in June 1899, the Boers were portrayed as stolid and stubborn, but still undisciplined 'untrained farmers'. They were merely 'masses of men' with a lack of higher organization and trained staff. More important for the authors of the report was the almost total absence of effective, qualified command as none of the field commanders were believed to have had significant military experience. Despite the large sums of money spent on the military in the Transvaal and Orange Free State from 1896 to

1899, the War Office felt that 'they have made but little progress towards improvement of their primitive organization'.[46]

The newspaper depiction of the Boers reflected this official view, as they were seen to have 'no organization whatever, and cannot remain concentrated for an unlimited period' because their ranks were made up of farmers who would rather sow seeds for their crops than be in laager. They were, indeed, a mere 'mass of burghers' and 'a huge guerrilla mob of 20,000' which could not remain concentrated for more than a month without bankrupting the Boer forces of men and horses.[47] Yet, success on the battlefield led to recognition that the Boers were not simply an uncivilized, disorganized mob of farmers. By the end of 'Black Week', the *Daily Mail* published an illustrated map showing the Boers hiding in the hills around Colenso, scattered and with no apparent organization, wearing civilian clothes and top hats. The text which accompanied the illustration stated that combat with the Boers was like 'fighting rather shabbily-dressed businessmen', but because of their military success, 'the comparison begins and ends with the clothes'. Similarly, by the end of 1900, the *Daily News* recognized that the commando under Christian De Wet was not a mere rabble nor were they seen as marauding bands without aim or purpose, but as a fully organized army with De Wet in control.[48]

A similar tendency was in operation regarding the non-European enemy in the Empire, such as the reports of the expedition to Tibet. Before the invasion, the Tibetans were compared unfavourably with the North West Frontier tribes, for while they were equally savage in battle, the Tibetans were not as warlike, nor were they 'reckless or daring'. They were seen as 'uncouth, unkempt barbarians, but in normal times are good natured and harmless...'.[49] None of the papers recognized or admitted the possibility of the rather complex military organization which Preman Addy has outlined.[50] The *Manchester Guardian* made this point clear when it compared the Tibetan and British armies after the capture of Gyantse Jong where the victory was celebrated, though expected, for it set 'trained troops with guns' against stone walls and 'uncivilized defenders'.[51] Here, the absence of recognized military training accounted for their lack of civilization, particularly when compared with the 'trained troops' of the 'civilized' British army.

The Tibetans, like the Boers, were initially seen to lack basic military organization and were frequently referred to as a 'mob'. At Guru, for example, where the Tibetans were easily surrounded by Gurkhas and Sikhs, huddling together behind their defensive wall, they were an 'undisciplined mob' and a 'surging mass'. This image was reinforced by drawings in the illustrated press, such as H. W. Koekkoek's 'Colonel

Younghusband's Mission to Lhasa: the Punishment of the Recalcitrant Tibetans at Guru'. The uncivilized Tibetans were a faceless mass, an unmilitary mob, while the Sikhs firing over the wall were ordered, regimented and disciplined; their degree of 'civilization' higher because they benefited from the martial influence of the British officers who were also depicted.[52]

As with the Boers, the view of the Tibetans changed as their skill on the battlefield became evident. Though the Tibetans were not successful and never did defeat the British forces, they were close to doing so on several occasions. The papers were confident of ultimate success, but were never able to dismiss the possibility of a 'reverse'. As the Tibetans became more militant in their operations, the press began to differentiate between groups in the 'mob' of Tibetans. After the near defeats at Karo La and Gyantse camp in May, 1904, and the stubborn stand by pockets of Tibetans at the Niani Monastery in June, a form of organization became discernible. By the time of the battle at Kangma, the press recognized that the attack was undertaken by 700 Kham warriors and 400 men from the Lhasa Regiment.[53] This was a result of the increased familiarity the reporters and army officers had with the Tibetan forces, but also of an awareness that in order to fight the British successfully, the Tibetans needed to have recognizable, British forms of military organization, and in doing so, they must have achieved a higher level of civilization.

Like the British forces in the Empire, the Japanese military were seen to bring civilization to foreign backward lands. Japan itself had been portrayed in the middle decades of the nineteenth century as a barbarous and uncivilized nation, but open to the influence of Western civilization. A letter writer to *The Times* called attention to this trend in September 1904 when he mentioned that Japan's adoption of Western ideas, customs and organization – its progress towards a civilized nation – began with the imitation of the 2nd Battalion XXth Regiment in 1864. The Japanese forces consisted of soldiers in Chinese armour with swords and bows and arrows, but under the drilling of Lieutenant William Glencross the concept of the modern effective fighting force was initiated.[54] It was felt that this contact was the origin of the modern Japanese army and the start of a trend towards higher cultural development.

The first fruits of these initial labours were not seen to have been promising. Sir Ernest Satow described a display held on behalf of the Mikado on 26 November 1868 as less than splendid. The Japanese army was made up of 'horribly untidy soldiers with unkempt hair and clothing vilely imitated from the West'.[55] After the restoration of the Meiji, military reform was given a high priority in the belief that modernization depended on loyal conscripted soldiers rather than clan-based Samurai. Even the many reforms to civil aspects of life have been seen as having possible martial application, such as the telegraph system, telephones, and the creation of modern railways.[56]

The newspaper press in Britain emphasized the connection between the Japanese adoption of European drill and uniforms through military reform, and the concept of 'civilization'. One of the most striking examples of this tendency was a set of nine illustrations showing the development of the Japanese army published in the *Illustrated London News*. Entitled, 'Japan's Leap from Barbarism: A Generation of Military Progress' (Plate 1), the full-page collection showed the rapid change in the dress and drill of the Japanese army, moving from traditional garb to modern European military uniforms based upon the French, German and British patterns. The first panel showed a wild and undisciplined warrior with a whip, emphasizing the brutality and barbarity of the service, while the last panel showed a modern, disciplined and well-armed European-style soldier.[57] Similarly, two full-page illustrations in the same issue showed portraits of Nicholas II and Emperor Mutsuhito and emphasized the equal status between the leaders by presenting them both in European-style ceremonial uniforms. The captions published with the drawings, however, stressed the civilized nature of the Japanese. The caption with the portrait of the Japanese Emperor stated that he was the most practical of monarchs, having 'brought his country from semi-barbarism to the status of a first-class Power' in only 40 years. Even the notes with the portrait of Nicholas presented this idea, suggesting that his lifespan coincided with 'the period of Japan's remarkable leap from barbarism towards modern civilization'.[58]

The martial nature of these drawings, reinforced by the captions, highlighted the interconnection between military development and 'civilization'. In contrast to the Tibetans who remained aloof and shunned the gifts of 'civilization', the Japanese adopted and adapted Western ways primarily, though not exclusively, through acquiring European military practices. Indeed, the Japanese had learned to become civilized over the previous 20 years and displayed 'qualities of the highest order' by building a first-class army along European lines with a General Staff and highly trained officers and men.[59] They were compared not to the Tibetans, but to the Gurkhas, another Asiatic nation which benefited directly from the adoption of British martial practices. Yet the modern Japanese did not need British officers to lead them and were thus described as 'Ghoorkas with brains', a sentiment which indicated their superior development.[60]

This sentiment stemmed not only from the perception that the Japanese were able to arm and lead themselves,[61] but also from their application of modern technology on the battlefield. The use and application of technology was a common means for Western societies to gauge the level of 'civilization' in their own and other cultures, particularly since the Industrial Revolution.[62] The Japanese successes depended upon their skill in military science and 'scientific preparation', and their use of 'every modern appliance', such as motorcars 'clothed in armour' and 'field telephones' which stressed 'Japan's scientific warfare'.[63] The success of the Japanese during the Russo-Japanese War led to the conviction that Japan, like Germany, was a 'paragon of National Efficiency'.[64]

Several papers were prepared to see the Japanese as more than just a nation which had acquired the 'garb of civilization', but one which had actually become 'European'. *The Times* felt that since the Japanese had adopted 'our civilization', 'their standards of conduct are in practice as high as those of the most progressive Powers in Europe', a statement proven by their actions during the Boxer Rebellion as well as the war against Russia. For this reason, the paper felt that Europeans should not exclude 'this last recruit from the sisterhood of civilized peoples'. The Japanese had demonstrated on the battlefield that they were a 'free, enlightened, chivalrous and highly educated people' who possessed a morality which was 'at least as high as anything we can show on this side of the world'.[65] The significance of these images is that the Japanese were seen to become civilized only when they adopted Western military practices and dress, and that they were seen as uncivilized before contact with Europeans. Thus, it was military development along Western lines which acted as a gauge to determine levels of civilization.

'The verge of over-refinement': the display of martial virtues

While those belligerents who displayed the ideals of British standards of civilization through their armed forces were admired, there was a perceived danger in being *over*-civilized. The Japanese were admired for not having yet reached the point where 'the primitive virtues of man begin to decay', as they were still 'climbing towards the high-water mark of modern civilization'. The British, however, were seen as having passed their peak, having reached their zenith as a 'fighting race' during the struggle against Napoleon. Indeed, one commentator in *The Times* suggested that the 'luxury of the age' had 'sapped the patriotism' of the rich and the 'unwholesome amusements of the cities' had ruined the backbone of the masses in Britain. The writer wondered whether the British could have carried out the campaigns Japan had won in the first six months of the war, and whether public opinion would have countenanced such losses, implying that he rather doubted it.[66] For Field-Marshal Wolseley, writing in his biography in 1903, war was 'the greatest purifier of the race or nation that has reached the verge of over-refinement, of excessive civilization'.[67] War was felt to be the antidote to the decadence and luxury which had been prevalent in late-Victorian Britain, seen by those such as Alfred, Lord Tennyson as 'poisonous honey spread from France', manifest in, for example, the writings and trial of Oscar Wilde, the reaction to Henry Vizetelly selling the novels of Emile Zola, and Impressionist painting.[68]

In this regard, the idea of the natural warriors, those cultures or 'races' that were seen to have, either through breeding or environment, natural instincts and affinity for fighting, induced a high degree of approbation. The Japanese were portrayed in this manner, praised for their 'dash and daring, great personal activity and natural instincts for war', where at Liaoyang, they were seen to have 'crept forward like Red Indians', the ultimate natural warriors.[69] Colonial troops were portrayed in a similar fashion as possessing natural instincts for war. *Punch* published a cartoon which showed William St John Brodrick, Secretary of State for War during the Boer War, refusing an offer of 2000 mounted troops from 'Canada', an attractive white female figure in native Indian clothing and moccasins, with feathers in her hair.[70] The cartoon equated the white settlers of Canada, primarily of British stock, with the native Indian warriors who had been perceived as natural and instinctive fighters. Through contact with the wilderness of the Canadian frontier, the British immigrants were felt to have survived the harsh environment and acquired an affinity with nature which ensured that they had not lost their natural instincts for war. While the Boers, particularly successful leaders like De Wet, were seen as born military men, the colonial troops were given higher praise because they were 'as cunning as the Boers and more daring', owing to their British background, freedom from decadence and their exposure, though not *over*-exposure, to army discipline.

Indeed, it was this combination of a natural talent for war and British blood which was esteemed. The *Daily Mail* attempted to explain 'why our colonial troops are so well qualified to meet the Boers' in an article entitled 'Sons of the Empire'. The paper explained that British defeats were due to the lack of training regular troops received over rough ground. It was implied that those skills belonged to the Napoleonic age and were forgotten by British troops, but that the Colonials were 'disciplined by the stern fight against an unkind soil' and feared by the Boers. To Colonial scouts, for example, 'the signs of nature are an open book . . . and they will by instinct know the likely spots for hidden bodies of the enemy'. Therefore, the country needed Yeomanry unhampered by over-drilling, taught to forage for themselves and to know the lie of the land in order to be more like the Colonials. It was thought that this type of soldier would most likely be found in the hunting classes, where riders were thought to 'read' the ground and lead a hearty outdoor life. The idea that the British troops could learn to become natural warriors from their colonial brethren was echoed by Kipling when, in his poem 'The Parting of the Columns', he praised the Colonial troops from 'Calgary and Wellington and Sydney and Quebec'.[71]

It is this praise of military acumen that leads to the second source of ideas which arise from an analysis of the depiction of belligerents in the press, which was related to the idea of civilization. It concerns the degree to which participants in warfare possessed a range of martial virtues. Those who displayed these virtues esteemed by the British and cherished in themselves were accorded a high level of approbation. These virtues covered a diverse number of characteristics and had multiple origins as identified by recent scholarship. Revered martial virtues include ideas of honour, chivalry, duty, self-sacrifice, discipline, gallantry and pluck, which have been traced to the teachings of the public schools which changed their emphasis from scholarship to character-building in the last third of the nineteenth-century. They combined with a renewal of neo-chivalric codes, such as those outlined by Mark Girouard, and the growing numbers of youth groups designed to inculcate these values into children of all classes.[72] The importance of these martial virtues was, as Michael Howard suggests, that they were considered to be 'the essence of an Imperial Race'.[73]

These virtues were clearly displayed by the British forces in descriptions found in the press. Glorious victories, such as the storming of Gyantse Jong, were occasions where martial virtues came to the fore and were celebrated. Almost all of the newspapers felt that the capture of Gyantse Jong, a strongly held fort on a cliff top, was a triumph of British arms. The usually staid *Glasgow Herald* printed reports which described the officer leading the attack, Lieutenant Grant, as a 'daring officer', stating that 'there is no more stirring story in the annals of Indian frontier warfare than that of the capture of Gyantse Fort, held by 7,000 Tibetans, by a mere handful of British and Indian soldiers today'.[74] The *Penny Illustrated Paper* demonstrated this display of gallantry with a drawing showing the British forces, mostly European with a few Gurkhas following an officer who beckoned his men, carrying a bloody sword. A sergeant in the foreground supported a wounded trooper, indicating that compassion and care for a wounded comrade was also seen as a necessary virtue. The text of the story published in the same issue emphasized the image of the illustration, for it reported that the Fusiliers, Gurkhas and Pathans 'carried it [the jong] with a glorious rush, Lieutenant Grant being the first through the breech'. It was, indeed, an action where 'our soldiers displayed the most conspicuous bravery'. In a story entitled 'The Union Jack at Lhasa', the *News of the World* described the entire expedition as a 'triumph over difficulties which might baffle a less highly disciplined or less spirited army'. Those difficulties included not only the 'several severe engagements fought', but also the environment and climate which were 'inhospitable and perilous'.[75]

Even in defeat, British soldiers were seen to have displayed these highly valued characteristics. The *News of the World* described members of a British patrol after 'Black Week' as 'outdoing each other in heroism and self-sacrifice'. It explained that the failed attacks were 'not due to any lack of bravery on the part of those who made it', but that 'the conduct of both officers and men, under the withering fire to which they were exposed for so many hours, was, indeed, beyond praise'. *Lloyd's* followed suit when it saw the 1st Battalion of the Gordon Highlanders at Magersfontein as having 'made a gallant but equally unsuccessful attempt to reach the Boer trenches'. They advanced with 'utmost gallantry' but the task was impossible, 'even for these troops' who did 'all that the Bravest Troops in the world could do'.[76]

The problem of British soldiers surrendering or, as in the case of the Highland Division at Magersfontein, panicking,[77] was pointed out by *Justice*, a paper deeply critical of the war. In a front page report entitled, 'Our Valiant Surrenderer', the paper commented on ' ... the plucky (of course "plucky", everything that a British soldier does is plucky) exploits of Tommy Atkins in hoisting the white flag'. The report emphasized surrenders such as those during 'Black Week' made by soldiers other than 'those of the valiant British race, would be called cowardice of the most abject type'. On the second page of the same issue, however, the paper explained that it did not want to be seen as 'down on' the average British soldier, but wanted to make the point that the support and devotion which came from people who 'wouldn't touch him with a pair of tongs under ordinary circumstances' was 'disgusting', a sentiment reminiscent of Kipling's poem 'Tommy'.[78]

This image of the British soldier lent itself to what John MacKenzie has termed 'heroic myths of Empire'. Elite military figures, primarily high-ranking officers, represented the martial values of the post-Mutiny era.[79] However, the image of both officers and rankers within and beyond the British Empire presented in newspapers before the First World War represented similar heroic and positive elements. This can be seen most clearly in advertisements published in the press, where the increasingly positive image of the soldier came to be used to sell products. The South African War influenced a move whereby products were given a 'patriotic glow' by association with images of the war, thus capitalizing on popular sentiment and increasing sales. For the first time on a large scale, both famous and ordinary soldiers were used to sell products for there was 'value in the testimonial of a humble warrior'.[80] However, the link between product and advertising image was not simply due to 'patriotism'. This association played upon the idea of the British soldier as full of health, determination and pluck, representing the opposite of decline, decay and decadence.

The product which used these soldierly images most frequently in advertising was the cigarette. Introduced during the Crimean War, the cigarette was seen as exotic and slightly effeminate and 'schoolboyish' until increased sales among males in the late 1860s began to counter this view.[81] By the Edwardian period, cigarette smoking was firmly associated with masculine activities and advertising showed how the image of martial characteristics helped sell cigarettes. Images associated successful or popular British generals such as Buller and Roberts with different brand names. Ogden's 'Guinea Gold' was one of the most heavily advertised brands and used Field Marshal Roberts in several advertisements. One showed him taking a break from a chess game with President Kruger, and while smoking, reflecting with a smile that 'Guess I have time to enjoy an Ogden's "Guinea Gold" Cigarette', while a worried Kruger contemplated his next move. The image of the ordinary soldier was also used to promote sales of cigarettes. Ogden's once again associated the two when it stated 'Both Keeping Up Their "GREAT REPUTATION"', while below a British soldier stood to attention next to a package of Ogden's 'Guinea Gold'. Similarly, the arrival home and parade of the popular City of London Imperial Volunteers gave rise to an advertisement combining the positive image of the CIVs and Ogden's cigarettes, showing that the company responded to popular perceptions.[82]

Yet it was not only cigarette companies that used these types of associations. Machonochie's, a food-processing firm, exploited its enviable position of being mentioned by Baden-Powell, the 'hero of Mafeking', in his book *Aids to Scouting for N.-C.O.'s and Men* where he stated 'an army can go anywhere and do anything so long as it possesses morale and Machonochie'. The advertisement used this quote and stressed that it supplied 'millions' of rations to the War Office. It suggested that it could 'relieve the housewife of anxiety' by providing an 'emergency meal'. The advertisement thus tied domestic consumption by the housewife's 'army' to the image of Baden-Powell and the recent relief of Mafeking. It also shows that females of the aspiring middle-classes were seen to be just as susceptible to these kinds of image as were males.[83]

In addition, testimonials by ordinary soldiers appeared in advertisements which brought an association between product and the positive image of the ordinary British trooper. Dr Tibbles' Vi-Cocoa was one product which used personal testimonials by named soldiers serving in South Africa. These advertisements were presented with a drawing of an appropriate soldier, for example a Highlander or a Dragoon, depending on the testimonial, looking healthy, courageous and contented while shells burst around him with no effect. The emphasis was on 'nourishment and vitality' and, like the British soldier, the product was 'for all who face the strife and battle of life'.[84]

Similar images were used during the Russo-Japanese War, where the positive perception of Japanese soldiers was used to promote the sale of goods, mostly the cigarette, but also other products such as mouthwash. The fall of Port Arthur offered a suitable moment for celebration not only for the Japanese but for those using their image, such as Cope's 'Bond of Union' smoking mixture. In a position of prominence, one advertisement showed a Japanese soldier with a Rising Sun flag standing on a map of the Laio-Tung Peninsula. In an outburst of verse that probably sounded more poetic in Japanese, the soldier shouted

> 'Banzai! Banzai! Banzai!
> We've captured Port Arthur todai!
> Yes we had taken the fort –
> Our "Bond of Union" had run short –
> And we captured all the Russians had –
> Hoo-Rai!'

The text emphasized that Cope's 'Bond of Union' was the 'victor in the contest for universal favouritism with the great army of smokers', thus identifying not only the product with the Japanese, but their customers as well, and the beneficial image of the victorious soldier.[85]

Cope's went so far as to launch a new brand of cigarettes which emphasized the desire for identification with the Japanese and their image. Readers of the boy's journal *Comic Cuts* were told of the virtues of Japanese soldiers and Cope's 'Jap' cigarettes. One example of this association occurred when a Japanese soldier was depicted smoking a cigarette with the slogan 'He's Alright! Smoking Cope's "Jap" Five a Penny Cigarettes'. Thus readers were encouraged to identify the virtues of the Japanese soldiers with 'Jap' cigarettes, and by smoking them would be 'alright' as well.[86]

Just as the colonial and native troops were praised for retaining their 'natural instincts' for war while benefitting from the influences of civilization, so too were they admired for their possession of martial virtues. The Canadians, for example, were praised for their role in the victory at Paardeburg, where they were thought to have 'won general praise again by their bearing under the hottest fire'. It was not just the tangible actions such as capturing Boer trenches, but intangible ones like bearing under fire, which found approval and were described as gallant. It was felt that 'to the Canadian Regiment belongs the honour of having hastened the inevitable', the defeat of Cronje, merely because of its presence in the front line when he surrendered. This might be an example of sensitivity to fragile Dominion sensibilities, or a desire to maintain Imperial unity against a hostile world, but singling out the Canadians meant also evoking images of hearty white colonials who had not yet degenerated with exposure to over-civilization and had retained their desirable martial qualities.[87]

This perspective was reinforced by the coverage of the actions of native soldiers, particularly the Gurkhas, a group praised for its extraordinary military characteristics. Recent scholarship has dealt with the issue of 'martial races', mostly concluding that soldiers act in a manner expected of them and that a 'race' is only 'martial' if it is seen to be so.[88] However, while this assertion is almost certainly correct, it is the *perception* of the Gurkhas as a 'martial race' and the approbation accorded to them which is important. The press, and indeed most contemporary and modern commentators who lived and fought with native troops, presented them, particularly the Gurkhas, as naturally warlike. The widely reported instance where one Gurkha faced 700 fanatical Tibetan warriors taking five of them before being killed was just one example where the bravery and determination of the Gurkhas was celebrated. Indeed, the Gurkhas were seen in the same romantic light as another 'martial' group of hillmen with whom the British were familiar; the Scottish Highlanders. They were seen to possess the same qualities of 'dash, endurance and unconquerable courage' and to be 'one of the best fighting men in the world'.[89] Like the Highlanders, the Gurkhas were portrayed as natural fighters who had only recently been tamed and assimilated into the British military system.

The display of these martial virtues by the Imperial enemy similarly acted as a source of respect and approval. Initially, the Imperial enemies were derided for being too disorganized, ineffective and timid to be able to mount an effective opposition. However, after the initial clashes, the press recognized that the opponents were not going to prove easily defeated, and as a result, their respect and admiration for 'the foe' rose accordingly. In its initial coverage of the Boer War, the *Daily Mail* was confident of a quick British victory. Their lack of recognizable organization, a sign of a lower level of civilization, was also an indication of poor martial qualities. The Boers were seen to have no capacity for offensive warfare, no organization 'whatever', and would be unable to remain concentrated for a long period of time. Moreover, they were said to be 'corrupt and dishonest men' who attempted to bribe the press and manipulate a large secret service, the most ungentlemanly organization. Their commander was Piet Cronje, which was felt to be significant as he was 'the man who funked at Potchefstroom' in the first Anglo-Boer War. The Boers themselves were seen as good horsemen, and inured to hardship, but lacking in discipline and organization at all levels, and it was thought that they would be unable to stand up to British artillery. Indeed, a Boer invasion was seen immediately prior to its actual occurrence as merely 'an act of insolent defiance' rather than a major threat, as an assault on General White and his 6000 troops would have 'only one result – a crushing defeat for the Boers'.[90]

Yet after the serious defeats at Stormberg, Magersfontein, and Colenso the *Daily Mail* began to portray the Boers as a more menacing enemy than first suspected. By the end of 1899, the paper felt that it would be 'foolish not to recognize that we are fighting a formidable and terrible enemy'. It was the Boer Governments that were 'vile and corrupt', while the individual Boer, mounted and armed with modern rifles, was worth several 'regular soldiers'. Even Cronje, no longer the man who 'funked at Potchefstroom', became a leader of men who 'have revealed a heroism never supposed in the history of our race' in their 'courage' and 'desperate' resistance at Paardeburg.[91]

Admiration for the Boers grew when they were seen to display perhaps the highest martial virtue: chivalrous behaviour towards an enemy. *Justice* was at pains to stress this as it suggested that one of the major battles of 'Black Week', at the Modder River on 28 November 1899 could have been much worse but for the magnanimous behaviour of the Boers. It was thought to be consistent with the 'chivalrous conduct' of the enemy, in contrast with the 'butchery' of the Boers captured at Elandslaagte. So chivalrous were the Boers, they prompted G. W. Steevens to jest during the seige of Ladysmith, that 'they make war like gentlemen of leisure', where Sunday was a holiday from the war, lunch was half an hour exactly for riflemen and gunners, and they hardly ever fired their guns after teatime and never when it rained.[92] Not only did this perception of the Boers as 'gentlemen of leisure' add weight to the idea that the British were fighting a chivalrous, honourable foe, but also the fact that Steevens was able to portray the enemy in a humorous manner indicated that there was affection, even admiration, for the Boers.

Similar changes were seen with the Tibetan enemy, as what was thought to be a 'mob' of undisciplined savages using old fashioned guns and bows and arrows became more formidable. *The Times* reported that the Tibetans were a timid people and cited unnamed 'expert opinion' to assert that there would be no armed resistance. The *Daily Express* thought they were not as warlike as the North-West Frontier tribes, being savage in battle but not reckless or daring. The Tibetans were 'uncouth, unkempt barbarians but in normal times are good natured and harmless'.[93]

When the Tibetans made their stand behind a hastily erected wall on the Tuna Plain, they were easily outflanked by the Gurkhas and Pioneers. They bunched up and were crowded around their general when the battle began. They were easy targets, virtually unable to fight back, and the estimated death-toll ranged from 300 to 700. Yet the first battle at Tuna revealed a courage and tenacity which the British admired. The majority of the papers reported that the Tibetans displayed great courage and that their defeat was not due to a lack of bravery but to the poor quality of weapons. While those papers opposed to the Expedition saw this as an indication that the use of force was a mistake, those that supported the mission felt that given Tibetan 'treachery', a strong escort for Younghusband's mission was only prudent. However, the image remained constant throughout, that respect for the Tibetans increased when they attempted to resist the British expedition. The Tibetans were admired when a small group actually climbed over the wall and 'died like heroes'. Their courage was confirmed when some of the Tibetans were found to have as many as eight or nine bullet wounds, and when they retired out of range it was in a sullen manner rather than in a panic.[94]

While the Tibetans were unable to inflict a heavy defeat on the Expedition, they came close several times such as at Palla, Kangma and the
Karo La. For example, the stand made by some Tibetans at the Niani
Monastery provoked widespread approbation when they 'obstinately'
refused to surrender despite being shelled from a range of only 300
yards. This action encouraged the *Daily Express* to remark that 'the
Tibet trouble is developing into a serious war. The Mongolian Moun-
taineers are displaying martial qualities little suspected'. In a change of
attitude towards their enemy, the paper suggested that they fought 'with
the most reckless daring, and severely though they have suffered ... it
seems to make no difference to their morale'. Even *The Times* grudgingly
accepted that the Tibetans 'continue to conduct their operations against
us with more courage and perseverance than intelligence'.[95] Indeed, the
martial qualities of the Tibetans were admired to such an extent that,
though they were 'ignorant and benighted', they showed admirable
gallantry and dash. They were 'Our Brave Enemy' and were directly
compared to British officers, proving themselves 'an enemy worthy of
our steel'.[96] There might have been an element of making the enemy
appear more formidable than they were in order to make the rather easy
victory not appear as harsh, but the images are consistent in that an
enemy that put up a fight was more admired than one that did not.

The war in which both combatants displayed martial virtues to the
greatest extent was the Russo-Japanese War. Both sides were seen to
display the utmost in courage, discipline, self-sacrifice, honour and
chivalry. The Japanese were, in particular, singled out for approbation
for their efforts during the war, while the Russians showed similar traits
but were let down badly by their poor leadership. The Japanese were
admired for the way in which they took risks and did not flinch at
attacking apparently impregnable positions. They were not seen as the
aggressor in Manchuria or Korea, but as having war thrust upon them by
the Russians. Therefore, though they fought well, they were not seen as
provoking war, despite their pre-emptive strike at Port Arthur. They
possessed the qualities of 'patience, pluck and patriotism' and were
seen to know no fear of death, which appealed to the British and
fostered sympathy.[97] The Russians were similarly admired, but with
qualifications. The average soldier was portrayed as stoical and strong,
disciplined and determined. The *Morning Post* described the average
Russian soldier as 'not a beef-and-cocoa individual', meaning that they
were hardy peasants not requiring modern luxuries. They were brave
and had the British soldiers' characteristic of not knowing when they
were beaten in battle.[98]

A further martial virtue which was greatly admired was the show of chivalry and honour which was displayed by both sides throughout the war, but particularly during the siege at Port Arthur. *The Times* highlighted this perspective when it declared its admiration for the Japanese who were felt to have displayed 'not only the highest fighting qualities, but also chivalry and humanity'. The 'hard fight' at Port Arthur where there were over 100,000 casualties, meant not bitterness between belligerents, but 'mutual respect and esteem which often arise between chivalrous combatants after hard blows given and received'. But the Russians too were praised for their behaviour at Port Arthur, where General Stoessel was seen to have followed the 'most exacting code of military honour'. He organized 'a right gallant and soldierly resistance which will live when the memory of much that is less noble has passed away'.[99]

These ideas of nobility and chivalry also appeared in publications bought by the lower classes of British society. The *News of the World* was slightly surprised to discover that the Japanese were the equals of the Russians in chivalry, stating that no European gentleman could show finer spirit regarding the captured enemy commander, General Stoessel. The *Penny Illustrated Paper* indicated a similar view when it applauded the Mikado for 'magnanimous chivalry' in allowing the Russian officers to retain their arms and parole them, while the soldiers marched out of the garrison with full military honours.[100]

Conclusion: 'the torch of culture and progress'

Though active participation in both the regular and part-time elements of the army remained relatively unappealing for large numbers of Edwardians before the First World War, the popular image of 'the soldier' had improved greatly. The reasons for this improvement were far-reaching and occurred over the whole of the century, involving domestic reforms and developments overseas. By 1914, 'the soldier' had come to be equated with ideals of advancement and to be perceived as a harbinger of civilization. British troops took law and order with them to the far reaches of the Empire, bringing the 'light' of civilization, lifting those they found from the 'Dark Ages'. For, as Frederick Lugard saw in West Africa, the British brought 'to the dark places of the earth, the abode of barbarian and cruelty, the torch of culture and progress, while ministering to the needs of our own civilization'.[101]

'The soldier' was also seen as the opposite of 'the crowd', being disciplined, regulated and orderly, where 'the mob' was unruly, dangerous and primitive, with its own peculiar irrational psychology.[102] While the fear of the crowd was not new, linked with the rise of the irrational and overbearing urbanization, it indicated that for Edwardians, mobs and crowds were signs of social decay and the very essence of modernism. In this way, 'the soldier' was seen to represent an antidote to degeneration and decadence, as the way in which society could avoid *over*-civilization through the possession and display of martial virtues. Those who found a balance between following rules of warfare as well as adopting Western modes of military organization while retaining or fostering natural fighting instincts, were the ones who received the most approbation. It was felt that the attainment of this equilibrium was a means by which Britain would retain its status and remain a great imperial power.

Indeed, 'the Soldier' became a model figure in the late-nineteenth century, but most particularly, in the Edwardian period. Most groups that wished to improve society utilized military imagery for their own purposes. This tendency not only encompassed the various paramilitary youth and interest groups, but also influenced movements as disparate as the suffragettes and the trade unions. Even advertisers capitalized on the perception of 'the Soldier' in order to sell goods, a sure testament to the positive nature of the image.

As an analysis of advertisements in the press reveals, it was not only the officers who were seen as heroic, but also the ordinary rankers. While officers such as Henry Havelock and Charles Gordon attained the status of mythic heroes, the average soldier or 'Tommy' also became a popular heroic figure. Along with the 'idolized generals', 'Tommy Atkins emerged as a particularly British embodiment of the military virtues', especially when seen in the words of Rudyard Kipling.[103] These perspectives were confirmed in advertisements which played upon the saleable image of the private soldier.

The admiration of an ability to strike a balance between military development fostering civilization and the possession of martial virtues fending off the ravages of over-civilization, was not limited to British or colonial soldiers. The Japanese were a 'paragon' of virtue, a model to be emulated out of admiration, a perspective reflected in the fashion for all things Japanese which was particularly intense during the Edwardian period. Military development and victory on the battlefield were seen as the crucial indicators of the successful adoption of 'our' civilization by the Japanese. That the Japanese were seen in a positive manner can be demonstrated in the way that their generals and rankers were described in the press. Readers identified with them in the same way that they identified with British heroes. The Japanese General Kodama was described as the Lord Kitchener of Japan, the 'brains' of the army who thought while others slept, and, though perhaps slightly less favourably, General Oyama was the 'ugliest, wittiest and most popular man' in the country, seen as the 'Bobs' of Japan.[104] Similarly, Japanese troops were frequently referred to as 'Tommies' or 'the Japanese Tommy Atkins', and seen to possess the same martial virtues.[105]

Furthermore, these newspaper images of 'the soldier' reveal that the representations of civilization and martial virtues were not fixed. A nation or 'race' such as the Tibetans could display their admired martial qualities and indicate that they were a much more complex enemy and therefore a sophisticated civilization. Similarly, the adoption of European military dress and drill could illustrate the 'leap' from barbarism to civilization, fostering a deep admiration and desire for emulation. In addition, military success could change attitudes towards an enemy, showing that what appeared to be madness was quite sophisticated and rational military organization. The implications of this would have been that if military development and activity could act as a means for other 'races' to improve and avoid decay, they could also be employed at home, thus avoiding the fearful fate of Rome.

As a result of the changing image of 'the soldier', those volunteering for duty in 1914 and 1915 would have had few intellectual dilemmas in becoming soldiers themselves. Those who encouraged both their own sons and the sons of others would also have had little difficulty seeing them 'in a red coat'.

3

'The Woof and Warp of the Web of Life': The Depiction of the Use of Force

Introduction: 'Condy's Fluid'

In his examination of the way in which war was 'imagined' in 1914, Samuel Hynes cites Edmund Gosse, the Edwardian novelist and Librarian of the House of Lords, who wrote in October 1914 that war was 'the sovereign disinfectant, and its red stream of blood is the Condy's Fluid that cleans out the stagnant pools and clotted channels of the intellect'.[1] Hynes uses Gosse's perspective on war to indicate that the view of war as purifying and cleansing, and thus beneficial for decadent and lethargic England, was a 'widely held' belief in 1914. Hynes shows successfully that literature published during the early stages of the war indicated that, with all its privations and self-sacrifices, war was seen as the physical and spiritual opposite of Edwardian luxury. This, according to Hynes, was not simply the view of the 'Old Men' who spoke and wrote of war, but also the view of the young men who fought and died on the battlefield.[2] Rupert Brooke, one of those 'young men', supported this idea by writing in his famous poem, '1914', that the war had 'wakened us from sleeping' and enabled his contemporaries 'To turn as swimmers into cleanness leaping, Glad from a world grown old and cold and weary'.[3]

This view was not only held by the literary élite who wrote fiction and poetry concerning war. Military thinkers, both professional and others, also expressed these views in the years leading up to 1914. In studying the pre-1914 *Weltanschauung* concerning the degree to which society considered the use of military force as necessary or desirable, it is necessary to examine areas such as popular fiction and the ideas of duty and self-sacrifice passed on to students at schools and universities. In addition, attention should be given to the 'serious' non-fiction literature of military thinkers, and their attempts to assess the fundamental nature of war. In doing so, it is clear that by the late 1890s two arguments had arisen, both of which derived their impetus from the theories of people such as Charles Darwin. The first was that war was a natural state, and attempts to end it or suppress the instinct for warfare would be useless. In addition, warfare had become an integral economy and the end of war would be devastating, as armaments were a key industry and soldiers were a large body of men in employment. The second was more dependent on the laws of natural selection as applied to the advancement of nations. These thinkers professed the notion that nations, like biological species, needed to struggle in order to survive and become stronger, more advanced. The unfortunate side-effects of warfare were more than compensated by the benefits to society.[4]

However, assumptions that the ideas of these 'technical' writers simply spread downwards and outwards into other sections of society carry less weight. The dispatches of war correspondents were an important conduit for the expression of cultural ideas about warfare before 1914. War correspondents were able to authenticate their images of war through the belief that, as eye-witnesses, they conveyed the 'reality' of actual warfare, and that they therefore 'knew' of its beneficial nature.[5]

Yet, in order to study the way in which war correspondents conveyed ideas of actual warfare to readers and how they understood its utility, it is necessary to examine their accounts of war first-hand as they appeared in the pages of the newspapers, along with other sources of war imagery. A study of this form of imagery in the press will go some way to showing the prevailing perception of the use of force in Edwardian Britain, and the deeply entrenched image of war that European pacifist groups had to counter. These groups, which to a degree formed a growing and successful international movement from 1899 to 1914, were opposed to the dominant view of warfare. However, although their existence revealed that 'not everyone was engaged in creating the long and short-term causes of the Great War',[6] the main perception of war conveyed in newspapers was that war was a natural event, that it was beneficial, and that it was also desirable to the societies engaged in it.

'Elementary human nature': the image of war as natural

The debate instigated by the Tsar of Russia's call for a peace conference in 1898 involved a discussion of the position of armed conflict as a reflection of unalterable human nature, and as a natural part of human activity and interaction.[7] While the press took an active role in the debate itself, these same perceptions were utilized in the reporting and general discussion of warfare before 1914. War was seen not simply as an organic component of the human condition, something which could not be denied, but also a way of reinforcing the nature of masculinity and countering the 'infection' of effeminate values. In addition, weapons of war and their effects were also seen in terms of meteorological events found in nature: violent, yet a part of the natural world.

Part of the perception of warfare as a component of the human condition involved an image of war as an acceptable or at least natural form of personal interaction like an argument, physical violence or even bullying. These images were used as a basis for describing and accepting the conduct of states, personified through the creation and manipulation of metaphorical national figures. These figures enabled a direct comparison to be made between war and the way in which people naturally behaved. In this way, warfare, described by the *Illustrated London News* as the 'last argument of kings',[8] was seen as an extension of the diplomatic posturing conducted before hostilities. *Punch* gave visual expression to this perception in October 1899 in a cartoon entitled 'A Word to the Un-Wise', where a martial figure with a lance representing the Orange Free State stands between a bearded Transvaal farmer-figure with a rifle and a uniformed John Bull with a sheathed sword. In the caption, a stern John Bull says to the Orange Free State, 'Stand aside, young man – I've no quarrel with you!' This cartoon illustrated that the initial dispute between Great Britain and the Boers was thought to concern only the *Uitlanders* in the Transvaal, but the Orange Free State figure was depicted with his hand on the shoulder of the Transvaal farmer, showing the degree of solidarity between the Dutch Republics.[9] Yet the significance of this cartoon was not so much the degree to which it portrayed the alliance between the Republics, as that the relations between the Boers and the British which were soon to turn into full-scale war, were merely seen as a 'quarrel' between neighbours. Similarly, the pre-war phase of the disputes in conflicts as diverse as the Russo-Japanese War and the British invasion of Tibet, were also summarized on the outbreak of hostilities in articles headlined 'History of the Quarrel' and introduced as 'the story of the quarrel with Tibet...'.[10]

While the pre-war diplomatic phase was seen as interpersonal bickering between states, the actual conduct and pursuit of war was also depicted by newspapers as 'quarrelling'. In describing the Japanese surprise attack at Port Arthur which inaugurated the Russo-Japanese War, the *Clarion* felt that 'this quarrel is only the beginning of a struggle whose upshot no man can foretell'. Even large-scale battles fought with knowledge of the carnage were similarly depicted: *The Times* believed that Kuropatkin was 'determined to stand his ground and to fight the quarrel out to the finish' at Liaoyang. The issue here is not whether Kuropatkin did indeed make a stand to the finish at Liaoyang – he did not and retreated towards Mukden – but rather that a large-scale battle between modern armies set amid the enormous losses at Port Arthur could be seen as a mere 'quarrel' between countries or personalities. Even *Justice*, the paper which described the Italians as having a policy of 'brutality and violence', earlier saw that country's 'Tripolitanian adventure' as an 'international squabble', while similarly depicting the Second Balkan War as a 'quarrel among thieves'.[11]

This reduction of warfare to a minor interpersonal dispute was reinforced by other images, both visual and written. Cartoons in the press often extended the image of the diplomatic 'quarrel' and depicted war as a fist-fight between allegorical male figures representing nations. They were portrayed as either discarding coats and rolling up their sleeves or as having knocked an opponent down and given him a black eye. When the Boer War began, *Punch* depicted the change from diplomatic manoeuvring to actual warfare by showing Boer and British allegorical figures no longer merely 'quarrelling' verbally, but actually indulging in fisticuffs. The cartoon 'Plain English', published on the day war broke out, showed John Bull and a stereotypical Boer, both with their hats and coats removed and their sleeves rolled up, preparing for a fist-fight (Plate 2). In March 1900, the cartoon 'A Handsome Offer' showed the results of recent fighting by depicting the same two figures, but with John Bull standing over a 'considerably damaged' prostrate Boer. The Boer was made to say, 'I didn't like to mention it before, but now that "you've recovered your prestige", give me everything I want and all shall be forgiven!'[12]

War, like a fist-fight among men, was an acceptable means of regaining 'prestige' and 'honour' for the wrongs inflicted upon the protagonists. It was a method of showing the pre-war tensions and the wartime conflict, and, like fist-fighting, was acceptable and legitimate when all other options had been explored. Yet these cartoons showed only British victories in this manner, there being no comparable examples of John Bull receiving a black eye or a bruised body during 'Black Week', for example, as this would have trivialized the deaths of British soldiers and depicted the country as receiving a 'severe beating' from the Boers. However, while it was not acceptable to show the British losing their prestige in this way, it was allowable to depict them regaining it through pugilistic success.

This movement from verbal quarrel to physical brawl, representing the swing from the reporting of diplomatic to military activity was emphasized in written imagery. The *Penny Illustrated Paper* made this clear in an article concerning the developments in Manchuria just before the outbreak of war in February 1904. The article, entitled 'A Row But No Fight', compared the Japanese and the Russians to two individuals in a street row. The paper defined a 'street row' as the 'wordy' or diplomatic phase, where one of the protagonists 'expresses anxiousness to "knock corners off" his opponent or to "chaw him up"', and to grow increasingly loud and more verbally aggressive. However, the paper noted that a change occurred as 'the chicken-hearted one becomes quite transformed. A cold look comes into his eye and his lips press together as very deliberately he removes his coat and proceeds to roll up his sleeves.' This, then, was seen as the moment where war was most likely, as the Japanese no longer accepted the 'bluff threats' and 'absurd claims' of the Russians and 'took off their coats and rolled up their sleeves', indicating through this imagery that they were preparing to fight a major war in the Far East, and, just like the urban brawler, were displaying a 'regular fighting attitude'.[13] In this example, the natural breaking point of individuals, no matter how rational or peace-loving, where violence was most likely was used to explain the actions of states, personified as allegorical individuals, as they pursued their interests through the use of force.

In this regard, the perception of the British invasion of Tibet needs to be addressed. The expedition was seen by both critics and supporters as an example of a large and powerful military display of force. Justifications centred on border transgressions and the Russian threat, but the perception of the use of force in Tibet as personal interaction gave rise to the image of the Empire acting like a bully, particularly given the one-sided nature of the first encounter. It was an image and an awareness of themselves that the British needed to address. Edmund Candler, war correspondent for the *Daily Mail* in Tibet, saw the conduct of Britain as similar to the dilemma of a big boy at school, who submits to the 'attacks' of smaller boys rather than incur the reputation of a bully. The situation, according to Candler, would be intolerable, but when the big boy gives the little boy a thoroughly deserved 'thrashing', he is 'remonstrated' with by spectators who had no knowledge of the whole interaction.[14]

The perception of warfare as a physical fist-fight between individuals, whether equals or bullies, was reinforced by the extensive use of the term 'blow' to symbolize a variety of military activity, from a small engagement of troops to a significant large-scale battle, with the severity of the 'blow' indicating the deadliness and destruction of the encounter. In this way, the relatively unopposed landing of Italian forces in North Africa was announced as simply 'the first blow' in the war with Turkey, while the Japanese assault on the key Fort Erhlung was the 'most deadly blow yet delivered to Port Arthur', despite R. M. Connaughton's belief that it was a disastrous failure for the Japanese.[15] Here, a range of military actions were depicted as inflicting a 'blow', a form of physical violence, suggesting that the use of force held no more terror or destructiveness than a punch from an opponent in a fist-fight. Just as in a brawl, the tenacity and skill with which the opponents 'struck' each other on the battlefield was seen to be disruptive, but also natural and expected.

The representation of warfare as a part of human nature incorporated suggestions of its necessity and also its irrationality. The *Illustrated London News* reflected upon what it saw as the 'anti-war lobby' during the Boer War, seeing it as 'this blindness to elementary human nature'. The paper went further and suggested the necessity and acceptability of warfare in the extension and preservation of the Empire, as opposed to 'pacific chatter and brotherly love'.[16] While accepting that boys expressed natural 'fighting instincts' in buying war toys, *Lloyd's* felt that human beings possessed an irrational and indefinable instinct for warfare. The paper attempted to explain why the Balkan states, newly liberated from Turkish domination, fought one another in July 1913, but confessed to being 'at a loss'. It felt that the Balkan states could be compared to bees that go mad with 'swarming fever', and swarm together for no apparent reason, or to the example of a Sioux native North American who gave up his education and position in 'civilized society' to go 'raging away with his folk on the war-trail'. This 'swarming fever' theory was, according to the paper, a sudden and intense desire to fight, which was 'the only reason that would appeal to any sensible person'.[17] In this way, war was portrayed as an irrational event, but one which was part of nature and instinctive. Moreover, 'swarming fever' was a mass event, one which caused large numbers of people to engage and acquiesce in war with no apparent individual free will.

The idea that warfare was a natural part of life was present in the discussions of war found in the works of war correspondents. Bennett Burleigh, for example, asked rhetorically whether conflict was not 'the woof and warp of the web of life, and abiding peace but a dream of the idle nirvani?'[18] This might be seen as special pleading on the part of a man who derived his living from the reporting of conflict, justifying the voyeuristic nature of his profession, but his colleague and contemporary, Maurice Baring, expressed a similar view. Baring saw warfare as a gender-specific event, as if it affected only the direct participants, and saw it as a natural masculine exercise. He suggested that war 'is perhaps to man what motherhood is to woman, a burden, a source of untold suffering, and yet a glory'.[19] Thus fighting a war, though an event that could be painful and even deadly, was seen as the natural male equivalent of the female role in childbirth, both being natural and glorious. Men thus derived their function in society by fighting in wars just as females found their natural roles as producing and raising children.[20]

While warfare has been seen as the ultimate gendering activity informing the masculinity of the participants and the femininity of non-combatants,[21] it also defined the state of the nation. The concern was that effeminacy was 'infecting' the male population, creating a generation of 'degenerate' unmanly males who were either unable or, worse, unwilling to defend the honour of their country, due to a loss of masculine martial spirit. For military men like Field-Marshal Wolseley, participation in a war was a 'manly, elevating aspiration'. Indeed, in referring to the state of the country, Wolseley felt that 'war can alone revive its former manliness and restore the virility that had made its sons renowned'.[22] Masculinity could be reasserted and emphasized only through warfare after the legacy of the 'decadent' 1890s, characterized by the scandalous trial of Oscar Wilde in 1895 and the appearance of the decadent periodical, *The Savoy*, in 1896 further contributed to the anxiety that Britain was becoming increasingly feminized.[23] Both of these events remained central to the British consciousness through the 'cult of Oscar Wilde' in 1914 and well into the 1920s.[24]

The perception of war as a defining masculine activity, however, was most clearly expressed in the lengthy and regular feature articles written by 'Linesman', pseudonym for Colonel Maurice Grant,[25] in the *Daily Mail* during the Balkan Wars. 'Linesman' described the tense weeks before the war as the 'calm before the storm' when men waited for the 'trumpet call' of war, which was answered in a variety of ways: 'the veteran' packing his kit calmly, 'the coward' waiting like Fagin for the hangman's footfall, and 'the young man', presumably the majority of respondents, listening 'for the blast [of the trumpet] as for his wedding bell' making his participation in war a rite of passage into masculine adult life, a positive ritual to which he should look forward. Thus, the way in which men reacted to warfare, either with the calm experience of the veteran, the recreant reaction of the coward or the excitement of the young man, defined their level of masculinity.

In the feminine 'other', 'Linesman' saw a group unaware or unable to grasp the significance and beneficial role of warfare, and, indeed, one which sought to bring an end to war to the peril of society primarily because of its inability to understand it. In 'the wife', he saw a type able to grasp the idea that war was an important event, but was concerned solely with the safe return of her husband. For her, 'capitals and dynasties may fall like leaves so long as a certain broad-shouldered wight come back upright', indicating that 'Linesman' saw women as concerned with their own individual relationships rather than the 'important' issues and benefits of war. This was made clear in his discussion of 'the maiden' whom he said 'pushes her lover forth with one hand and holds him back with the other – pity that he cannot win the fame she wants for him without quite so much peril'. The capricious nature of women, as 'Linesman' saw it, was contrasted with the expected reactions of men. Women wanted their menfolk to gain fame and honour in a larger campaign whose 'significance' they barely understood, while also returning home safely. Just as women failed to see the significance of a particular war, they were equally unable to see warfare as a necessary and natural rite of passage.[26]

This was one aspect of what Samuel Hynes has called 'The Trouble With Women'. This 'trouble' not only included the most visible campaign for female suffrage, but also touched virtually all aspects of Edwardian society, including the perceived rise in the number of illegitimate children, the declining birth rate, and the increasing use of contraception. Hynes suggests links between these elements of Edwardian anxiety and the problem of Imperial Defence, making women, in the eyes of men, responsible for the decline and fall of England.[27] More specifically, 'Linesman' saw war as not only a gender-defining activity, but as the sole factor in preventing women from gaining equality with men. In his article, 'Women and War', he noted the female voice of 'rage and fury' raised against war, which was seen by women as pure 'folly'. Yet this voice of opposition to warfare, while initially futile, signified what he called 'the subtle infection of womanishness which is bringing nearly the whole of the world's manhood to womanish points of view on manly matters'.

This 'infection' of anti-war sentiment, symbolized by the Hague Conferences of 1899 and 1907,[28] would not only end war, but would emasculate men by reducing the significance of their gender role and end their 'superiority' to women. For 'Linesman', when women stopped war, they would gain true emancipation, 'for they will have annihilated the only thing that bars them from equality or perhaps superiority to the fighting man'.[29] The desire to see the end of war was seen to be set against the nature of masculinity; men defined themselves in terms of participation in warfare, a rite of passage and that which separated them from the feminine 'other'. Attempts to end warfare were perceived to be not only undesirable, but also contrary to nature.

'Linesman's' fears were well founded, as – associated with the rise of the 'New Woman' – was the increasing number of national and international councils of women in the 1890s, with England's founded in 1895. All of these groups used parliamentary procedures, which have been seen as legitimizing women's roles in politics. These groups were linked with democratic pacifism, for as Anne-Marie Käppeli has noted, the 'women question' and the 'peace question' were inseparable for contemporaries, since both were seen as 'a struggle for the power of law and against the law of power'. The first international demonstration of pacifist women was at The Hague in 1899 during the international peace conference.[30] If warfare can be seen as the ultimate gendering activity, as for the most part men do it and women do not, then the desire for the pacific settlement of disputes must be essentially emasculating.[31]

The perception of warfare as a natural component of life and identity was reinforced by the description of war and the effects of weaponry as meteorological events. Richard Holmes gives these terms only cursory attention, but he does demonstrate their ubiquity as similes used by soldiers to describe the effects of battle and bullets.[32] These same images were utilized extensively in the press to report battles. The approach of war was depicted as the 'gathering storm clouds', the geographic location of the battle was the 'storm centre', and the ending of hostilities as war clouds rolling away from the horizon.[33] The *Daily News* made this correlation clear when describing the final assault at Paardeburg in South Africa in a lengthy two-column article entitled 'With Lord Roberts'. The paper described in detail the lightning and thunder of 'one of the most wonderful storms ever remembered by old campaigners' which passed over the British positions. The paper stated that the rainstorm 'added an awe of its own to a scene already made awesome by a conflict of another kind'. Here, both storm and battle were seen as 'conflicts', with the meteorological event being overshadowed by the awe-inspiring battle, making both appear to be violent but natural and anticipated phenomena.[34]

These written images of storm and war clouds were supported by visual imagery found in the cartoons of *Punch*, and the *News of the World*, and the allegorical drawings of the *Illustrated London News*. They show gathering clouds and darkening skies to denote the approach of war, allegorical figures such as Britannia sheltering from the 'storm' of war, and the clearing skies and brightening landscapes of imminent peace.[35] These illustrations and cartoons implied that though the 'storm of war' was violent and harrowing, its destruction was minimal, in that the allegorical figures always survived the storm, and its duration fleeting, as the storms always gave way to bright sunshine and calm.

In a similar manner, the effects of weapons were also described in terms of natural phenomena. Readers were told of a 'hail of shrapnel', the 'rain of bullets' and the 'thunder of artillery' in reports of battle. Thus in its article 'The Fight on Spion Kop', the *Daily Mail* reported that the 'top of the hill was a perfect inferno, a hailstorm of bullets falling on it'.[36] More sublime were reports that 'an incessant rain of shells covered the entire line' or that there was an 'incessant shower of shrapnel' during the early stages of the Battle of Liaoyang.[37] These terms, like those discussed by Holmes, represented the intensity of the battle, the comparison to rain or hail signifying a high rate of fire. Yet, through the association with meteorological phenomena in nature, they also conveyed the impression that, like the weather, a battle was a violent display of power, and that it was natural, fleeting and, though possibly inconvenient, ultimately beneficial.

'We are not a decaying race': the image of war as beneficial

Much of the discussion and debate on the nature of war before 1914 centred around the ideas and theories of Charles Darwin, modified to include nations and military activity within the concept of the 'survival of the fittest'. This popular Social Darwinism propagated the idea that in order for civilization to advance and for nations to survive, they must compete with other nations, just as biological organisms must compete in the natural world. Furthermore, this competition was the only way in which nations could avoid the effects of 'over-civilization' and the ravages of 'racial degeneration'. While this debate occurred among military thinkers in specialist journals and books, the perspective of warfare found in newspapers prior to the First World War also conveyed the idea of warfare as a beneficial activity. They did this surreptitiously through latent imagery, both written and visual, and more directly through overt references to the positive benefits of war.

Historians who have recently examined the origins of the First World War have found space for discussions of the contributory role of these pervading Social Darwinist theories. Michael Howard listed the ideas of popular Social Darwinism as one of the pre-1914 trends which, though difficult to document, must be taken into account in determining the origin of the war.[38] Benjamin Kidd, exponent of Social Darwinism, wrote in his influential work *Social Evolution* in 1894 that the 'law of life has always been the same from the beginning – ceaseless and inevitable struggle and competition, ceaseless and inevitable progress'.[39] Stress has been put on the widespread belief in 'war as a test of national power and natural superiority' and Neo-Darwinian ideas as being common in Britain.[40] The ideas and observations of H. F. Wyatt, Honorary Secretary of the Navy League in 1905, have also been used to demonstrate the influence of Darwin's theories.[41] Wyatt's book, *God's Test By War*, published in 1912, highlighted his belief that competition was 'the process of the universe [which] made the fundamental condition of advance' and through which the 'higher and nobler' nations secured their superiority. He saw the culmination of international competition as warfare, 'the machinery by which national corruption is punished and national virtue rewarded'.[42]

The event which crystallized the idea that warfare was a test of national fitness was the Boer War. It was not simply the fact that the Boers put up a determined and partially successful resistance, but also the amount of time taken to subdue a 'handful of farmers', the high number of surrenders during battle and, perhaps most significantly, the alarming number of rejected volunteers. General Sir Frederick Maurice estimated that 60 per cent of those who volunteered were unfit for military duty. The fear that the British 'race' was deteriorating became a major concern and led to the creation of the Inter-Departmental Committee on Physical Deterioration. The Committee's report, submitted in August 1904, intended to allay the fears of 'racial deterioration' by emphasizing the influence of environmental conditions and poverty as the main engines of poor health. Yet, as Samuel Hynes has mentioned, the mere existence of a report on 'physical deterioration' gave the idea more immediate currency in Edwardian society.[43]

Newspaper reports of war throughout this period displayed similar perspectives on the utility of warfare not simply as expressions of struggle and competition, but also as a means to curtail the ravages of racial degeneration. In this way, the manner in which war was presented was informed not only by the defeats in the Boer War, but by the resulting discussion and anxiety represented by the Inter-Departmental Committee's report. Newspapers depicted warfare in ways similar to Kidd and Wyatt: as a form of 'struggle', a 'tremendous struggle', a 'great struggle', where two combatants met to determine which was the better led, the most efficient nation, and the most spirited side.

The *Daily News* referred to the Russo-Japanese War as the 'titanic struggle' not simply because of the scale of the war, but also because of what was seen as the significance of the war with its racial, political and martial overtones. The paper suggested that defeat at Mukden revealed that 'the simple, unvarnished truth has been forced home at the point of a bayonet', showing the extent to which Russia had become corrupted.[44]

The redemptive nature of the idea of struggle was discussed in the *Daily Mail* in the fourth month of the Boer War. The paper linked war and economic competition, labelling them 'the trials through which the Empire is passing' and suggesting that war was indeed beneficial as it led to national unity and inculcated ideals of self-sacrifice. This redemptive quality was developed further in a leading article entitled 'The Blessings of War', in which the paper felt that the war was a double blessing 'if it makes us re-examine the bases of our national life, ruthlessly dig away all that is decayed or doubtful, and place things on a sound footing'. While the long years of 'peace and tranquillity' had resulted in a slothful lack of preparedness, 'out of the present strife and conflict shall emerge an Empire stronger, more fully prepared, amply equipped against the worst our foes can do against us'.[45]

The idea that warfare was the one event which could halt the advancing and terminal state of deterioration was commonplace. *Lloyd's* suggested that while the Boer War was the most formidable war Britain had ever fought, the test had been beneficial in that it showed that the country's sense of security had been misguided and the degree to which the 'great heart' of the Empire had been suffering 'from fatty degeneration'.[46] The *News of the World* concurred in a reflective leading article soon after the pronouncement of peace, ending the war with the Boers. It felt that Britain had entered the war 'with a light-heartedness born of ignorance and too much prosperity', but had soon found itself 'compelled to put forward every energy, to send our bravest and best to the seat of war, and battle for very existence'. The result was that 'we have emerged not only triumphant, but stronger and more fitted for the duties of Empire'. With victory over the Boers, 'the inevitable had come to pass, however, only after a struggle which tested severely the character of the race'.[47]

These papers echoed and reinforced the ideas of Karl Pearson, the leading Social Darwinist and eugenicist, who, speaking later that same year, said that the struggle for existence involved 'suffering, intense suffering'. For Pearson, the redeeming feature of warfare was that without it, 'mankind will no longer progress', for 'it is the fiery crucible out of which comes the finest metals'. In countering the early Social Darwinists who concentrated on the struggle between individuals rather than social groups, Pearson stated that the nation 'kept up to a high pitch of external efficiency by contest, chiefly by way of war with inferior races...'.[48]

The *Daily Mirror* made the connection between participation in warfare and racial health in an article which appeared five months before the Inter-Departmental Committee's report was published, entitled 'Our Three Little Wars'. The article stated firmly that 'England's' military interventions in Tibet, Nigeria and Somaliland were proof that the British were in fact not bereft of the martial spirit. Its leading article concluded: 'that England is at war shows an amount of energy and superabundant spirits that go a long way to demonstrate that we are not a decaying race'. Despite the fears of degeneration, the Boer War had 'not tired us of fighting, and this shows that we have the elasticity of a great people'.[49] Notwithstanding the protests to the contrary, like Hynes's assessment of the Inter-Departmental Committee, the very existence of an article such as this and the repeated denial of deterioration, suggests that the fear of racial decay was current. Indeed, the idea conveyed is that these commentators protested too much, attempting to convince themselves and to reinforce their readers' perception that though Britain had been blind to the corrupting influence of prolonged periods of peace and prosperity, the Boer War had been a timely reminder to beware of racial decay and over-civilization. Most importantly, however, these articles indicate that war was perceived as an activity which was beneficial to society and the 'race', and an acceptable and necessary antidote to degeneration.

While thinkers such as Jean de Bloch, Norman Angell, and Jacques Novicow predicted 'the natural decline of warfare',[50] newspapers covering wars in the Edwardian period did not perceive warfare as a dysgenic activity. Warfare was not seen as having a negative effect on the 'race' by exposing the young and the healthy to death and disease, despite Paul Crook's contention that 'peace biology' flourished in the western world before 1914.[51] The *Daily News* came close on one occasion when the siege of Port Arthur was developing and the Battle of Liaoyang beginning. It described the war as 'the ghastly and dangerous struggle in the Far East', commenting on rumours of a peace negotiation that 'we should have nothing but praise for any attempt to stop this hateful and meaningless struggle'.[52] H. F. Wyatt would have disagreed, for he believed that all wars had a purpose, as the test of ethical and moral superiority. He stated that even on the battlefield, 'where horrors piled high with the dead, the dying and the wounded', the ethical quality of soldiers tended always to produce military efficiency, and thus victory.[53] Even *Justice* thought that there were 'not un-numerous wars that have been beneficial to mankind'.[54] Though these 'benefits' of war discussed by the paper were political and not 'racial', it nevertheless did not see warfare as a 'genetic disaster', and it used common terms such as 'struggle' found in other newspapers to describe war.

The association between warfare and health was frequently made in the press. The *Daily Mail* saw the conduct of war in the early stages of the Boer War in the same way as early medical practices. Formerly, doctors who knew nothing of influenza would merely treat the symptoms rather than the causes of the disease, just as the British were fighting the war piecemeal by attempting to raise the sieges of Ladysmith, Kimberley and Mafeking separately with 'special treatment' or 'powder' for each one. This strategy was seen to improve once 'Dr. Lord Roberts' had 'been called in', demonstrating that he would ease the symptoms by relieving the garrisons, but would 'go to the root of the matter and attack the microbe' by conducting warfare successfully and scientifically.[55] Thus, war itself was not the microbe to be attacked and eliminated, but rather the inefficient conduct of war. In this way, soldiers, like doctors, were not seen as eradicators of contagion, but merely professionals who should conduct their operations more scientifically and effectively.

This written image was reinforced by visual images, such as a cartoon published in the *News of the World* just prior to the outbreak of war in October 1899. In this cartoon, entitled 'Violent Diseases Require Violent Remedies', in which Colonial Secretary Joseph Chamberlain was portrayed as a doctor holding a large pill labelled 'reforms', taken from the 'cabinet meeting pill box', and offering it to his patient, President Paul Kruger of the Transvaal. The patient, surrounded by medicines and looking nervous, said, 'Why Doctor, that's a much bigger pill than the one I wouldn't swallow last week!', to which the Doctor replies, 'Yes, I know, but your case is getting worse, and unless you swallow it at once, it may mean an operation.'[56] Thus, the reforms demanded by the British Government to allow equal rights to the *Uitlanders* were portrayed as a bitter, almost impossible pill for the Boers to swallow, as to acquiesce to the demands would cause more disruption than they were willing to sanction. The threat of war, neatly referred to by both the medical and the military term, 'operation', was seen as the only alternative to the ill-health of the Boers. In this way, war was linked to a positive undertaking, a necessary medical operation, rather than to a negative destructive military campaign.

In a similar vein, the war correspondent for the *Daily Telegraph*, Bennet Burleigh spoke of war as a positive medical operation in his book, *Empire of the Sun or Japan and Russia at War 1904–5*. In describing the war, Burleigh looked at the beneficial nature of war through the example of the war in the Far East, suggesting that war, 'terrible and cruel as it is, which shocks all civilized senses in England, may, like the old priest's sacrificial weapon, or, better, the modern surgeon's knife, be the means of saving men and races'.[57] Here Burleigh reasserts the perception that warfare was perceived as having beneficial repercussions, and that it was necessary to see beyond the destruction and the horror to witness the facets of war which were to the benefit of a culture or society.

The concept of warfare as a disease to be studied and treated was also proposed during the Balkan Wars by 'Linesman', who compared the inevitability and frequency of war to the regular outbreaks of pestilence. 'Linesman' felt that war, like plague, must be studied and understood as natural and periodic, for he believed that it was a continual and popular misconception that the previous war was to be the very last war. Furthermore, he believed that the total eradication of war and disease was perhaps not as beneficial as it might appear, using the introduction of rabbits to Australia as support for his argument. He seemed to offer a Malthusian approach to the roles of war and disease, seeing them as ways of stabilizing the population and thus improving the quality of the species, be they rabbit or human. For 'Linesman', it was a matter of incontestable fact that: 'peace may and has ruined many a nationality with its surfeit of everything except those tonics of privation and sacrifice. But the severest war wreaks little practical injury.'[58] Thus, the eradication of war was not the aim, for its purpose, though destructive, ensured a stronger, more vibrant nation. Like plague and pestilence, warfare was seen as a natural and periodic outbreak which kept populations down and acted as a 'tonic' to prevent the ruin of nations.

Advertisers were not slow to utilize this imagery of warfare as a healthy, medicinal activity. It seems that 'the enemy' was seen as a suitable metaphor for influenza in particular, as Bovril used it as an image in an advertisement three days after the Japanese attacked Port Arthur. The advertisement capitalized on the undeclared surprise attack, suggesting that the stealthy but relentless Russians were akin to the onset of influenza and that precautions should be taken in order to prevent the illness from developing. The advertisement stated that ' "Twice armed is he that hath his quarrel just. Thrice armed is he that gets his blows in furst": Bovril enables one to get in the first blow at influenza, without waiting for the enemy to attack.'[59] War was thus seen as having medicinal qualities in that, like Bovril, it countered the actions of the enemy, leaving the body strong and disease free. In addition, the impression made by comparing war to Bovril was that war, like Bovril, was to be seen as a helpful, familiar home remedy, and a good element to use against ailments and to prevent deterioration.

'A much needed lesson': the image of war as desirable

Closely aligned to the image of war as beneficial, was the perception of war as desirable, in that not only was war to be seen as good for the nation and the 'race' because of the rewards of competition and struggle, but it was also a desirable event for other, more practical reasons. There were many references to the assertion that warfare was an acceptable and desirable method of settling disputes between nations and that military action constituted suitable forms of retribution or punishment of transgressors of laws, treaties, or what was perceived to be acceptable behaviour. In this regard, warfare was seen as a legitimate means of exercising coercive power, comparable to other, more familiar institutions of social control, such as the police and schools. Yet warfare was also seen in a more positive manner, as methods of generating a sense of identity through the rewards of labour and an awareness of history.

The idea of war as the legitimate means by which states conducted their policies regarding the use of force had as one of its major proponents Carl von Clausewitz and his theories. Like Darwin, his ideas were modified and interpreted in the late-nineteenth century in order to suit the purposes and perceptions of his readers.[60] Indeed, his famous dictum that war was merely the continuation of politics by other means, proposed in his book *On War*, was seen by at least some late-Victorians and Edwardians as a means by which war was made acceptable as a method of settling differences.[61]

The perception of war as an acceptable arbiter of disputes between nations was also made obvious in the newspaper reports of conflict before 1914. The *Daily Mail* published a leading article on the day of the Boer invasion asking 'Who Will Rule South Africa?', believing that the choice was clearly divided between either the British or the Dutch, but that the question was to be 'committed to the arbitrament of battle'.[62] The *Illustrated London News* agreed in a comment made a few days later, putting the onus squarely on the Boers, stating that 'the Boers court the arbitrament of shot and shell. They must take the consequences'. The paper did not change its views on war as an acceptable arbiter, despite the horrors it produced. In a double-page drawing entitled, ' "The Savage Arbitrament of Arms": Turkish Troops Under Rapid Concentrated Shrapnel Fire at Lule Burgas', the Turks were shown retreating as the Bulgarians pressed their attack, causing large numbers of casualties. Later, the paper published a similar drawing, stating in the caption that the modern battlefield 'cannot but be filled with distressing scenes which mark the stern arbitrament of war'.[63] In this way, warfare was perceived as a 'stern' but acceptable arbiter between disagreeing parties, with the associated horrors and destruction as merely 'the consequences' of the process of settling disputes. The use of force in this manner was seen as acceptable because, given Wyatt's concept of God's test by war, those who were successful at war were those who possessed the morally correct virtues. It was seen not as a matter of 'might makes right', but rather as 'right always tended to create might'.[64]

Those who lost in the arbitration of war were seen to have been punished for challenging their superior opponents and losing. Death and wounding of the vanquished was punishment, not only for the transgressions of the rules of war, but also for more simple actions such as occupying an exposed position, thereby showing a lack of military efficiency. Thus the *Illustrated London News* believed that the burning of a farmhouse and the removal of cattle by Canadian troops was a correct and proper means of 'punishment' for the Boer 'perpetrators' who abused the white flag. Similarly, after a 'brief tussle' with Major-General Horace Smith-Dorien, the Boers who moved into open positions were 'severely punished' by rifle fire.[65] While there was some debate regarding the appropriate degree and circumstances of 'punishment', the idea itself was acceptable. For example, *The Times* believed that the British expedition to Tibet acted with 'determination and firmness' in its dealings with the Tibetans who hid behind the wall at Guru. However, the *Manchester Guardian*, while not challenging the general legitimacy of the use of force, felt that the killing of 300 poorly armed Tibetans was a 'very heavy penalty to exact for blowing off a Sikh's jaw', the incident which instigated the battle.[66] Yet, as the *Glasgow Herald* reminded its readers, the goal of the operation was to inflict punishment and to inculcate a 'wholesome dread of the power of the invader', and thus initiate a change in Tibetan behaviour.[67]

In addition to individual battles being considered a form of punishment, they might also be seen as more serious examples of chastisement, depending on the degree of suffering inflicted by the victor. The Oasis Massacre, where the Italians committed wide-scale atrocities against the Arabs outside Tripoli, was seen by the *Daily Mail* as 'A Terrible

Retribution', a significant form of 'punishment' inflicted on the Arabs for almost defeating the elite Bersaglieri Regiment. Though the paper condemned the Italians for not taking the correct military precautions, thereby showing themselves to be inefficient soldiers, it was clear in its vision of military force as a form of punishment. Similarly, the defeat of the Tibetans was described by the *Daily Express* as 'Swift Retribution', as the paper considered 'how the Tibetans wrought their own undoing'. The paper described how after 15 years of negotiation, the British were going to advance to Gyantse. When the initial shot was fired at Guru, 'all the Tibetans drew their swords and rushed at the troops'. It was for this defiance that they were 'punished'.[68]

The image of punishing a vanquished enemy because they displayed a lesser form of military efficiency and challenged the morally superior victor, was extended to include the concept of criminalization. John Gooch has mentioned how military thinkers attempted to avoid the suggestion that war was to the nation what crime was to the individual, that war was, by its nature, a crime.[69] Yet images of crime and the criminal were pervasive in the press, the vast majority viewing military force as desirable and comparing the military forces to the police in the use of coercive powers against recalcitrant enemies portrayed as criminals. War itself was not seen as a criminal activity, but as a positive, desirable enterprise used to encourage and ensure correct behaviour. In the early stages of the Boer War, the British presence in South Africa was portrayed as such a policing activity. The *Daily News*, believing that the army would be conducting a 'piece of police work', interpreted the intervention as a desirable, stabilizing organization of law and order, with the Boers as the criminals. After their victories, the Boers were lauded for their display of martial prowess, but nevertheless, the idea of them as 'criminal' was still current. The *Daily Mail* professed admiration for the Boer stand at Paardeburg, yet still declared that further resistance was 'criminal'. Indeed, the paper quoted several captured Boers who commented on General Cronje's persistence, stating that they felt it was 'simply murder'.[70]

Military force was justified by several papers through the perception of the enemy as criminals. The *Daily Express* did not describe the Tibetan general who opposed the British forces at Guru by his rank or position, but as the 'ringleader' who paid the penalty for his crime of inciting the 'mob' of Tibetans to fire on the British. The *Daily Mail* concurred, justifying the British expedition by comparing the Tibetans to burglars who had been entering Indian territory without permission. The paper explained that 'we do not pardon the burglar or criminal because he is of puny stature or weak in health'.[71] Thus, both papers justified the invasion of Tibet and explained away the one-sided nature of the war in Tibet by showing that the natives were criminals with whom the British forces had to deal. The fact that the forces of law and order were overwhelming in comparison was of little consequence, just as the relationship between the criminal and the police was weighted in favour of the police. For as the *Daily News* argued in explaining the initially unequal nature of the war against the Boers, 'the contest between law and order is often an unequal one; the organized forces of the police are immeasurably the stronger...'. The paper explained that, just like the conduct of the police, the British in South Africa were 'employed not for glory, but of necessity', pointing out that the war was not to be seen as a 'prize fight', but a matter of 'police work', where the size and strength of the perpetrator did not matter – only that transgressions had been made.[72] This opinion changed, of course, when the Boers were seen to be more than a match for the British forces.

The image of the Imperial enemy as criminal was emphasized by the description of battle. The Highlanders at the Modder in South Africa were said to have suffered 'murderous fire from the Trenches' where the Boers were hiding, and elsewhere, British troops were inflicted with 'murderous musketry fire'.[73] While the term 'murderous' here referred to the intensity of the fire from the enemy and its effect, it also suggested indirectly that the Boers were criminals, for only murderers inflict murderous fire. Thus the use of force was once again justified and seen as desirable to subdue criminal or anti-social activity.

Yet there were no calls in the newspapers examined for a supernational or international police force. Individual states were seen to perform the role of policeman adequately, especially in their Imperial setting, and there was thought to be no practical alternative to 'civilized' states making war on each other. The *Morning Post*, commenting on the Russo-Japanese War after the Japanese victory at the Yalu, criticized the Belgian economist Gustave de Molinari's suggestion for an 'international policeman'. De Molinari believed that though warfare had had a positive benefit in the past, defending settled, civilized societies from attack by barbaric hordes, it had no place in a modern, secure Europe. The race for armaments was therefore unnecessary and threatened to drain the accumulated capital that the states of Europe had struggled to acquire. But the paper dismissed the idea, maintaining that states were not like individuals, and it defended the idea of war as beneficial to racial development, hinting that to police war would be to limit its beneficial influences. The paper declared that 'if [states] shall quarrel, there is nothing for it but that they should fight it out'.[74]

However, even the pacifist community was opposed to the concept of an international police force, despite support for the idea from the Dutch professor of international law, Cornelius van Vollenhoven. Pacifist groups feared that a 'police force' of this type if sent into a European country, would initiate the major war it was intended to stop.[75] The hostility to de Molinari's ideas in the conservative, middle and upper-middle-class *Morning Post* might have arisen from his views that the longevity of the desire to 'fight it out' depended upon the entrenched class interests of the military, political and civil servant caste who represented interests opposed to the end of war. To break the dominance of this class, according to de Molinari, required the elimination of elites, not through revolution, but through the creation of an 'international order', a proposal which the *Morning Post*'s readers would find unpalatable.[76]

Similar to the perception of war as a relationship between policeman and criminal, was the depiction of war as the desirable conveyance of instruction in the manner of a teacher–pupil relationship in schools. Like the concept of crime, warfare was not seen as a destructive or anti-social activity, but as the desirable inculcation of proper behaviour and reason, acting as a positive means of social control. Gillian Sutherland, quoting Emile Durkheim, has noted that the activities of schools in general can be seen, in essence, as means of socialization.[77] However, the late-nineteenth century saw changes in emphasis and increasing militarization which formed a link between the desirable benefits of education and the use of military force. In mid-century, the emphasis in public schools changed from scholarship to the creation and formation of 'character', through rigorous discipline, a spartan environment and ideals of self-sacrifice. Thus, pupils were learning that discipline and punishment were means by which their 'character' was formed. In addition, the increasing popularity of cadet corps also showed that military training and activity were acceptable means of exercising character-building.[78]

Similarly, the Church and Board schools have been described as seeing themselves as 'disciplining institutions *per se*', where discipline was compared to that found in the military itself. This connection between school and military discipline has been made, citing compulsory sitting, standing still, taking up pens 'by number', and the increasing use of military drill as a form of physical exercise.[79] It is not only that the increasing militarization in schools was influential in the pre-Boer War period, but that the desirable activity of instruction fostered and inculcated in schools was used as an image of military force.

At the same time that schools were increasingly militarized, military activity was perceived as a desirable form of education. It was in the Imperial setting where natives were seen as children requiring the attention of the Imperial power, where the image of war as 'lesson' was most prominent in the press. The actions on the Tuna plain and at Guru in Tibet were seen by the *Glasgow Herald* as a use of force that 'may have taught the Tibetans a much needed lesson . . .'. The paper interpreted the British 'victory' in reaching Lhasa as a lesson which 'will receive its appropriate interpretation from peoples who understand the "strong man armed", even if they do not love him'.[80] That 'lesson' taught to the Tibetans through military force was outlined by the *Daily Express*, which felt that the 'Lamas of Lhasa', who displayed their 'arrogant ignorance and overweening folly', 'must learn that they are not beyond the long arm of the British raj', and that their seclusion was not due to British fear or weakness.[81]

The opposition press also used the image of the 'lesson' to denote military activity, mocking the notion that the Tibetans sought or required instruction, while also re-emphasizing the image's currency. The *Manchester Guardian* was critical in a leading article published after the Karo La and Gyantse attacks, stating that 'the Tibetans are not quick at learning the folly of defending their native country, and the British mission has had to give them another sanguinary "lesson" '. Indeed, the paper went on to state that: 'the assumption that one or two experiences of the superiority of maxims to leather cannon would reduce the Tibetans to a peaceful submissive acknowledgement of the pleasures of Anglo-Indian friendship and the blessings of Anglo-Indian trade, continues to be falsified by the course of events.'[82] The indemnity imposed upon the Tibetans in the Anglo-Tibetan Convention, set at Rs75,000,000 (£500,000),[83] was also ridiculed. The *Clarion*, with characteristic irony, stated that the overwhelming indemnity was only 'right and proper', for 'one learns the value of wisdom when it has to be paid for. They ought to have known we were doing them good'. The *Lancaster Guardian* concurred, noting that: 'we make them pay for the lesson we have taught them, unwilling recipients of instruction though they were.'[84] These statements of opposition to the expedition and the uneven nature of the use of force in Tibet show that the image of war as a lesson was widespread and inadvertently reinforced the very image which they were attempting to counter through their irony.

The image of the field of battle as classroom where military lessons were given to the enemy was also conveyed visually in cartoons. The *News of the World* depicted Lord Roberts as a friendly figure leading two small boys, the Orange Free State and the Transvaal, off to Madam Britannia's Boarding School, saying, 'Come along now my little fellows, and don't be silly; you'll learn all kinds of nice things you never knew before...'. Here, the idea of inculcating the Boers with British values through assimilation was suggested, but in addition, the basis of that desirable process was the 'lesson' taught by military force.[85]

These images of school lessons taught to an Imperial enemy were not limited to the British. While the *Daily Mail* condemned the Italians for the manner in which they were unprepared for an attack by the Arabs and Turks, it nevertheless believed that 'the [Italian] General Staff had no alternative but to give this horrid lesson'. That 'lesson' was widely denounced as the Oasis Massacre. Similarly, for the *Illustrated London News*, the execution of Oasis Arabs who were thought to be in breach of international law by attacking the Italians, was 'a most serious lesson to the Arabs...'.[86]

Just like an educational institution, the purpose of these military engagements or 'lessons' was to teach the opposition reasonable behaviour. Before the invasion of Natal, the *Daily Mail* was confident that if war did break out General Buller would be able easily to bring the Republics 'to reason'. Similarly, the paper discussed the value of 'military promenades' in Somaliland to bring the 'Mad Mullah' 'to reason'.[87] Thus war, an activity which was seen to be as irrational and inexplicable as the sudden swarming of bees, was the means by which 'reason' and correct behaviour was instilled into an enemy. In this way, it was seen as a positive activity to be sought rather than as a destructive one to be avoided, desirable for the edification and improvement of the enemy.

Yet warfare was not just desirable for its effects on the enemy, for it was seen to have similarly positive influences on the British soldiers as well. In the *mentalité* of the Victorians, next to 'God', 'work' was the most popular word in the Victorian vocabulary. This, in a commercial society, is not surprising, for through 'work' lay the path to success and prosperity, idleness being an 'unforgivable – economic – sin'. However, 'work' was also seen as a virtue in itself, as it was the means by which one developed natural talents, and was the measurement of advancement towards 'human perfection'. Indeed faith in work almost superseded 'actual faith' in religion for many Victorians.[88]

In this way, the term 'work' as applied to the use of force can be seen to have had several meanings. At one level, describing the conduct of soldiers as 'work' conveyed the impression of intense labour; soldiering as a difficult physical activity. However, combat as 'work' also signified a belief that a desirable influence was in operation on those indulged in it. The Shropshires, after having been relieved by the Gordon Highlanders, were said to have done 'good work' in the days before Cronje's surrender at Paardeburg. Their efforts were seen not only as successful in contributing to the first major British victory of the war, but also as having positive effects on the soldiers themselves.[89]

Moreover, the various images of work utilized in newspapers tended to correspond to the forms of labour familiar to their readers, particularly in conveying visual images of warfare. The working class *News of the World*, for example, used the image of a building-site carter and a gardener to represent the labours of Kitchener in South Africa, particularly in the British attempts to capture Boers during the guerrilla phase of the war. In a cartoon entitled 'Re-Assured', the paper depicted John Bull and Lord Salisbury, as 'Head Ganger', on a building site, watching Kitchener dumping cartfuls of miniature dead Boers into a pit, while the 'Head Ganger' said, 'Bless yer 'eart sir, there's no call to worry. The job's a going on just as fast as it can, and our carter there is a-doing all as mortal man can fur to get through with it.' While the visual image has significant and disturbing resonances for the late-twentieth century observer raised on images of the Holocaust, the cartoon represented the contemporary obsession, particularly and strongly stressed in the *News of the World*, with counting the number of Boers captured and 'carted' off the battlefield to camps or exile. This emphasis on numbers of Boers caught was conveyed in other specifically labouring forms of work portraying Kitchener as a short-order cook whose many pots are boiling over, a master of a fishing smack pulling in full nets, and as a rat-catcher with a record catch for the week.[90] A more positive image of war as a form of labour was presented when Kitchener was transferred to India after the end of the Boer War. The paper depicted this move as being similar to a gardener doing 'spade work' in another part of the 'estate', indicating that military activity was a difficult form of labour, but one which was creative and brought 'wild' areas of the world under controlled 'cultivation'.[91]

The same tendency to use work imagery can be found among the middle and upper-class papers, reflecting not so much an image of physical labour as one of business or office work. In its description of the early phases of the Russo-Japanese War, the *Morning Post* praised the Japanese for conducting 'a business-like campaign' on the battlefield, indicating that the paper believed this to be similar to the way in which its readers conducted their affairs as a desirable and profitable operation.[92] *Punch*, like the *News of the World*, saw Kitchener as a person employed in an occupation, but, as in the *Morning Post*, not in a form of physical labour. A cartoon published in August 1901 showed warfare as the opposite of leisure, with Kitchener, reading the latest news from England outside his tent, lamenting, 'House up! Grouse plentiful! Yacht-racing in full swing! I wonder when *we* shall get *our* holiday?' The traditional events which symbolized the beginning of the summer holi-day season for the middle and upper classes, recess for Parliament, shooting season, and boat-races, were contrasted with the 'work' Kit-chener and his soldiers, represented by a sentry standing nearby, were still undertaking in South Africa. Similarly, the place of employment was expected to be an office behind a desk, as a cartoon, 'Incorrigible', suggested.[93] The idea of war as 'work', a term associated with the con-veyance of positive effects on those who were employed in it, reinforced the image of war as a desirable activity, and was presented as modes which were most familiar and acceptable to readers, irrespective of their position in society.

A similar perspective which contributed to the image of war as a desirable activity was the belief that war was an important factor in the formation of historical consciousness. Readers were aware that when they saw reports of battle in the paper, they were observing the forging of 'history'. Significant battles were seen to fill chapters in a country's or the world's history book, either because of the strength of character and resolve they displayed or because they represented a victory which was felt to be of future significance. The siege at Port Arthur, for example, was described in *The Times*, through the corres-pondent of the *New York Herald*, as an historical event. The article cited General Heinsmann who wrote of the Russians that 'even if they can no longer defend the walls crumbling about their ears, the defenders of Port Arthur will have written one of the most glorious pages of Russian history'.[94] Despite the fact that Port Arthur was a defeat for the Russian army, its defence, believed initially to have been conducted with honour and with great privation, was seen as significant enough to contribute to Russian history.

The Russo-Japanese War itself was similarly seen as of historical importance, because of the scale of casualties and the way in which it was fought, but mainly because of the significance of a non-European victory over a large and powerful European Empire. The perspective was not only military but also political and racial, as it was feared that the effect of a Japanese victory would end the illusion of white superiority over the other races and mark not only the beginning of a Japanese Empire, but also the end of the white Empires, particularly the British in India. Japanese victories were more than simply military events, for they signified a shift in the power structure in the Far East. Even before their commencement, the papers recognized that particular battles, such as those at Liaoyang and Mukden, were going to be of significance, because of the scale of the conflicts and the potential for destroying the Russian armies. As Kuropatkin retreated from the rapidly advancing Japanese, the *Daily News* predicted that a 'fierce historical battle is certain', and indicated that its historical importance rested not simply on its ferocity but on the impact a Japanese victory would have on issues beyond the war. The *News of the World* described that same battle as 'The Battle of an Epoch', suggesting that the battle might contribute to the 'world's annals'.[95]

Yet it was not simply large-scale battles conducted in wars of great importance which were seen to be of historical significance. Smaller frontier wars also contributed to the annals of a nation through the display of determination, loyalty and bravery of the participants in both victory and defeat. In a leading article, the *Daily News* described Plunkett's defeat at Gumburu in Somaliland as a 'disaster which everywhere created profound disquietude'. Yet an article by A. G. Hales in the same issue proclaimed that even though the British knew of the vast concentration of the enemy's forces, they still attempted to cross the desolate stretch of desert to confront the Mullah with 'a handful of men'. This, for Hales, was a source of amazement and though the pursuit led to a major British defeat, he stated boldly, 'that is how we make history'.[96] For this reason, victory and defeat had the same impact. A force could be annihilated, such as that under Plunkett, but if it did not panic and died to the last man, displaying those qualities which were deemed important and valuable, then the action, even though a military blunder and defeat, would be considered 'historic'.

Conclusion: 'as swimmers into cleanness leaping'

It is clear that the view of warfare as natural, beneficial, and desirable was not merely a minority view held by the 'Old Men', who wrote about war from the distance of their advancing years, or the amateur and professional military experts. These views found expression in a range of representative newspapers written for diverse social classes, indicating that readers from a myriad of social backgrounds perceived warfare in similar ways. Their images might have varied to take into account their experiences, such as the various images of war as 'work', but the essential perspective of conflict and its desirability was, as Samuel Hynes suggests, widely held before 1914. By that time, war was seen as a means to escape the ravages of luxury and sloth, and to brush away the cobwebs of a crusty, somnolent society. Gosse's concept of war as disinfecting the 'stagnant pools' of the intellect was supported by those 'young men', like Brooke, who volunteered for active service.

While examinations of pacifist activity throughout the nineteenth century are correct in suggesting that there were organizations that did not contribute to the origins of the First World War, their impact in relation to the reporting of war in newspapers was minimal. Their message concerning the uselessness of war, its horrors, and its economically catastrophic potential did not alter the essentially positive image of warfare. Similarly, movements which stressed the dysgenic nature of combat were equally unable to influence the perception of war as beneficial to the racial, biological and mental health of participants and their societies.

Those who considered and read reports about Imperial and 'civilized' war in the Edwardian period, saw it as a positive experience for both sides engaged in it. It was not a genetic, cultural or nihilistic disaster, but the opposite. The images in the newspapers convey the perception of the use of force prevalent in 1914, as young men willingly sought to indulge in the activity, and as the remainder of British society acquiesced and encouraged them. The dominant perception of war was that it was not such a terrible event and that it would likely bring with it positive benefits to those engaged in it individually and as members of a nation.

4
'The Great Game of War': The Image of War as Sport and Hunting

Introduction: 'a sort of glorified football match'

The anti-war campaigner Norman Angell noted in 1910 that the British saw 'the spectacle of war [as] even more attractive than the spectacle of sport. Indeed, our Press treats it as a sort of glorified football match'. In doing so, Angell touched upon not only the common perception of warfare as a game, but also the role of the newspapers in propagating that image.[1] The image of war as a sporting event or as hunting has a long and persistent history, as both war and sport have been seen as similar and intertwined, with one of the most obvious connections being the depiction of sport as suitable training for warfare. The elements of these associations have existed in Britain at least since the reign of Richard I and the importation of the French practice of staging tournaments. The '*mêlée*' has been perceived as virtually indistinguishable from actual combat, and continued to be used as a description of warfare well into the nineteenth and twentieth centuries.[2] The medieval tournament and its accompanying ritual significance enjoyed a revival in the form of nineteenth-century neo-chivalry, which showed how 'gentlemen' were expected to live and die, based upon such diverse influences as the Eglinton Tournament in 1839, the concept of 'muscular Christianity', the character-forming public schools, and the paintings of the Pre-Raphaelites.[3]

Hunting was another activity which was seen to associate war and sport. It too was portrayed as suitable training for military operations by encouraging not only proficiency with horse and weapon, but also a martial temperament where the vital characteristics of courage, calm and coordination were inculcated. While fostering an ability to shed blood guiltlessly, hunting also played a role in the maintenance of

Imperial rule by acting as a highly significant ritual. It demonstrated that not only were the Imperial rulers able to resort to force, but that they were willing to do so as well. In addition, these rituals were seen to have 'quasi-feudal' elements, where the authority of Imperial rule was reinforced and enhanced through shooting and hunting parties.[4]

The increasing use during the nineteenth century of images of war as a sporting practice was encouraged by developments in sport and the reporting of it in the press. The move to codify the rules and regulations of traditional sports can be seen as analogous to similar attempts to remove the excessive barbarities of armed conflict. The result was a move towards agreement on rules of warfare which culminated in the Hague Conferences of 1899 and 1907. Similarly, as the reporting of battle by war correspondents increased and became a regular and necessary feature for newspapers, so too did the reporting of sport. The mid-century developments in the newspaper industry, such as the repeal of the 'taxes on knowledge' and technological improvements, combined with changes in sport, like the creation of organized leagues as well as the increased leisure time and economic power of workers.[5] Because of this increasing interest in sport, Britain was able to support three national sporting daily newspapers by the mid-1880s: the *Sporting Life*, the *Sportsman*, and the *Sporting Chronicle*. These journals catered to a diverse audience, reflecting their interests and tastes, but at a cover price of 1d, could not have been representative of 'the masses', the majority of whom would have found the expense prohibitive. A far more important development in the sporting press by the end of the nineteenth century was the increased coverage in the non-specialist daily and, in particular, the weekly press. These utilized an average 10 per cent or more of available news space in daily papers like the *Daily Mail*, and up to 14 per cent in Sundays such as the *News of the World*. This attention to sporting news led to the development of the sports page and the sports editor, both of which became almost universal by 1900, with *The Times* the only notable exception.[6]

In looking at the sporting and games images of war reports in the press, it must be kept in mind that they are not simply useful descriptions, but carry with them real meaning in the context of the times. The association between sport and war went deeper than the simple correlation between similar activities. They were both seen to be methods to combat the onset of racial degeneration, a major fear particularly after the Boer War and the publication of the report by the *Inter-Departmental Committee on Physical Deterioration* in 1904.[7] Participation in sport was seen as one way to increase fitness and defeat the ravages of increased urbanization, and was propagated as a virtue through youth movements and the public schools.[8]

Similar perspectives relating to the utility of warfare were based upon popular misreadings of Charles Darwin. Social Darwinist thought, while confusing the term 'fittest' with 'strongest', presented war as not only natural and endemic in advanced civilization, but also beneficial. War, like sport, eliminated the weaker states and assimilated them into the more vigorous, stronger and supposedly virtuous ones. The disadvantages of war were seen to be outweighed by its progressive influence on science, art and learning.[9] Even the pre-war 'peace eugenicists', while seeing war as dysgenic, believed that physical training for war had 'racial benefits' and once acquired, could be transferred, in a Lamarckian sense, to offspring.[10]

Yet the similarities between sport and war were not simply that they both were expected to contribute to the physical health of society, but that they also inculcated desirable attitudes and values.[11] Ideals of perseverance, self-discipline, co-operation and *esprit de corps* were the qualities fostered by sport and games, and recognized as necessary for victory in war. The most obvious example of this type of connection occurred in the public schools, where an increasing emphasis on 'character', rather than 'scholarship', corresponded with a growing association between militarism and sport. The public schools have been seen as centres of militarism, which diffused these ideas into the larger population. There was a clear relationship between sport and militarism at the public schools. Team games, it was felt, inculcated schoolboys with officer qualities such as leadership, manliness, self-discipline and the ability to coordinate with others, in addition to providing them with simple physical fitness.[12]

It has been suggested that this ethos, of which the sporting imagery of warfare was a major part, percolated downwards through a combination of factors to such a degree that the public school 'entered the national consciousness'. The dissemination of public school ideals operated through literature, boys' magazines, East End 'missionaries', youth movements and 'martial verse'.[13] There is some debate concerning the degree to which upper-class and middle-class ideals were imposed upon the lower classes, particularly in the area of sport and the 're-invention' and codification of traditional games.[14] Yet the popularity of youth movements and literature suggests that this ethos was at least acceptable to the lower classes, if not imposed upon them. The images utilized in works such as Sir Henry Newbolt's popular poem '*Vitäi Lampada*', where both schoolboy cricketer and adult soldier continue to 'play the game' despite certain defeat, fused the positive perception of war as sport set to counter the ravages of degeneration with the importance of sporting ideals and values in the development of character.[15]

Descriptions of war found in the newspapers can be divided into two distinct groups: those invoking images of particular sports or games, and those using hunting imagery. The implementation of specific images raises questions as to the way in which they were applied. Whether specific images of war were class-based and dependent on the sports and activities popular within particular classes reveals much about their perceptions of war. Similarly, the particular types of sports which lend themselves to comparisons with war, whether team sports or those which are overtly 'martial', are useful in determining contemporary views of conflict. Lastly, it would be of interest to determine whether these images were dependent upon the kind of warfare described, whether Imperial wars or those between 'civilized' opponents.

'Like chess players in a tournament': images of war as a game

In looking at the images of sport and games used by newspapers in describing war, several issues invite further study. The first is the description of warfare and its conduct as an actual game, implying that it was not only a suitable activity for children to play, but was followed and discussed as if it were an entertaining game. Following this idea is the use of sporting terms and phrases which were seen to be appropriate and gave particular meaning to war reporting. An examination of the types of sports employed and their relationship with gambling fleshes out the image of war as a sport or game, and can show how some activities were thought to be appropriate in describing warfare while others were not. Lastly, other imagery reveals how warfare could be seen from above and at a distance, through the use of associated board-games and maps.

The most obvious way in which games imagery was used to describe war was to compare warfare with the activities of children, almost exclusively boys, and the perception that it was itself a game to be played by soldiers and watched by others. Several papers published photographs, drawings and articles showing how children indulged in playing at war, which implied that this type of play was not only common but natural and cross-cultural. The *Daily Mail* published photographs at the beginning of the Russo-Japanese War which compared the activities of Japanese boys in 1904 with those of English children during the Boer War. Both groups of children 'showed an interest in no other game' but that of 'soldiers'. These photographs were featured alongside photographs of Japanese soldiers in actual combat, making them appear as if they were playing at 'real' soldiers. *Lloyd's Weekly News* made this point clearly when it mentioned how it was interesting but not surprising that the sale of war toys increased during a conflict. This was due, the paper felt, to the natural 'fighting instincts in boys', which some 'born soldiers' never outgrow, going on to become leaders of armies. The increase in the number of advertisements for these war toys during the Russo-Japanese War, such as the 'Japanese Monster Cannon', firing a 1.5 inch 'harmless' projectile, and the 'Little Jap Rifle' with 1000 rounds of ammunition, 'Entirely Free of Danger', attest to the idea of war as a harmless game and give an indication of the popularity of these toys.[16] This was also an image reinforced by descriptions of certain military activities which were perceived to be less dangerous or exhausting than others, as 'child's play'.[17]

Other ways in which war was portrayed as a game were emphasized through phrases and images which created a correlation between the two activities. Echoes of Newbolt encouraging soldiers to 'play the game' reverberated throughout the press coverage of war in the period. A *Daily Mail* leading article explained how one of De Wet's more spectacular escapes was due to officers not following orders issued by Field-Marshal Roberts. In a direct association of war and sport, the paper suggested that 'if our cherished games teach anything, it is the value of combination and the necessity to follow the captain's orders', and that while De Wet was 'a sportsman of high powers', 'our side have not "played the game" '.[18] This was a call for team spirit and co-operation which Baden-Powell extolled in his book *Aids to Scouting for N.-C.Os and Men*, where he compared scouting to a game of football in which the scout, like the forward player, was encouraged to play not for personal glory, but to simply 'play the game; play that your side may win'.[19]

This use of games imagery could occasionally give the impression that warfare was not necessarily a serious or deadly event. For example, the *Daily News*, a respectable liberal newspaper, reported on the defeats during Black Week. Of these defeats, the paper stated that 'war is a game of ups and downs. Nobody ever wins all the moves'. After Spion Kop, it announced that defeat was 'one of those incidents common to war which one has to accept as part of the rough-and-tumble of the game'.[20] Here, defeat was part of playing at war just as it was in games, while the suffering of troops and the disappointment of abandoning hard-fought positions were by-products of participation, rather like the knocks and bruises of a tough match or the loss of field position.

The relationship between war and sport, and the image of war as another form of games, was further enhanced by the use of sporting terminology to describe military events. The use of such phraseology highlights the congruity with which both activities were perceived. While the use of sporting phrases to describe war was not unique to the Edwardians, it was the intensity and conjunction with other factors which made these images significant. For example, it is important to examine the increasing militarism in the public schools and to determine the degree to which the post-Arnoldian period was one where the relationship between war and sport intensified, particularly after the Boer War. Much of this relationship depended on the growing use of sporting terminology. It is felt by some that the dissemination of the public school perspective, including the description of military activity through sporting terminology, was imposed from above onto a receptive population.[21] However, newspapers must also be seen as important disseminators and reinforcers of sporting ideals as they utilized sporting terminology widely and frequently to describe military operations. These images were not found exclusively in the upmarket broadsheets, but also in the 'Yellow Press', the working-class papers, and the radical and socialist press.

The idea of war as a sporting activity was strengthened and expanded through the perception of military objectives in terms of sporting terminology. The papers presented belligerent armies as having 'scored' over their opponents when they experienced a military success. General Manning's pursuit of the Mullah in Somaliland during the Third Expedition could be described as a 'Forward Move', while the Boer Mounted Infantry and the Bikanir Camel Corps were presented as having 'scored on several occasions'.[22] Thus not only is the entire operation perceived as a game in which the British executed a 'forward move' reminiscent of Baden-Powell's scouts or a football team, but the method of establishing success was to count the number of victories 'scored'.

It is in this sense of keeping score that the practice of recording the number of Boers captured every week must be seen. The *Daily Mail* was one paper that kept a tally of the number of Boers who were captured or surrendered to the British forces in South Africa. These numbers were compared to the previous two weeks and analysed rather like the scoring performance of a sports team.[23] Yet, a further way in which these recorded tallies can be viewed arose when the guerrilla phase of the war is considered. With the fall and occupation of the major Boer cities, definable military objectives became obscure, and the only way to gauge military victory was to count the number of Boers captured, the sole tangible 'trophies' in the last phase of the war. More conventional forms of warfare utilized the image of military objectives being 'prizes' to be 'won' by the victorious army which also suggested a sporting or games perspective of warfare. In this way, the objectives of Port Arthur and the destruction of the Russian army at Liaoyang were presented as 'prizes' sought by the Japanese; one of which was 'won' while the other was not.[24]

The use of sporting terminology in describing warfare was a facet of public school education, but its presence in a wide variety of newspapers suggests that this perception was much more widespread and that the lower classes perceived warfare in similar ways. However, it is necessary to temper this analysis by examining the specific types of sporting imagery present in the newspapers of different classes. There were certain sporting images of war which were found in specific class-based newspapers and not found in others. Equally, there were other images which were present in a wide range of papers. Thus, those sports which tended to be class-specific were found mostly, though not exclusively, in newspapers that catered to those classes, reflecting their interests, experiences and tastes. The more universally popular sports were used as images of war by several papers, irrespective of target audiences.

The image of war as a 'duel' or 'fencing' match between two belligerents evoked an image of gentlemen settling a point of honour in a well-established, traditional and understood manner. These images were present in the upmarket papers, such as the conservative *The Times* and the liberal *Daily News*, but also in the self-improving middle-class papers, like the *Daily Mail*. Readers of the *Daily Mail* were described as representing a new self-improving and respectable social group, and thus the presence of the image of war as a gentlemanly duel in the paper is unsurprising.[25] The paper published a regular column by a military expert under the pen name of 'Linesman', a *nom de plume* which itself evokes an impression of commentary or judgement from 'the sidelines' regarding the 'rush of war' in 1912. According to 'Linesman',

> there are none of the elaborate graces and courtesies of the foil-play of yore, when the duellists were even accused – as Marshal Saxe was – of prolonging hostilities for the sheer enjoyment in them. It is now a case of 'One! Two! and the third in your bosom!'[26]

While the *pace* of war had changed, the image of war as a duel with swords remained, combining war with sporting ideals and acceptable gentlemanly means of settling disputes.

Duelling imagery was not completely absent from the working-class or socialist press, but the few examples found indicate that the image conveyed a different meaning. The conservative working-class *News of the World* used the image to represent diplomatic wrangling, and contrasted it with actual warfare. The months before the outbreak of the Russo-Japanese War were full of preparations for 'the great game of war' by both sides, but might still be disappointingly restricted to the 'choice of words in a petty but wearisome diplomatic duel'.[27] The 'duel' here referred to the diplomatic negotiations undertaken by upper-class government officials, which was wearisome and petty, directly opposed to the exciting and important 'great game of war'.

An example of a singularly working-class sporting image which occurred numerous times in the *News of the World* was that of fishing or angling. While angling as a whole has been seen to be a pan-class leisure activity, coarse fishing, the most popular and widespread type of fishing, was overwhelmingly working class. The clubs which promoted coarse fishing and organized working-class anglers, stemmed from the public houses and the 'street milieu', rather than being imposed from above by middle-class reformers.[28] Thus descriptions of wars in working-class papers that utilized coarse-fishing imagery, played upon perceptions and experiences of working-class people for whom angling was a popular pursuit.

Specifically, these images gave the impression that warfare was similar to an angling competition or leisure pastime. Just as the selection of the correct bait was crucial in order to catch the desired fish, so too were the correct methods and policies needed to capture the largest number of Boer troops, as the *News of the World* cartoon 'The Two Baits' emphasized. The cartoon represented the debate between those who held out for 'unconditional surrender' and those who advocated 'favourable terms'. Similarly, the guerrilla phase of the Boer War required a great deal of patience, with very little activity before results were to be manifest; an attitude directly comparable to the virtues required of those who fish and understood by them. The paper quoted a speech in Liverpool by Lord Roberts who, in supporting Lord Kitchener's policies, stated that 'the greatest, sublimest power is often simple patience', and associated it with a cartoon where Lord Roberts and John Bull, the British Public, watched as Lord Kitchener fished. Success in pursuit of fish was equated with success in the military sphere in a cartoon entitled 'Return of the Angler', where a smug British lion in khaki returned from Lhasa with a large fish labelled 'Treaty'.[29] These cartoons were located on the front page of the paper and formed a major part of the visual layout of the most important page of each issue. Thus they had to capture reader attention and hold it, which suggests that the use of such imagery was significant, for it had to play upon preconceived perceptions of warfare already present and familiar to the audience.

While these two examples, 'duelling' and 'fishing', tend to suggest that there were some class divisions in the sporting imagery of war, the majority of the images that were used frequently were found in a diverse variety of newspapers. These images represented sports which were popular with all classes from the most wealthy to the poorest, and show that certain sporting images were near-universal. The most obvious and natural sporting image was that of boxing, and the related pursuit of wrestling. In the later nineteenth century, boxing took over from the former working-class sports of animal-baiting and cock-fighting, establishing a firm hold on working-class culture through the upper rooms and court-yards of the local pubs. This was a natural extension of typical pub activities and, indeed many of the bouts were merely regulated street fights.[30] Yet boxing was also popular with the middle and upper classes, where it was seen as part of the 'muscular Christianity' movement, inculcating not only strength and fitness in young men, but also a sense of discipline and sportsmanship, characteristics required of gentlemen.

Comparisons between war and boxing or wrestling, along with accompanying terms such as 'blows' to denote successful military attacks, created a common impression of war which corresponded to pan-class forms of sport. Reports of the first battles in the Russo-Japanese War utilized these images effectively. The *Daily News* described the Battle of the Yalu in these terms by suggesting that 'blow after blow has befallen them [the Russians] until they give the impression of a clumsy giant at the mercy of a fierce and nimble foe'. The *Penny Illustrated Paper* went further by stating that 'pugilistic metaphor' was more than appropriate to describe warfare and saw the surprise attack on Port Arthur as 'round one', with Japan drawing 'first blood', and the two competitors subsequently retiring to their respective 'corners' for a rest.[31]

Further indications of classless sporting imagery included the use of such activities as cricket, football and horse-racing. Both cricket and football were seen as appropriate analogies for warfare by those conveying upper and middle-class ideals, as Newbolt's '*Vitäi Lampada*' and Baden-Powell's *Aids to Scouting* show. Yet these images were appropriate not only for the newspapers read by these classes, but also for those of working-class newspapers. There is a particular duality of cricket and football: the former being 'holiday entertainment' while the latter acted as 'the staple diet' of popular sports.[32] The presence of cricket and

football imagery to describe warfare is thus not surprising. They combine to emphasize the need to 'play the game', follow certain set rules,
and combine and coordinate with others, qualities essential to both
games and warfare. Yet these images also show that, like sport, warfare
was an exciting spectator pastime and a source of harmless amusement.

Cartoons such as 'The Last Wicket' in *Punch* stressed the notion that
warfare was a sporting activity. Here, Lord Kitchener as wicket-keeper
and captain admitted that his 'team' had been 'in the field' a long time,
but confidently expected that the new tactics of 'closing in for catches',
the blockade system created to facilitate the 'catching' of Boers, would
soon end the 'game'. *Lloyd's Weekly News* campaigned for an early end to
the first Balkan War by suggesting on its leader page, that 'we have had
enough' of the game, and awaited the intervention of the great umpire
among the Powers to call 'over'. The paper suggested that the Bulgarians
have been 'bowled', the Turks were 'stumped' and the reservists 'all out',
announcing that 'we want a new game'. The article, entitled 'The Passing Show', expressed not only the paper's plea to end the war on behalf
of the 'weak and helpless', but also on the grounds of its being a game
which had become tedious to watch.[33]

Of these three examples, however, horse racing was the sport which
combined exclusivity and popularity across the social spectrum. This
appeal grew in the late-nineteenth century because of increased leisure
time and the development of rail and motor transport, and was reflected
in the founding of the specialist, national racing newspapers. The non-
specialist newspapers played upon the popularity of horse racing, the
Derby in particular, in their reporting of warfare. Thus, the Boers were
described as conducting themselves in going into battle like gentlemen
riding in carts to the Derby, while the Cossacks were seen to be like
American jockeys in their riding styles.[34] In addition, horse racing was
used to denote a breakthrough or pursuit to particular objectives after
earlier disasters or the end of a long-drawn-out encounter. For example,
the British victory at Paardeburg was one of the major turning points of the
Boer War, ending a string of disheartening disasters. Days before Cronje's
surrender, the *News of the World* published a cartoon entitled 'A Thaw!
Sport At Last "Bobs' is Up!" ', where Field-Marshal Roberts was depicted as a
jockey setting off on a racehorse to cheering crowds in the 'Bloemfontein
Stakes'. The 'thaw' referred not only to the change in military fortune for
the British, but also to the change in the weather which signalled the
resumption of racing. Similarly, *Punch* portrayed the war in the Far East
as a horse race in which Japan took an early 'lead' in the 'Manchurian
Stakes'.[35]

Horse-racing was an appropriate image because of the perception of war as a race between two armies for specific goals, with all the excitement, tension and suspense of a horse race. Both were popular spectator activities, with the audience out of the reach of danger, and both had an element of unpredictability. Something of this excitement was conveyed by Ellis Ashmead-Bartlett, war correspondent for *The Times*, when he compared a great battle to the end of an exciting race. He thought that the two events were similar, except that the course was packed with armed men and the 'grandstand' was filled with half a dozen shabbily dressed men of the General Staff. He suggested that in order to capitalize on the excitement of the end of a battle, 'grandstands' should be erected 'close to the scene of hostilities and filled with kings, ministers, fashionable crowds, eager multitudes – all ... who are going to gain or lose by the issue'.[36] Thus the excitement felt by those who watched the battle could match those who eagerly read about it in their papers, just as those who followed horse racing were excited by a spectacular finish. From his point of view as a war correspondent, far from the ravages of the battle looking down upon the scene, the image of spectators in a grandstand seemed appropriate. By association, and due to the similar but extended distance from the danger, his readers would have perceived the battle just as he did.

The activity which made the excitement of sport more intense was the practice of gambling on the results, the two pastimes having a lengthy association. Horse racing in particular was the one sport which attracted the attention not only of gamblers from all classes, but also the middle-class reformers anxious to rid the working classes of this particular vice. It was under their influence that off-course betting was made illegal in 1853 as an attempt to leave only those with the money and leisure to gamble at the track itself, though large crowds of working-class 'punters', particularly at important meetings, were an increasing source of frustration for reformers.[37]

Warfare was also portrayed in the newspapers as a gambling venture, where armies put up 'stakes' to ensure victory, making it more interesting and exciting to follow. In this way, the Japanese were seen by the *Morning Post* as 'playing for a great stake' in their approach to Mukden, while the *Daily News* felt that the Japanese were 'inclined to stake everything on the throw against Port Arthur.'[38] This was an image repeated by the war correspondents themselves in their later book-length accounts of battle where the Japanese were portrayed as gamblers who, having 'spent' more than they could afford by way of casualties, were determined to recover their losses. Similarly, General Kuropatkin, the Commander of the Russian Armies, was 'either ordered or permitted to stake the *maximum* upon the gaming-table of war' thus fully committing his forces. [39]

These images were reinforced by further ones which portrayed warfare more specifically as a card game, where armies with the advantage or initiative over their opponents were seen to possess 'a strong hand' or to have all the trump cards. Charles à Court Repington, *The Times'* military expert, elaborated in his book on the Russo-Japanese War based upon his published articles, when he stated that 'war is a game in which there are two players, of whom one may rise and leave the table whenever the fancy takes him to forfeit a stake'. A *Daily News* cartoon entitled 'A Strong Hand' emphasized this perspective during the first Balkan War by showing four cards from the point of view of a card player, all kings and labelled 'Servia', 'Bulgaria', 'Greece' and 'Montenegro'. [40]

The image of war as a sporting or gaming gamble thus capitalized on the unpredictability of the outcome. The higher the 'stake', as at Port Arthur or Mukden, and the less predictable the result, the more the spectator interest. Yet portraying warfare as a gambling game also abrogated the human element in its conduct, further divorcing the spectator from the reality of warfare. Luck played a strong role in determining who was to win the larger stake, and who was to lose. The idea of the unpredictable nature of warfare and thus the abrogation of human responsibility was highlighted in a *Punch* cartoon entitled 'Which Wins?' In this cartoon, the Angel of Peace, encapsulating beauty, youth and light, was depicted throwing dice with the Angel of War, representing ugliness, old age and darkness, to determine whether to end the Boer War. These figures emphasized a denial of responsibility for military and political leaders and the population at large, suggesting that the decision for war or peace was 'in the hands of the Gods'. The use of the female figure also suggested a denial of male culpability in an essentially masculine activity. [41]

This sense of denial or distance can be discerned when examining images which play upon more cerebral pastimes, such as the traditional game of chess. One historian of chess, writing in 1913, emphasized that chess had to be seen as a 'game of war' where two players directed a conflict between two 'armies', both of equal strength and with only their reason and skill to guide them. [42] Chess is a *strategic* game, where the perspective originates from the highest level and where the reality of 'battle' is overlooked. Newspaper reports, with the aid of strategic maps, took a similar perspective, a fact recognized in the *Daily Mail* during the Balkan Wars. Here, in an article entitled 'What Battle is Like', 'Linesman' described strategy as 'chess play' and tactics as 'bludgeon work'.[43] This distinction is significant, for strategy was seen as clean and cerebral 'play', whereas tactics were its antithesis, bloody and violent work. The emphasis in reports tended to be on the strategic, with the messy and distressing tactical details receiving little concentrated attention. In describing the conduct of battle, chess imagery contributed to this 'higher' perspective, and was such a powerful image that it was used by several classes of newspaper, regardless of whether readers would have been likely to play chess themselves.

Similarly, generals were seen as chess players, positioning the 'pieces' of their armies and countering the moves of their opponents. While the Russian General Stackleberg was seen as one who 'directed the affairs of the fight as a chess player the pieces', the Japanese leader Field-Marshal Oyama was 'moving his men like pawns on a chess board ... the real moves are taking place on both sides of the board'.[44] The *News of the World* combined several images when it described the fighting at Liaoyang, 'The Battle of an Epoch', in the first leading article. It felt that both sides 'plan evolution and counter-move like chess players in a tournament, with the wide world for an audience, and, for stakes, the lives and happiness of millions of men and of generations unborn'.[45] This description emphasized the high-level perspective readers had of the conflict, but also reinforced the idea of war being a game where the spectators watched with interest and found entertainment. The 'game' was made more interesting when stress was put upon the importance of the result.

While the image of war as a chess game between two opposing but equal armies applied most easily to 'civilized' warfare between Western-styled belligerents, it was also used to describe elements of Imperial warfare. Descriptions of both the Boer War and the expedition to Tibet employed images of the game of chess, but close examination reveals that they were not strictly speaking images of an uncivilized war. Thus when the *Daily News* used chess imagery, it was being critical of the cavalier attitude of the British leadership and its disregard for the principles of warfare during 'Black Week'. The paper suggested that a chess player who had not seriously studied strategic openings and endings, no matter how talented, would be at a disadvantage when playing an opponent who had. Also, these images occurred during the 'conventional' phase of the war, before the cross-veldt hunts, when the British still talked of 'rules of war' and the irregular obedience of them by the Boers.[46]

This particular use of chess imagery in Imperial warfare was made more clearly when looking at the ways in which it was employed to describe British manoeuvres in Tibet. The chess imagery in newspapers, both supportive and critical of the British Expedition, used it not in relation to the Tibetans but only when discussing the Russians. The 'Great Game' was not only to be played on the North-West Frontier, but on the North-East also. It was a game of chess between two great Empires using smaller and weaker states as 'pawns' or other minor pieces. Once again, battle in Tibet was perceived in its larger, strategic sense by readers, through the use of chess imagery. As Lord Hamilton, Secretary of State for India remarked, Tibet was merely 'the smallest of pawns on the political chessboard, but castles, knights and bishops may be all involved in trying to take that pawn'.[47]

The publication of maps to enable readers to follow the military action on the ground allowed them to generate particular perceptions of the war which were similar to that of a chess game. By following lines of advance or retreat, with symbols representing items or events of geographical and martial interest, readers were able to assume the role of opposing generals and leaders in order to anticipate, contradict or question 'moves' made. In such a way, readers would become distanced from the ravages of war, ensuring that conflict was perceived as a clean, strategic game.

Newspapers further contributed to this perspective not only by publishing maps to coincide with reports of battle, but also by offering readers the chance to purchase large and detailed maps of the war zones specifically commissioned by the paper. Almost all newspapers printed large maps and encouraged their readers to 'cut it out and keep it by you' in order to refer constantly to it while reading their war reports.[48] Several other newspapers offered large maps for sale, and there is evidence to suggest that these maps sold well. The *Daily Chronicle*, for example, produced a 'war map' of the Balkans shortly after the allied invasion of the Ottoman Empire. Ten days after the initial invasions and several major defeats for the Turks, an advertisement stated that the map was already in its fifth edition. Prices ranged dramatically, from 6d, 1s 6d or 3s 6d for the *Daily Chronicle*'s map to 1s or 2s 6d for a *Daily Mail* Russo-Japanese War Map and 5s for a similar map offered by *The Times*.[49]

These two images of warfare, those of strategic map and chess game, combined to reinforce the high-level perspective of readers and create the impression of actual warfare as an entertaining board game. The practice of moving military pieces along a map of a real area was relatively new, with games such as 'Gordon-Kitchener', 'The Conquest of the Sudan', or ' "Bobs": The Great War Game' becoming popular during the last decade of the nineteenth century. The concomitant development of the toy soldier industry characterized by William Brittain's famous hollow-cast toy soldiers patented in 1903, added to the illusion of war as a game where 'players' acted as 'generals' moving 'pieces' across a strategic 'board'. In addition, the attraction and entertainment value of war games was demonstrated by inventors such as H. G. Wells and Jerome K. Jerome who developed a sophisticated game called 'Little Wars' in 1913. Designed to be more amenable than the 'Real Thing', players could devise strategies, and thrill in the 'strain of accumulating victory of disaster', with 'no smashed nor sanguinary bodies, no shattered fine buildings nor devastated countrysides, no petty cruelties...'.[50]

These perceptions that war would make an interesting game were shared by newspapers that published their own 'War Games'. Readers were encouraged to cut out a map provided by the paper and move flags or cut-out soldiers to represent opposing armies. The object of the newspaper, like that of the publication of 'programmes' or glossaries, was to ensure that readers kept referring to a board map with the paper's name on it and continued to buy the paper for military dispatches in order to make their own 'moves'. The commercial interests of the papers played upon the entertainment value readers found in the 'game', the word used here to describe the activity, rather than an alternative, more educational or instructive term.

These cut-out games were only found in middle-class publications, while references to them were made in more 'respectable' journals. The *Illustrated Mail* and the *Daily Mirror* both published one of these 'War Games'; the former during the Boer War and the latter for the Russo-Japanese War.[51] Yet other more upmarket papers discussed or illustrated their pages with references to these games, suggesting that their readers too were also keen game players, or at least knew about the practice. These references also include evidence to suggest how this method of following the course of war was a family event, with children and women actively involved. Interviews with wives of men in South Africa showed that not only children were playing soldier-games, but that whole households were active. One wife was found to have tacked up a map of the war area and was 'evidently taking the cheeriest interest in the grim game at the Cape'.[52] The middle-class ideal, found in the full-page *Illustrated London News* drawing 'Follow the Flags', where father read despatches while the children eagerly placed flags on a mounted map, was the object of parody by *Punch* in cartoons entitled 'The Enthusiast' and 'The War Game and How it is Played',[53] These illustrations

1. 'Japan's Leap from Barbarism' *Illustrated London News* 16 January 1904, Supplement VII.

2. 'Plain English' *Punch* 11 October 1899, p. 175.

3. 'Theatre Royal, S. Africa, Feb 1, 1901' *Punch* 6 February 1901.

4. 'War As it Is' *Illustrated London News* 11 November 1911, pp. 770–1.

5. 'War As it Is' *Illustrated London News* 11 November 1911, pp. 770–1.

AS THEY REMAINED ON THE ROAD FOR TWENTY-FOUR HOURS: THE BODIES OF TWO ARABS WHO WERE BAYONETTED
BY THE ITALIANS AT TRIPOLI

6. 'War As it Is' *Illustrated London News* 11 November 1911, pp. 770–1.

7. 'Ammunition Against the Enemy' *Illustrated London News* 17 February 1912, p. 268.

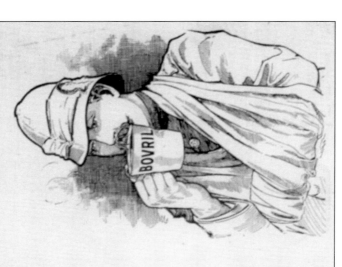

8. 'Bovril to the Front in Peace and War' *Illustrated London News* 24 February 1900, p. 275.

demonstrate that the practice of following troop movements on a board-mounted map was widespread, at least among certain classes, for they could not have been successfully depicted or ridiculed if the 'game' had been unusual or uncommon. In addition, it was seen as a 'game' where readers became involved in the strategic nature of conflict, but were able to avoid the 'bludgeon work' of actual combat.

The association between war and sport was also part of the marketing strategy of selling newspapers. While this technique can be seen as manipulative on the part of newspapers, marketing must play upon the interests and preconceived notions held by its target audience, such as the fascination for war news expressed by their readers. The *Daily Mirror* published a series of 'War Glossaries' which it encouraged its readers to cut out and keep, so as to be better able to follow the course of the war. The commercial advantages of having the paper's name on a glossary to which readers constantly referred is obvious. But its similarity to programmes sold at football matches is striking, as both were designed to fulfil the same function of informing spectators by giving details of participants and their performance.[54]

A further example of the commercial function of the association between war and sport in the minds of readers occurred when it was recognized that news of both activities increasingly sold newspapers. The *Penny Illustrated Paper* thus combined both in its promotional headlines designed to capture the attention of readers and encourage them to buy the paper. The importance of both war and sport was made clear in headlines such as 'War, Sport and All the News in Pictures' and 'Special War Pictures and Football Photographs'.[55] While in these examples war news was given priority, its association with sport in the headlines and on the photograph pages emphasized the popularity of both events and their similar nature. Furthermore, there appeared to be no contradiction in the minds of readers in associating these two activities.

'A contest between the skill of man ... and the intellect of some wild creature': images of war as hunting

The other major way in which war was depicted in the press was through hunting imagery, which, like that of sport, reveals much about perceptions of specific forms of warfare. Imperial warfare seemed in particular to lend itself to these images, for the enemy encountered was, for the most part, 'uncivilized' and not expected or thought able to follow 'rules', a requirement necessary to play 'games' or 'sport'. Newspaper images of Imperial wars as a hunt reflected the attitudes of the military, both professional thinkers such as Callwell and Baden-Powell, and those more directly and closely involved in operations. Firstly, hunting was seen as a pleasurable pursuit, one in which officers and men indulged throughout the Empire, both on active duty and in garrison. Secondly, the idea of hunting as suitable training for warfare, prevalent in military circles, was also current in newspapers. Furthermore, military operations into unknown areas of the Empire were depicted as 'expeditions', where 'civilization' crossed over to meet 'barbarism', and where the concept of 'hunting' the enemy was easily transferred from the idea of hunting game. Lastly, newspaper depictions of operations in Imperial warfare utilized to a great extent the language and imagery of hunting which reinforced perceptions of war as a glamorous, safe and guiltless activity.

For the officers involved in the various military expeditions, the rigours of campaign life were eased by the opportunity of conducting hunting expeditions. Somaliland, for example, provided an ideal hunting ground, and officers, despite the pressures of staff and other duties, were able to go hunting for several days on end while preparations for the move inland were under way.[56] This 'hunting for pleasure' attitude of officers was officially sanctioned: the *Military Report on Somaliland*, giving hints to officers on what kit to take there while on duty, included the suggestion to 'bring any rifles and guns that you have, with a moderate supply of ammunition' and added advice on what types of rifle were best suited for the game available.[57]

While officers perceived warfare in this way, the newspapers also conveyed the idea of Imperial conflicts being a sanctioned occasion for soldiers to indulge in hunting. In many ways, the military nature of expeditions seems to have been subsumed by the amount of hunting that would be available once the force arrived. The *Illustrated London News* published a lengthy article by Major Bonham Christie which anticipated the pleasures awaiting the officers preparing for the Third Expedition to Somaliland, and the extreme variety of animal life to hunt. He went so far as to tell readers that Somaliland would be 'the pleasantest and most interesting of all the countries in Africa they have soldiered in', making the whole experience seem like a holiday safari rather than a serious military operation.[58]

In addition to hunting being a pleasurable experience for officers and men while on active service, it was also seen as a worthy activity for training purposes. The use of firearms, an ability to forage in the woods or jungle and familiarity with the lie of the land were all skills which fostered military excellence. Hunting was seen to be exceptionally practical training, particularly for British officers, as it gave 'a genuine, permanent education' rather than 'a form of ephemeral instruction'.[59] The impression was clear that hunting as a form of training was far better than lessons in the classroom, as officers learned more from the practical demonstrations in the field than second-hand from an instructor. Also, the animal hunted, particularly the boar, was unpredictable, brave and possibly dangerous, exactly like the Imperial enemy. This meant that soldiers had to be as sharp in the hunting ground as on the battlefield, thus blurring the distinction between the two activities.

The newspapers recognized that hunting was an important element of military training and nurtured the idea of developing and fostering an informal military reserve. Yet this enthusiasm was stimulated by the fear that the hunting instinct among the British had become diluted. This fear combined with the trauma of major military setbacks during the Boer War, poor organization and the substandard health of recruits, along with the more general feeling of social and martial degeneration. In association with the release of the *Inter-Departmental Report on Physical Deterioration* and the impressive Japanese victories in Manchuria, the *Daily Mail* published an article entitled 'Decadent English Sportsmen', asking the question 'Is He Any Longer A "Military Reserve"?' The 'true spirit of sport', which made the Empire what it was, was to be found in the individuals who 'suffered real hardship in pursuit of his game, were it grey goose or an armed foe'. The activities of hunting and war were complementary, in that one provided the skills and endurance needed for the other. The essence of hunting was also that of warfare, 'a contest between the skill of man and the craft or intellect of some wild creature'.[60] Whether that 'creature' was man or beast was left unclear. It was felt that this type of sportsman, who made an excellent military reserve, was diminishing, while those who 'shoot' merely have the birds driven towards them, and, by inference, were not far from the picnic basket or the company of ladies.

Yet hunting was not the sole type of training for military men. The activities of hunting and Imperial warfare were similar to such an extent that they could easily be transferred. Just as hunting was seen to be admirable training for Imperial warfare, skirmishes on the frontier were felt to represent adequate training for future wars. Baden-Powell, writing in 1915, stated plainly that the British were fortunate to have the 'valuable training ground' of the North-West Frontier in India, where there were 'real life enemies always ready to oblige in giving us practical instruction...'.[61] Future victories in the war Britain was currently fighting, would be due not to the playing fields of Eton but to the more practical battlefields of the North-West Frontier.

The newspaper reinforced this idea that Imperial warfare was important and valuable, because it showed not only that the Boer War had *not* sapped the ardour of the British, but also that this type of warfare was excellent practice, rather like the use of live ammunition in modern military exercises. The *Daily Mirror* reflected upon the three colonial conflicts that Britain was then conducting in Tibet, Nigeria and Somaliland. In the first leading article, that paper stated that these 'little wars' 'keep our officers in practice and prevent our men from getting "stale" through too long inaction'.[62] The value of these expeditions, then, was that they were seen to be a good substitute for 'real' combat, and rather like 'hunting expeditions' where, with almost military precision, they reached deep into 'hostile' territory in search of their objective.

Indeed, these perceptions of military expeditions penetrating into isolated regions of the Empire and beyond as being like hunting expeditions was firmly rooted in the initial descriptions of them in the press. In this way, the delineation between hunting and military expeditions was further blurred. The initial descriptions of the British Expedition into Tibet read like those of a well-armed exploration of new lands, rather than a military invasion. Drawings, illustrations and travellers' tales dominated much of the early coverage before the dispatch of the Expedition. The *Daily Express* showed photographs of life, customs and native women in Tibet in the early stages of the Expedition. As the force progressed into the country, reports of flora and fauna, as well as climatic conditions and geographical descriptions, gave the impression of a journey of discovery. This was emphasized in article headlines such as 'Into Unknown Tibet' and 'In Unknown Land', where readers were told that 'no living European has hitherto travelled along the route between Chumbi and Tuna'.[63]

It is in this sense that the newspaper reports of military force in the Empire supported the view of hunting as an activity where hunters moved between 'civilization' and 'barbarism'. Like the big game hunter, the military expeditions were seen to represent the dominance of 'civilization' over 'the darker, primeval and untamed forces at work in the world'.[64] Descriptions and images of military operations utilized those of hunting to the extent that the 'enemy' was portrayed as the object of a hunting expedition, rather than military opponents. Thus, the popular sport of pig-sticking could be used as a metaphor for Imperial fighting, particularly when the images of 'Boer-Boar' were fused and used almost interchangeably.[65]

The pleasures and challenges of hunting and the 'ecstasy' of the migration from 'civilization' to 'barbarism' were easily transferred to descriptions of Imperial warfare found in the press. For example, a letter from a private in Methuen's force explained: 'you can't believe how happy I was fighting against the Boers.' His happiness while on active service was based upon the fact that the British troops got 'some sport in – chasing Boers'. Somaliland was similarly seen as 'the happy hunting ground of sportsmen who seek big game', which had become the scene of 'a sterner chase' during the operations against the Mullah.[66] In these examples, the Imperial enemy was portrayed as the ultimate 'game', implying that Imperial warfare was the ultimate hunting expedition. In this way, the papers echoed Baden-Powell's sentiment in advising soldiers from the other ranks that 'hunting an enemy is like hunting game'.[67]

The specific images used in the description of Imperial warfare played upon these perceived similarities between hunting game and fighting an enemy. Thus the pursuit of Christian De Wet during the guerrilla phase of the Boer War, the phase most like the Imperial wars with which the British were familiar, was almost universally described as the 'hunting' of De Wet. This image implied much more than just a search for a leader and his forces, but was seen as an actual 'hunt', with De Wet as the 'fox' and British generals, such as Knox, as the huntsman.[68] The image itself was not class-specific, appearing in working-class newspapers, both radical and conservative, as well as in journals read by those who hunted foxes in the same manner themselves. In this way, the press depiction of warfare as hunting expeditions can be seen to act as a mechanism for the dispersal of ideas of hunting to a wider audience that were inextricably linked with English culture.

A further reason for the use of hunting imagery was that it adequately conveyed the excitement often found in Imperial warfare. For the working-class readers of *Lloyd's Weekly News*, the thrill of the encounter with De Wet was related in what the paper itself described as a 'vivid narrative of a wonderful chase'.[69] However, it was not simply the thrill of the chase that made warfare in the Empire exciting. In dealing with an Imperial enemy, the danger of being attacked and suffering severe setbacks or having a force annihilated, such as Plunkett's column in Somaliland, extended the exhilaration. One never knew when or if the hunter was to become the hunted. Pig-sticking was seen as a similar activity, because the boar was an animal with a fierce reputation for fighting back, never giving up and fighting bravely to the bitter end.[70] The press presented this perception in their reports of warfare. De Wet was the model Boer, who represented those who 'stalked' his enemy 'patiently, silently and warily as he would stalk any wild animal', his 'game' being the British columns, acting both as hunter and hunted in the ultimate hunting expedition. Similarly, the chasing of the Mullah was made all the more exciting because he was 'a crafty old fox' who could 'bite back'.[71]

The use of hunting imagery to describe Imperial warfare illustrates another important factor; the application of what has been called 'the perfect image of war without guilt'.[72] Soldiers could use the image to assuage feelings of guilt in killing fellow human beings with impunity, but the appropriation of the hunting imagery by readers was a further way in which they were distanced from the realities of warfare. They were thus able to concentrate on the thrilling aspects of Imperial conflict and see it as an exciting event.

Conclusion: 'kick-off at zero'

In looking at the Edwardian depiction of warfare in the press, it becomes clear that images of sport and games were used extensively. This practice not only reflected developments in leisure pastimes, such as the codifi-cation of rules and the increased interest in sport, but also attitudes and values attached to ideas of sporting activities. Both sport and war were seen as beneficial to individuals and societies as they postponed or overturned the ravages of physical deterioration and increased a nation's chance of survival. Social Darwinist thought was applied to warfare despite its recognized dysgenic nature. Warfare, like sport, infused participants, and by extension readers, with moral values that were seen to be desirable traits. They 'played the game' of war like good sportsmen and women, cooperating and always doing their best. They played by the rules, either those explicitly made or those of honour. Lastly, they died without giving up, playing to the end in the face of certain defeat with good grace, determined that their team revenge a 'loss' and 'win' next time. Also, warfare was presented as an activity which was 'fun' and 'exciting' – thrilling for both participant and spec-tator. These perceptions were combined with a sense of adventure, which made the reports of war correspondents, themselves seen as glamorous adventurers, 'a good read'.

For the most part, these images were not class-based. Although there were some examples of images being of relevance to particular groups, most of the allusions were familiar and pertinent to the majority of readers. Also, they played mostly upon images of sports where individuals were set against each other, seeing warfare mostly as a game between two allegorical figures rather than as groups or teams of players. This made the depiction of warfare simple and avoided complex digressions into strategy and tactics. Warfare was recognized as complex, as the comparisons to the game of chess showed, but sporting images concentrated on the personalities and skills of leaders rather than deep discussions of how the game was played.

The type of warfare also influenced the kind of images used. Sports and games imagery was most relevant in describing war between Western-style armies, so-called 'civilized' warfare. Belligerents were expected to know and follow set rules, and could be criticized or praised accordingly, just as players were on the sports pages. Imperial warfare most suited the images of the 'hunt', where the opponents were unable or unwilling to follow 'rules'. Hunting imagery was most appropriate because of the nature of warfare in the Empire; it was conducted in unknown or exotic territory, had a form of 'ecstasy' unavailable in the modern world as 'civilization' moved into 'barbarism', and it represented a form of Imperial control demonstrating an ability and willingness to resort to force. More importantly, Imperial warfare and hunting were seen as excellent forms of military training, made all the more practical and exciting because of the ability of the 'prey' to 'bite back'.

More generally, sporting and hunting imagery can be seen as reinforcing a paradigm of detachment and denial of warfare and its realities. Sporting imagery related warfare as something other than what it was – it was depicted as fun, exciting, harmless and beneficial. But also it was presented as a distant activity, giving the impression of detachment. This can be seen in the use of maps and board-games, where not only were the events depicted far away, in the 'Far East' or in the 'far-flung reaches of the Empire', but they were also seen from above, at a high strategic level. Thus, the realities of warfare were masked by the taking of 'pieces', the removal of toy 'soldiers' or the movement of 'flags'. Armies or columns scored 'goals', they did not destroy, maim or kill, and they did so in a spirit of sport and entertainment which was essentially beneficial and positive.

The Edwardians, both those who participated and those who remained as spectators, went to war in 1914 with a particular sporting image of warfare. It contributed to the enthusiasm shown by those anxious to join-up themselves and those eager to see their friends and relatives do so. It was also a persistent image, as some of the East Surreys demonstrated on the first day of the Battle of the Somme in 1916 when they kicked footballs given to them by their company commander,

Captain Nevill, towards the German trenches. Painted on one was: 'The Great European Cup-Tie Finals, East Surreys v. Bavarians. Kick-off at zero.'[73] War on the Western Front had shown that Angell's concern about press treatment of war had been correct; it had indeed become a 'glorified football match'.

5

'This Wonderfully Lovely Theatre of War': The Imagery of Stage and Spectacle

Introduction: 'passive and detached'

The use of the term 'theatre' in describing warfare has become so common as to be unremarkable. Terms such as 'Pacific Theatre', 'European Theatre' or 'Theatre of Operations' to denote an area of conflict have become acceptable and have acquired their own legitimacy. Such usage can appear to be natural and commonplace to such a degree that the metaphor loses its impact and significance, deteriorating into a well-worn and rather hackneyed cliché. Yet, the challenge for the historian is to 'recover the impact of ideas and metaphors worn smooth by repetition'.[1] This concern focuses on theatrical metaphors in German politics, which can be seen as more than simply figures of speech. This is quite true, for they can be used to determine a particular mindset or *mentalité*. A similar approach can be made regarding the depiction of war before 1914. The very ubiquity of stage and spectacle imagery in the press indicates their importance and utility as a means to determine how Edwardians vicariously experienced war.

Paul Fussell has identified instances where the military use of language could be seen as ironic, such as the terms 'mess' and 'fatigue' and the command 'fall out'. He suggests that the image of the theatre was particularly appropriate as a metaphor for those in the military, for volunteers frequently saw themselves as 'playing a role' during active service with 'real life' pertaining to their existence as civilians. Further, uniforms could be seen as forms of stage costumes, military rank as displaying stereotypes or character types and even military training as a form of rehearsal.[2] While Fussell admits that the connection between theatre and war occurred even before 1914, citing the 1909 Guy du Maurier play, *An Englishman's Home*, his main aim remains to establish that 'memory' of war as theatre was initiated by experiences of the First World War. But this does not explain adequately how these metaphors came so easily to the minds of both military personnel and those civilians with whom they interacted. Part of the answer comes from an analysis of newspaper coverage of pre-1914 conflict, which reveals the way in which these individuals would have been exposed to discussions concerning actual warfare. It is in this sense that Fussell's findings need to be contextualized.

In addition, military thinkers were discussing warfare in terms of 'theatre' well before the outbreak of war in 1914. The *United Services Magazine* described the Chilean Civil War in 1891 in such a way that the fighting was a 'great drama', artillery acting as 'orchestral music' and the European powers as neutral 'spectators'.[3] A similar example of a military thinker utilizing this sort of imagery, but to a slightly wider audience, was Lieutenant-General Sir Ian Hamilton, who wrote about the Russo-Japanese War in his *Staff Officer's Scrapbook*. Hamilton had hoped to get to the area of operations early in order to study

> not only the actors but also the theatre of an impending world drama; a world drama more fascinating than any staged since the Greeks put measure to another ambition which had known no bounds until the curtain rose on the plains of Marathon.[4]

While these two examples seem to support the view that the military professionals saw warfare as theatre, they cannot give an accurate indication of popular sentiment concerning warfare, nor can they reveal whether theatre imagery extended beyond the realms of military experts.

As Edwardians used the theatre as an image of war, it will be fruitful to examine the state and development of theatrical entertainment from the late-Victorian period to 1914 in order to ascertain why the theatre was a suitable and readily used metaphor. Both the theatre and the press underwent significant changes in the last decades of the nineteenth century which enabled them to be seen as important cultural venues, and led to the ready use of theatrical imagery to describe warfare. However, in terms of style and setting the early Victorian theatre was little different from its Georgian antecedents, as early audiences tended to be made up of the rowdy lower classes who demanded simplistic but exciting and novel entertainments. The theatre lacked respectability, both as a place of ill-repute and for the low reputation of actors, while the style of acting was characterized by the melodramatic visualizations of stock emotions and with scenery composed of two-dimensional flats.[5]

This situation changed by the end of the third quarter of the nineteenth century to a point where the middle and upper classes began to patronize the theatre, which had acquired a new respectability. This trend was primarily due to the professionalization and raised social status of actors, which reached its apotheosis with the knighthood conferred upon Henry Irving in 1895, and to the increased comfort and luxury afforded to theatregoers, signalled by the refurbishment and building boom of the 1880s and 1890s. As a further indication of increasing respectability, the press, which had ignored or condemned the theatre before the 1880s, began to focus on it, a tendency commented upon by contemporaries who perceived more column inches devoted to the stage.[6]

Also in the 1880s there was a movement towards 'naturalism' in acting, where actors expressed themselves in ways appropriate to setting and dialogue rather than through a stock set of facial or arm gestures. Concomitant with this tendency was the increasing 'realism' of sets and props, which made theatre more convincing. William Telbin, Henry Irving's scenic painter, wrote in 1894 that 'the appliances connected with the stage have within the last twenty years greatly changed', indicating that the more efficient forms of lighting and increasing sophistication of audiences required modelled or 'built out' scenery to make the production more realistic.[7]

Despite this trend towards increasing 'realism' in some aspects of the stage, popular demand still required the prevalence of 'unreflecting optimism', happy endings, and the avoidance of 'psychological truth'. The increasing respectability of the theatre contributed to the 'falsification of life on stage', and a presentation which was 'more refined, but only offered an escape from life not an examination of it'. This was a development encouraged not simply by the stage censorship of the Lord Chamberlain, but primarily by the demands of public taste. The 'new dramas' of the 1890s which emphasized real plots, characters and settings, and focused on social concerns, the so-called 'problem play', did not take root in England as readily as they did on the Continent. Indeed, the Edwardian theatre represented a time of 'unrepentant make-believe', where even the powerful realism of the Barker-Vedrenne seasons with George Bernard Shaw as the principal playwright was, for the majority of theatregoers, of little significance; a 'fringe benefit'.[8] Thus the theatre represented not so much 'reality', but more 'realistic' illusions.

Just as the theatre developed and changed in the second half of the nineteenth century, so too did the music halls. From the middle of the century, they catered to those displaced from the theatres, and began to challenge them artistically and socially.[9] The audience of these 'theatres of variety' was a social mixture, which towards the latter decades of the century broadened from a working-class base to a wider 'mass' audience. The very nature of the music halls, with their 'review' style which promised 'something for everyone', ensured that acts, if not always universally popular, at least did not offend or alienate sections of the audience. Thus music hall managers had to ensure not only that they catered to a wide variety of patrons, but that they were also sensitive to the tastes of their customers. In such an increasingly commercial environment, success depended upon capitalizing on popular sentiment.[10]

Using these features of the music halls, a connection can be made between theatre and warfare which provides a background to Fussell's concept of First World War theatre imagery. The development of the way martial topics were presented can be traced to a change from what has been called 'liberating melodramas', where soldiers and sailors were seen as the defenders of native rights, to a more jingoistic belligerent nationalism, where those same natives were enemies to be subdued and incorporated into the British Empire.[11] Similarly, an increasing respect and interest concerning the British army has been demonstrated. While the music halls had always presented military material, the amount increased significantly after the 1870s, with attention to the rank and file growing by the mid-1890s.[12] Thus the overlap which Fussell has identified with du Maurier and the official response to his play, were well-established in the music hall well before 1914.

Newspaper reports which utilized images of theatre to describe warfare demonstrate the way in which readers experienced war in terms that were familiar to them. In consuming the accounts of war correspondents, readers were, like the military observer Sir Ian Hamilton, in a position similar to those who watched performances on stage, for they were the 'spectators' who watched, 'passive and detached', 'with rapt attention, the development of the drama'.[13] 'Stage' and 'spectacle', however, are more than simply metaphors, for they indicate the nature of a vicarious experience readers possessed concerning warfare, representing a discourse around which they 'constructed' their image of war.

'All the fascination of a great and uncertain drama': images of the stage

Fussell suggests that one of the most omnipresent images of the First World War was that of 'the theatre'. He cites the war memoirs of participants, where there is 'hardly a book about the war that at some point does not avail itself of a theatrical figure', and outlines the use of images such as 'theatre of war', 'performance', 'scenes', 'acts' and so on.[14] This is to be expected, as the conventions for using theatrical imagery were well established in both the up-market and 'new journalism' newspapers before the war. These include the portrayal of war as 'dramatic', in the way that surprising events and the image of war were described as a form of 'drama', and, more specifically, the presentation of war as a 'stage play' or comic entertainment with 'scenes', 'curtains', 'actors' and an 'audience'. Similarly, battles were seen as different types of stories and accompanied by 'music' or 'singing'.

One of the most obvious ways in which the reporting of warfare used theatre imagery was to convey the perception of military activity as dramatic. Just as the twists and turns of a playwright's plot surprise and delight audiences, so too did the dispatches from the war correspondent, for both audience and reader were unaware of how the 'story' would end. Military events, either as they occurred or were anticipated, were thus seen as 'dramatic' events, such as the surprise attack at Port Arthur in February 1904. The diplomatic attempts to avoid war combined with increasing interest in the situation, so that when the war eventually began, the *Daily Mirror* could state as its first line of a full front page story that 'The war has begun dramatically.' This statement, rather theatrical in itself, was not seen as an exaggeration, for the war was to continue in a similar fashion. During the Battle of Liaoyang, the same paper, again on the first line, but of a leading article, confirmed that 'The Russo-Japanese War has reached a height of supreme dramatic and historical interest.'[15]

While *Black and White* predicted that Liaoyang would eclipse the siege at Port Arthur in 'dramatic interest', it was the suspenseful and eventful fall of the strategic port that was thought by most papers to be the most dramatic. The *Daily News* emphasized this in June 1904, almost seven months before the actual fall of Port Arthur. In its first leading article the paper stressed that: 'the great drama that is being played out behind the veil of silence in the Far East approaches its climax. Any day may bring us the news of the fall of Port Arthur.' The dramatic tension was thus built up over the course of the siege and was increased as the weeks went by, despite the knowledge that Port Arthur's military significance actually decreased over time. The *Official History* of the war, however, concurred with the *Daily Express*, by suggesting that 'in a war which will always be remembered for the stubborn character of the fighting, this siege was the most dramatic incident'.[16]

War, however, was not simply seen as consisting of a series of events which were dramatic because of the suspense or surprise involved; it was a drama in itself. War was expected to contain elements of surprise, for this was part of the attraction for both practitioner and viewer, but it emphasized the imagery of the theatre. The pursuit of the Boers after the battle at Belmont in November 1899 was described in the *Daily Mail* as 'the rest of that day's drama', suggesting that the entire day had been a drama enacted in South Africa for its readers. For the *News of the World*, quoting a foreign correspondent, Tripoli was 'the theatre of one of the reddest dramas'. This idea was best portrayed in a *Daily News* leading article entitled simply and powerfully 'Tragedy' after this disaster at Gumburu. While the paper opposed the British efforts in Somaliland, it still presented the four expeditions as encapsulating an ideal drama, however 'tragic' it might have been. In this article the paper stated that 'the imagination of millions pictured the terrible drama enacted scene by scene upon the parched plains of Somaliland'. It then outlined the course of the 'drama' which encompassed 'the effort to find new wells, the preliminary alarm, apparently false, the bold dash of the relief party, the surprise, and finally the pitiless annihilation of the shattered fragments of a square'.[17]

These 'dramas' were made more accessible to readers through the introduction of personalities who acted in small manageable vignettes. In this way, the larger lessons of the war presented by the press, such as admired personal characteristics or the sacrifices made in the fighting, were stressed. Despite its opposition to the use of force, the liberal *Daily News* admired both the Japanese and the Russians for their display of bravery, loyalty and self-sacrifice. It emphasized this through the publication of 'dramas' or 'incidents', which told the story of individuals or small groups of individuals. In September 1904, the paper printed an article headed almost as if it were an advertisement for a stage production: 'A Drama of The War: The Russian Colonel's Sacrifice.' This article outlined the plight of Colonel Pokotilo, 6th Battery of the East Siberian Artillery, whose death was 'the touching epilogue of a military drama which began at the battle of Tuseutchen'. The Colonel had been repeatedly reproached by General Kuropatkin for the earlier loss of guns, despite the difficulties of the situation and orders to abandon them.

The *Daily News*, a middle-class organ, stressed the effect on the Colonel, which resulted in his 'inviting death' by gallantly standing in front of his battery and dying during a battle sometime later. Similar vignettes occurred in other papers such as the *News of the World*, a working-class paper which conveyed a report involving ordinary soldiers in 'an intensely dramatic incident'.[18] Here, a paper bought by a class of reader which identified with the rank and file, gave details of a story which was portrayed as a dramatic event, whose principals were themselves common soldiers. Thus both papers portrayed individuals or groups of soldiers in tales featuring characters with whom their readers could identify.

Sir Ian Hamilton, in the preface of the second volume of his *Scrapbook*, extended his 'drama' metaphor, and in so doing shed light on the perspective of the observer and the way in which that perspective influenced other writers. He compared watching the battle at Port Arthur with watching a play at the theatre, where the military observer and the theatregoer are initially occupied with similar small considerations: the checking of hat and coat, buying a programme and getting a seat. For both spectators, the curtain rises, the actors play parts, scenes shift and plots thicken through the course of the play/battle.[19]

Another observer watching the same 'play' from a similar perspective reveals that the point of view of the war correspondent matched that of the military observer. Ellis Ashmead-Bartlett, war correspondent for *The Times* and also present at Port Arthur, felt that all aspects of the battle he was watching seemed like a stage play, by being realistic and convincing. During the 'performance', the 'stage on which they are enacted, the setting, the actors, even the accompanying music, are all suited to the play.' Just like the theatre, watching the same or similar 'plays' regularly could make 'tragedy' seem commonplace and induce boredom in the theatregoer, for according to Ashmead-Bartlett, 'instead of "I shall not use my box at the opera tonight, I am tired of hearing Melba", it was "I shall not use my bomb-proof tonight for the assault this afternoon, I am tired of watching Ichinoke" '. For him, the reasons for boredom were similar: that the pattern of entertainment had become familiar and routine, but that 'the stage alone is different'.[20]

This conception of warfare as a stage play was conveyed in contemporary news reports also, operating at several different levels. One of the most striking examples of this image was written by Douglas Story, who wrote a very long article called 'The Play of Death', describing of the battle at Tashichao in July 1904. In this article, Story followed the course of the battle from sunrise to sunset, as if he were describing the unfolding of a play at a theatre from the moment he arrived to the end of the performance.[21] Others also used aspects of theatre imagery to describe elements of combat. For example, individual battles were divided into 'acts' to denote different phases within them, while the periods between these phases were seen as 'intervals'.[22]

Yet it was not only soldiers who were seen to be acting in 'plays', nor was it only the immediate fighting which was depicted as the 'stage'. Countries took on metaphorical stage personalities in order that war correspondents could explain their actions, thus further distancing readers from actual fighting. For example, 'Linesman' writing in the *Daily Mail* portrayed the Balkan War as a 'theatre of war' where countries 'act' out their political and military desires, with readers as 'audience'. 'Linesman' described the manoeuvrings of the Greeks and the Monte-negrins, where the former

> attracted from the casual spectator no more attention than a super upon the stage, though certain experienced critics in the pits, marking an unwonted vigour in her gait, look curiously towards Salonica and wondered if in a later act there might not be a very 'speaking' part for the old tragedian. Montenegro, too, though she had bounded onto the boards like a very demon, had seemed so to have exhausted herself with the capture of Berane and among the swamps of Scutari that she seems scarcely worth watching any longer.[23]

Here the actions of countries contrasted greatly, with the one showing the most aggressive military posture having the most arresting 'stage presence' and being interesting to watch, while the other was less so because of its military inaction.

This last example suggests that newspapers did more than report war news. By employing images of 'drama' and 'plays', they also published critical 'reviews' of military events as though they were discussing the merits of a play or form of stage entertainment. They had as their 'critics' the war correspondents who were present at the battle observing from a distance, writing their opinions on the course and outcome of the 'plot'. In February 1900, the *Illustrated London News* published an article entitled 'The Transvaal War Reviewed', where the reviewers stated that 'the story of the capture and evacuation of Spion Kop is a stirring if rather tragic one'. The article was written as if the reviewer were discussing the way in which a stage production evolved, as if the course of events were written out by a playwright for full dramatic effect. This 'review' was located within the published issue alongside other forms of 'reviews', such as the 'Parliament' section, the British equivalent of the idea of 'political theatre', and 'The Playhouses', which offered critiques of current stage plays.[24]

This kind of association emphasized the theatrical perspective of warfare conveyed by newspapers and therefore the critical role of war correspondents. More directly, newspapers such as *The Times* referred to correspondents as 'critics' speculating whether battles were to have a 'third act' or to end abruptly with a 'finale'.[25] This was the perspective of George Lynch, war correspondent for the *Daily Chronicle* during the South African War, who held that reporting a battle was like 'the first night of a play'. For him, a war correspondent's 'account of the performance is to some extent like that of a dramatic critic'.[26]

A further way in which warfare was conceived as theatre was through the application of ancillary theatrical images, such as 'scene', 'curtain' and 'audience'. Yet while these images add more weight to the portrayal of war as theatre, they also contain a significance of their own in conveying perceptions of warfare. The term 'scene' was used in two distinct, but related ways. The first seems initially to have little direct connection to the theatre, but in the textual context was of more relevance. These examples refer mostly to the landscape or areas where battles took place. Thus the *Daily Mail* described Paardeburg as the 'scene of the last day's fighting', an attractive area in which 'the river where General Cronje is ensconced and fighting for his life resembles parts of the Thames'.[27] While these types of images appear to have little direct connection to the theatre, they do nonetheless convey an impression of 'setting the stage' in which the action was to take place. Far more directly related to theatrical imagery were other descriptions of warfare which used the term 'scene' in conjunction with other theatre imagery to make the connection clear. The *News of the World*, for example, portrayed the fall of Port Arthur as 'the scene of the terrible drama just concluded', while the *Daily Express* saw the same event as 'The Final Scene', the last stages of which were 'dramatic'.[28] These examples show how descriptions of war were able to utilize various images of the theatrical 'scene': that of action in a play or variations of 'scenery'.

'Curtain' imagery used in war correspondents' reports extended the application of theatrical metaphor to describe warfare. Just as a play, tableaux or turn began and ended with the rise and fall of the curtain, so too did the portrayal of battles. Thus the *Daily News* used the image to announce the imminent outbreak of hostilities between Japan and

Russia by predicting that the 'curtain' would rise upon what it saw as a tragedy rather than a triumph. It called for an end to the war after the first battle at the Yalu River by suggesting that 'even the most thoughtless spectator must now desire that the curtain should fall'.[29]

Just as stage productions have curtains to denote the changes of scenes and acts, so too do they have audiences to watch the performance. War reports had as their 'audience' not soldiers, for they were participants or 'actors', but the correspondents themselves who relayed the stories to their readers, known also as the 'world'. War correspondents could watch quite calmly and observe the course of battle in the 'passive' and 'detached' manner of a member of an audience. Gordon Smith, writing about the battle at the Sha-Ho for the *Morning Post*, speculated about the different roles to be played by the various Japanese armies and then 'sat on a ridge to eat my mid-day meal and watch the battle'.[30] Significant events such as battles of the Russo-Japanese War were felt to be watched anxiously by a world audience. Thus readers related not only to a single observer watching a battle, but to a larger whole, waiting and speculating on the outcome of a 'play', which had an uncertain ending, like a large audience in an auditorium. In this way it was felt that during the battle at Liaoyang, there would never be another moment so 'deeply charged with the essentially great elements of tragedy... as that on which the world now gazes, waiting in tense excitement for the final curtain to fall on that far-off Manchurian battlefield'.[31] It is made clear here that the 'world that gazes' was seen as an audience watching a tragedy, until the end was brought by victory, symbolized by the curtain going down. In addition, readers were included in a larger community of observers, socialized like a theatre audience watching the same play.

While the mere use of these images adds weight to the contention that warfare was depicted as a theatrical entertainment, the scene–curtain–audience images also indicate a certain distancing from the realities of warfare. The 'curtain' represents the 'fourth wall' through which audiences watch the action on stage. It reminds them that the performance is illusory, no matter how realistic it appears, and that when the entertainment ends, they will resume their ordinary routine. Percy Fitzgerald mentioned the significance of the 'curtain' in his book *The Art of Acting*, written in 1892, suggesting that it represents 'the barrier between the real and the ideal world'.[32] The naturalness of theatre imagery as applied to war reporting suggests that the same ideas apply: that if the readers are the 'real' world, the war on the other side of the curtain is the 'ideal' or 'unreal' world. This indicates then that not only was war an entertaining piece of theatre which moved its audience, it was also not real. The 'actors', unlike the 'audience', inhabited an ephemeral, unreal world which lasted only as long as the 'curtain' remained up.

These theatrical images, of course, required an area in which to be staged. In this way, the 'theatre of war' became more than just an area of operations, it was a term to denote the physical place encompassing the 'sets', the 'acting' and the 'audience' mentioned in war dispatches. Douglas Story supported this perspective when he described the battle-field before a major assault: 'the theatre of battle had been admirably chosen, magnificently set' and with more than 50,000 soldiers, 'did not lack players'. Other war correspondents made more specific compari-sons to particular theatres, such as Ashmead-Bartlett's reference to the assaults on Port Arthur, which were for him perfectly staged, so much so that they 'could not have been better witnessed had they been mounted at Drury Lane'.[33]

The visual representations of warfare in the form of cartoons utilized a wide range of these images to portray warfare as 'music hall' entertain-ment. This was the case even in upmarket publications like *Punch* which frequently used the image of the 'music hall' rather than the 'straight' theatre with which its readers would have been more familiar, because it was easier to lampoon through a 'comic' medium than through a 'ser-ious' one. Anticipating George Lynch who wrote after the war that Elandslaagte was as an intricate 'military tableau', *Punch* depicted Kit-chener as 'stage manager' of the 'Theatre Royal, S. Africa, Feb. 1, 1901' (Plate 3). He was portrayed in top hat and tails at the edge of the stage and in front of the curtain, saying to the 'audience', 'Ladies and Gentle-man, on account of the elaborate preparations for the final tableaux, I must request your kind indulgence while the curtain remains down'. The different phases of the war were thus represented as different music hall tableaux, and the British public or 'audience' were asked to remain patient while Kitchener's blockhouse and flying column system was put into place.[34]

Similar images were used to criticize those involved in unpopular wars, such as the Turco-Italian War in North Africa. The *News of the World* cartoon entitled 'Tripoli or Your Life!' depicted Italy as a fat comic-opera highwayman in a uniform full of medals, a large sash, a feather hat (reminiscent of the elite Bersaglieri troopers' cap) and oversize sword, trying to rob a noble and brave-looking Turk. *Justice* used the 'comic opera' metaphor to criticize Italy and suggested that their 'victories' made them appear ludicrous. Francis McCullagh, war correspondent for the *Daily News* and the *Westminster Gazette*, felt that several instances persuaded the non-Italians that they were witnessing a 'comic opera or Christmas pantomime of some excruciatingly funny sort'.[35]

The sense that warfare was a light and entertaining theatre production was strengthened through the application of 'music' imagery. Accompanying musical pieces had the effect of intensifying events on stage, of making light of hardships or of highlighting particular points of emphasis. Music was for the late-Victorians and Edwardians an integral part of everyday life, and was used to convey moral and political significance.[36] It is, therefore, not surprising to see music imagery being employed in descriptions of warfare, particularly in the context of images of the theatre. The main application of this image was to compare the use of weapons to orchestral works. Primarily, this referred to preliminary bombardments before an attack was launched, which were described as the 'overture' or 'first movement' of a symphony.[37] Similarly, senior officers were often depicted as principal 'players' while commanders of forces were 'conductors'. For example, Repington described the unwillingness of Generals Sakharoff and Bilderling to cooperate with each other as two principal players, Sakharoff a piano soloist and Bilderling as a solo violinist, who refused to accompany each other in a 'fantasia'. This was, for Repington, 'one more proof of the indiscipline of Kuropatkin's orchestra and the incapacity of its conductor'.[38]

While the events depicted in the Russo-Japanese War were most easily seen as sombre dramas, those in the setting of the British Empire were stories of interest, containing both tragedy and romance. This perspective was primarily due to the habit of having adventure stories set in the Empire, particularly those designed for juveniles.[39] The Imperial setting and native enemy also influenced the way in which wars were perceived, both of which were seen as exotic. Battles such as those at Spion Kop and Gumburu were depicted as 'thrilling stories',[40] entertaining adventure stories set in the Empire. But the most obvious example was a story which was covered in most newspapers in similar styles concerning the storming of Gyantse Jong in Tibet. Most papers used Henry Newman's report which stated that 'there is no more stirring story in the annals of Indian frontier warfare than that of the capture of Gyantse Fort, held by 7,000 Tibetans, by a mere handful of British and Indian troops...'. It was seen as 'the finest feat of arms our Indian Army had accomplished since the gallant Gordons carried Dargai heights in the North West Frontier campaign' in 1897.[41]

Both British victories and defeats could be portrayed as tragedies, but the Imperial background added elements of mystery and romance which were lacking in the majority of non-Imperial wars. Thus the first encounter with the Tibetans at Guru was not portrayed as a great victory like Gyantse, but as a 'grim tragedy'. While not understanding why the Tibetans did not disarm peacefully but struck at the British forces which had them surrounded, the British admired their stoicism and courage under fire. Yet for the war correspondents, the battle still conveyed a sense of 'tragical romance', which was emphasized by the location of the battle. Thus the *Glasgow Herald* reported that 'the tragical romance' of the battle was 'heightened by the fact that it took place in the throne of the winds of the world, in a secret place of the earth under the shadow of the mighty snow-capped mountains'.[42] While the battle itself was 'romantic', that is, a hazardous conflict with a barbarous and mysterious enemy, the exotic location was able to heighten the sense of romance by giving it an element of adventure and mystery.

Even the correspondents themselves were said to have led romantic lives, mostly by the papers that employed them, thus showing that 'romance' in a reporter was a favourable attribute to be emphasized by papers attempting to promote their versions of war descriptions. The *Daily Mail* correspondent Edmund Candler was wounded at Guru and in reporting the event, the paper said that he was a young man 'whose life reads like a romance'. The same paper presented its military commentator on the Balkan Wars, 'Linesman', as someone who was able to convey the 'romance of stark-reality', and whose works combined the romance of his own adventures during the South African War with the romance of Rudyard Kipling.[43] Whether these claims are true is not at issue; their significance is rather that war was seen as a romantic event and that serious reporting combined that sense with the style of an arch-Imperialist poet.

'Unprecedented in history': images of spectacle

Style was also important for the way in which military activity was visually represented and discussed. The value of army spectacle in nineteenth-century Britain has been examined, along with its adoption by a wide variety of institutions. Spectacle was a necessary and inherent part of armies not only for the need to maintain morale and discipline within the ranks, but also to stimulate recruitment. Military commanders used martial spectacle in the forms of the review, of ceremonies and of popular entertainment to raise the profile of their units and make them more attractive socially. It was a spirit taken up by entertainment entrepreneurs who produced equestrian dramas, mock battles, panoramas and musicals. Military spectacle in this sense was widespread and popular, having been adopted in the course of the century by capitalists like Joshua Wedgwood and Robert Owen, and social reformers like Samuel Smiles and Baden-Powell.[44]

The paradox was characteristic of the mid-nineteenth century where at one level, soldiers were feared and despised as agents of authority and loathed for their ill-disciplined behaviour. Yet another level represented the public taste for military display, colour, fancy uniforms, synchronized drill and martial music, all free forms of entertainment readily accessible just as traditional forms of recreation were being suppressed.[45] By the end of the nineteenth century, much of this sense of display, spectacle and beauty was conveyed in the reporting of real warfare, having the effect of blurring the distinctions between entertaining displays of military spectacle, which would have everyday familiarity, and the deadly nature of actual combat. This blurring occurred through depictions of warfare as 'picturesque', the descriptions of military movement and manoeuvre as pretty and beautiful, the presentation of warfare as made up of amazing sights, the manner in which weapons and their effects were described, and the conveying of a sense of war as excitement or even as a leisure activity.

All of the wars examined here were seen to be conducted in exotic locations. Part of the power of the attraction of Empire was the wondrous sights and scenes which greeted pioneer and soldier. While the Imperial setting for armed combat was portrayed as beautiful and picturesque, battles found in other parts of the world were also seen this way. In setting the scene for a report on the fighting at Paardeburg, *Lloyd's* suggested that the location was 'one of the prettiest spots in South Africa'. There was no suggestion of the havoc or destruction which battle would bring to this charming, beautiful, English-looking location. The last line of defence for the retreating Turks before Constantinople, the famous lines of Tchataldja, was described in the *Illustrated London News* as a place where 'soldiers sleep peacefully' and 'the scene is very picturesque under the young moon, the crescent of the sky, and the warm glow of camp-fires is on the ground'. It was portrayed as a scene of tranquillity and beauty, yet the title announced that it was a sketch drawn on the battlefield, a statement which alleges the authenticity of the image.[46]

While the location of battle was seen as beautiful and attractive, the soldiers operating within that mental landscape could be depicted in similar ways. After the fight at Erigo during the Second Somaliland Expedition, the *Daily News* described the Somaliland Field Force as 'a most picturesque tag-rag', giving details of the collection of tribes and races of soldiers, their uniforms and their variety of weapons. This was, the paper announced in its headline, 'Picturesque Warfare', in which the commander of the force was said to have later 'won for himself the picturesque title of "The Man Who Moves With the Wind"' for his ability to move his forces rapidly over great distances in the desert.[47]

The movement of military forces, with the speed, colour and control inherent in manoeuvre was a major part of the descriptions of war as a spectacle. Military reviews capitalized on this aspect of military manoeuvres to emphasize the display and awesome beauty popular with the public in the nineteenth century. A similar tendency revealed itself in descriptions of movement on the battlefield, where emphasis was on the beauty and splendour of the troops instead of the grim, destructive nature of combat. The movement of British and native troops from Phari onto the Tuna Plain in Tibet, with a broad front and scouts fanned out in front, was described by the *Manchester Guardian* in detail as 'an imposing spectacle'. The operations in South Africa, particularly the chasing of De Wet, with the rapid movement of large numbers of men, horses and guns were described similarly. *Lloyd's*, for example, announced that the 'great chase after De Wet by four columns commanded by General Knox has been one of the most exciting operations of the whole war'. The crossing of the Caledon River, with all the horses, wagons, carts and men involved was to the paper's war correspondent, 'one of the most wonderful sights which I have ever seen'.[48]

This perception of military manoeuvre as being an impressive spectacle was intensified during battle. On several occasions, actual fighting was described as if it were a military exhibition for the entertainment of spectators, like those popular events held at Earl's Court. A rush of British soldiers in South Africa was described as exciting and akin to the spirit of a large military display, while the victory at Paardeburg was 'a beautiful spectacle and appeared to be as bloodless as manoeuvres'.[49] This was a spirit echoed by George Lynch who suggested that the vision of gunners advancing in limber 'was a pretty sight to see', which 'would have drawn ringing rounds of applause at an Islington tournament'.[50] Foreign soldiers fared just as well in terms of offering spectacular sights during fighting, for according to A. G. Hales, veteran war correspondent for the *Daily News*, 'one of the prettiest sights I ever saw was a regiment of Cossacks in full charge'. For Hales, the thunderous sound of the horses and the flash of drawn swords poised and ready was an awe-inspiring sight.[51] Thus not only the location of conflict and the movement of military forces was seen as fascinating and colourful, but elements of actual fighting were also portrayed as exciting and pretty.

Yet this essentially positive view of war as entertainment depended upon the way in which the effects of weapons were portrayed: if weapons were seen as engines of destruction, the illusion of 'bloodless manoeuvre' and colourful spectacle would be greatly diminished if not completely contradicted. However, the effects of modern armaments were portrayed in a way consistent with images of spectacle.

The most common way of describing the effects of weapons was to compare them to fireworks displays. The end of the attack, which Douglas Story outlined in his 'Play of Death', was described as 'closing in a pyrotechnic display', as the afternoon drew on and the artillery bombardment lit up the evening skies.[52] This particular image was not out of context for those describing military action in terms of entertainment, such as the phenomenon of 'pyrodramas', fireworks displays which told of current military events, particularly in the Imperial setting but also depicting major wars such as the Russo-Japanese War. These displays portrayed a wide range of military activity, including battles, sieges, mutinies, and artillery 'duels', and they were extremely popular as forms of entertainment, at amusement parks such as Belle Vue Gardens, where patrons waltzed with partners and promenaded with friends before fireworks lit up the sky in simulated warfare.[53]

The most spectacular event that captured the spirit of the 'pyrodrama', was that of an artillery bombardment. The bursting of artillery shells, while recognized in passing by some newspapers as 'deadly', was depicted primarily as noises and flashes characterized by puffs of white smoke, which enabled eye-witnesses to report that whole actions were 'awe inspiring to a degree'.[54] Yet most newspapers avoided mention of the deadly nature of 'artillery duels', preferring to concentrate on the visual and aural spectacle rather than on the actual effects of the bombardment. A pre-dawn exchange of fire between the Russians and Japanese was described as 'a magnificent spectacle' that 'was presented, the lurid sky streaked with the flashes of lightning and the bursting of shells across the rays of the searchlights, the crashing, roaring and flashing of the artillery, the thunder and dazzling of star-shells'. This description was published under the title 'The Story of the War' and might easily have been the description of a firework display representing a far-away conflict in a genteel setting such as a pleasure gardens.[55]

The connection between warfare and the activities conducted in a pleasure park was further enhanced by the leisurely manner in which war correspondents conducted themselves while describing aspects of warfare. Just as patrons of pleasure gardens watched 'pyrodrama' displays in a leisurely manner while promenading or consuming light refreshment in parks like Belle Vue, so too did war correspondents behave while witnessing real warfare. The Japanese had made such detailed catering arrangements for Western war correspondents who accompanied their forces, that one reporter remarked that 'one would imagine that we are embarking on a picnic or arranging with Messrs. Cook for a tour in Palestine'.[56] Yet this was precisely the image of warfare which was conveyed by the correspondents, such as Edmund Candler who described the assault on the Karo La in Tibet. He explained how the civilians watched the whole affair, 'stretched on a grassy knoll on the left, enjoying the sunshine and the smell of warm turf'. For Candler, 'it might have been a picnic on the Surrey Downs' with 'the tap-tap of the Maxim, like a distant woodpecker, in the valley, and the occasional report of the 10-pounder by our side, which made the valley and cliffs reverberate like thunder'.[57]

While these examples illustrate how the effects of weapons were celebrated as a stimulating spectacle, they do not capture the excitement and tension which infused the reports of war correspondents. They wrote their reports as their 'stories' unfolded, and in a style reminiscent of the adventure books which were so popular with readers. While all attacks on significant positions were characterized by this adventure style, the battles fought in the Empire were conveyed as the most exciting. The capture of Gyantse Jong in Tibet, for example, was seen as the climax of an exciting day's military activity. Newman's report for Reuters exuded this spirit when it mentioned that 'the excitement of a long day culminated in the scaling of a breach in the walls of the jong by Lieutenant Grant, of 8th Gurkhas, followed by a mixed company of Gurkhas and Fusiliers'. Newman told of how he and his colleagues 'watched with bated breath these heroic men climb a cleft in the rock in the face of a hail of bullets and torrents of stone'.[58] This was a spirit shared by Colonel Younghusband who admitted that 'we held our breath, and in tense excitement awaited the result of the storming party'.[59]

Specific events led war correspondents to convey a sense of excitement as they watched the proceedings of an attack from a distance, but warfare in general was also depicted in similar ways. After reporting the Turco-Italian War and the Balkan Wars, Seppings-Wright was still able to confess that initial nervousness at being under fire soon gave way as 'excitement and enthusiasm blazed in your heart. At times, indeed, one revelled in it' for 'your blood thrills through your pulse with mad excitement. Surely

there is nothing more awe inspiring...than war'.[60] With these senti-
ments expressed by war correspondents in the field, it is no wonder that
the same sense of excitement was conveyed to readers in their reports.

Conclusion: 'a seat in the dress-circle on the hills behind'

The use of theatrical imagery to describe warfare concerns more than
just the simple delineation of a geographical area where battle occurred.
These metaphors were not simply clichés, for they reveal the ways in
which war was perceived by correspondents and readers alike. In several
ways, these images of stage and spectacle served to distance readers from
the realities of war, and thus blurred the distinctions between the
amusing and the deadly. War being depicted as a form of entertainment
to be equated with a leisure activity, contributed to the trivialization of
combat and the insulation of readers from the less pleasurable aspects of
the soldier's experience.

The very use of theatrical imagery indicated a particular point of view.
Events in battle were 'dramas', 'staged' for the benefit and amusement of
the 'audience' and commented upon by the war correspondent or
'critic'. Reports of battle were similar to stage productions in that they
required a suspension of belief on the part of the audience and represented a 'falsification of life' in the manner of the Edwardian theatre.
Just as the curtain separated the 'real' world of the audience from the
'unreal' world of the stage, so too did the image of the 'curtain' separate
readers from the realities of battle. If warfare was a theatrical production,
then it too represented an amusement which was illusory; just as in the
theatre when the curtain rose, real life was suspended, but the moment
the 'fourth wall' descended was the moment when the play or battle
ended and reality returned.

In another way, the physical location of the war correspondent encouraged the use of theatre imagery and contributed to the effect of
creating distance between readers and warfare. War correspondents
were, for the most part, physically distant from the actual battle. They
observed from the relative safety of communication trenches or far-
away hills where their intention was to increase their perspective to
encompass as much of the battlefield as possible. As their sole purpose
was to *watch* a battle, and they did so from a distance, they could see
themselves as disinterested or 'passive' observers, looking upon a 'stage'.
For people like Hamilton or Ashmead-Bartlett, theatre imagery would
have come naturally, as the relatively static nature of the battles around
the siege at Port Arthur easily lent itself to these images. Observers

watched the passing events as if they were raised on a stage, where one could occupy the 'stalls' or trenches near the 'footlights' or 'a seat could be occupied in the dress-circle on the hills behind'.[61] With war correspondents occupying vantage points which physically placed them in such positions, it is not surprising that they utilized images of the theatre. This perception served to reinforce the idea of distance between reader and battle, for correspondents actually occupied positions akin to the theatre, and encouraged a perspective which gave resonance to their ancillary stage imagery.

The presentation of warfare as a spectacle in newspapers linked combat to leisure activities which were amusing and fun, further isolating readers from the realities of battle. Thus, just as the review, march-past or guard ceremony were colourful and entertaining public displays, so too were battles which combined the attraction of these displays with exotic or 'picturesque' settings. Battles were also similar to peacetime military spectacle in that they were seen as harmless, with weapons creating 'pretty' sights and impressively loud noises. War correspondents, like those enjoying entertainments such as 'pyrodramas', watched the events before them in a detached, distant manner, relatively unaffected by the destructive weapons and deadly assaults they were describing. Readers familiar with these forms of entertainment would have imagined war to be exactly what their 'eye-witnesses' described: an event which was pleasant and diverting to watch. This image essentially denied the destructive nature of warfare by representing it as an activity which could be enjoyed as one danced and promenaded in the warm, peaceful summer evenings.

Fussell maintains that the use of theatre imagery acted as a 'psychic escape' for participants in the First World War, enabling them to deny the challenges to 'real' life and their 'real' identity, and thus to assert that the world was still 'rational'. However, theatrical imagery was widely used in the press and therefore widely accepted by readers well before the outbreak of the war in 1914. The application of theatre imagery in these pre-1914 news reports of warfare had a different but related significance to those employed later. It essentially denied the reality of war and enabled readers to distance themselves from the brutal and destructive nature of warfare, and compared it instead with forms of mass entertainment and pleasant leisure activities. The *mentalité* was one which subsumed the 'real' into the 'unreal' and gave the impression that warfare was not such a terrible experience, encouraging a willingness and desire to actively become involved in warfare, rather than seek a means to escape it.

6
'A Withering Fire that Mowed Them Down in Heaps': Images of Death and Wounding

Introduction: 'masking and denying the actuality of death'

In examining descriptions of dying in British literature, Garrett Stewart boldly suggests that death is the ultimate fiction, an event which can only be described by those who have not experienced it. Descriptions of death are thus much more dependent on cultural perceptions and the imagination of the writer than any other literary event.[1] Newspaper representations of death on the battlefield similarly must be, by their nature, fictional. While the act of dying is a fictional event for authors, the way that death was portrayed in the press reveals much about Edwardian perceptions of warfare. Depictions which showed warfare with all its horror, pain and destruction would conflict with the image of warfare as beneficial, healthy and desirable. If, however, the reality of death and wounding were denied, suppressed or glossed over, the impression of readers that war's sporting, entertaining and adventurous qualities were not diminished by its horrors would be reinforced, and the positive images of war would remain. This does not necessarily demand a total rejection of the horrors of war, for the use of language can de-emphasize war's realities while at the same time purporting to be 'graphic'. Similarly, visual depictions of war can suggest the unpleasant side of battle while not contradicting its overall positive nature.

In order to interpret correctly newspaper depictions of death and wounding in war, it is necessary to examine the cultural context in which death was imagined: what has been called the 'Victorian Celebration of Death'.[2] This 'celebration' was not constant, but changed gradually towards the end of the nineteenth century, to lay the foundations of the twentieth-century 'death-denying' society.[3] Indeed, the late nineteenth century saw the creation of 'invisible death', as the psychological landscape was completely transformed to the virtual exclusion and denial of death, though less quickly among the working classes.[4]

Attitudes to death, of course, changed slowly. Ruth Richardson has outlined the importance of the 1832 Anatomy Act in altering the focus of attention among the better-off in society. Confident that they could avoid a pauper's destiny of becoming anatomical fodder for inquiring scientific minds, this Act, Richardson suggests, allowed attention and expenditure to shift from strong, solid coffins and elaborate tombs to thwart grave-robbers, to lavish funerary displays.[5] Others have identified these displays as expensive affairs which included intricate and complex mourning rituals, particularly for widows, lavish funerary processions, mourning cards, poetry and stationery, and the overwhelming predominance of the colour black to symbolize the 'deep' mourning of the individual.[6]

This 'celebration' of death reached its apogee in the 1870s but began to decline in the last quarter of the nineteenth century. The National Funeral and Mourning Reform Association, founded in 1875, campaigned to make funerals less expensive and mourning rituals less constraining. Similarly, the practice of cremation, long associated with pre-Christian pagan practices, also emerged in the 1870s to challenge traditional funeral and mourning rites.[7] The effect of these developments was to infuse and encourage a sense of removal and denial in social attitudes towards death. One major reform was the creation of large, spacious burial grounds outside of cities in order to rectify chronic overcrowding in urban cemeteries which constituted a significant health hazard in the nineteenth century. This effectively altered the landscape of death by removing the physical location of the dead.[8] Similarly, the destruction of the physical remains of the dead through cremation also changed basic perceptions of death, where the 'body' was no longer central or even present during mourning rituals.[9]

Other ways in which this denial of death became manifest were through the replacement of direct images of death, such as skulls, bones and cadavers in contemporary sepulchres with classical allegorical allusions, such as empty or cracked urns, willows and broken columns. This change of imagery in the late-nineteenth century represented a 'desire to swathe the reality of decomposition in a romantic aura, masking and denying the actuality of death'. In addition, this denial was extended further through the use of 'decorous language', where the word 'dead' was rarely found and replaced by euphemisms such as 'passed on', 'passed away' or 'gone to God'.[10]

The idea of 'going to God' or 'passing on' indicated that both Christians and non-believers were attempting to deny the reality of death. Christians sought 'theological denial' in a concept of heaven and, in the ultimate denial, the resurrection of the body, while non-believers looked to similar belief systems such as spiritualism in order to deal with 'loss'. What both groups of Victorian mourners were seeking was 'an effective system of denial'.[11] Indeed, Spiritualism can be seen as a 'private denial of death' which, while expanding greatly during the inter-war period, originated at a popular level in the 1850s, growing to a respectable 141 local associations of the Spiritualist National Union in 1914.[12]

As shown in other studies of death in the Victorian and Edwardian period, the twin themes of removal and denial can be traced in the newspaper descriptions of war casualties. Written images formed a language of suppression which removed the body and the unpleasant consequences of combat. Further images denied the reality of warfare by describing death and wounding with either vague terms or allegorical references. Visual images, which included illustrations, photographs, cartoons and advertisements, also removed and denied death by hiding the horrors of war and by presenting images which showed distorted realities.

'Melt away like solder before the flame of a blow pipe': written images

An examination of the written images of death and wounding in newspapers presents particular problems for the historian. Often, several distinct images were used in the same issue, the same article and even the same sentence in order to convey the consequences of warfare to readers. It is necessary to disentangle these images in order to subject them to meaningful analysis, to compare them to imagery found in a range of newspapers and to determine if these images conform to the dominant themes of 'removal' and 'denial'. An obvious way in which casualties were manipulated by written imagery was to remove the dead and wounded from both the battlefield and from discussions in the press. Other methods included the use of a language of suppression which effectively hid casualties from the imaginative gaze of the reader, and the use of a metaphorical language which, while seemingly emotive, was 'numbing and exonerating' in its use of terms such as 'slaughter', 'abattoir' and 'harvest'.

The most direct method of removing casualties from the consciousness of readers was to suggest that the soldiers no longer existed, that they had simply disappeared. In this way, the word 'annihilate' was utilized extensively and became a common method to denote the deaths of soldiers, particularly if on a large scale. It essentially removed the dead and the wounded from the battlefield and thus from further consideration regarding their fate. This image was reinforced by the tendency to group soldiers in 'parties', 'batteries', 'companies' or 'regiments' and suggest that it was merely the unit or group that was 'annihilated', further adding to the sense of complete removal and, in effect, distancing readers from the actual fate of individual soldiers. When the Arabs attacked the Italians at Sciara Sciat in North Africa, causing large numbers of casualties among the invaders, the press announced that 'three companies of Bersaglieri were totally annihilated', thus removing them from the scene and the discussion. In addition, casualties were said to have 'vanished' or to have been 'disposed of'.[13] Similarly, for Ellis Ashmead-Bartlett, Russians killed in the war against Japan simply 'cease to be soldiers of the Czar'.[14] This sense of 'ceasing to be' effectively removed the casualties from the psychological landscape of those reading about the consequences of battle.

Similar images which evoked a strong sense of removal were terms such as 'cleared out', 'swept back' and 'swept away'. Not only were the vestiges of death removed, but an element of sanitation was introduced reminiscent of the hygienic removal of corpses from seeping inner-city church graveyards to distant sanitary cemeteries. While the 'Dervishes' in Somaliland could only be temporarily 'swept back' because of the relentless nature of their attack, the Turks and the Arabs were easily 'swept away' by the Italians during futile and uncoordinated assaults.[15] Similarly, the Tibetans were 'cleared out' of sangars and other positions by British soldiers and Mounted Infantry, as if they were domestic dust or an infestation of vermin. The *Penny Illustrated Paper* suggested this image in its report on the assault of Gyantse Jong in Tibet, where 'it took hours to clear them out of nooks and crannies', rather like a domestic cleaner clearing the more inaccessible parts of a house.[16]

While *Lloyd's Weekly News* used the term 'annihilate' in a headline to describe Plunkett's defeat at Gumburu, it was more common to use other, softer images to describe the battle. Both this paper and the *Daily News*, for example, used the term 'wiped out', which still removed the dead from the imagination and continued to promote images of 'cleansing', but as a phrase, it was less total and complete than 'annihilate'. However, even the image of annihilation as an instance of removal was used with qualifications when applied to British casualties. The *Daily News* report emphasized the smallness of Plunkett's force of 208 men compared to the Somalis, as did *Lloyd's*, though the latter believed that the defeat was not as overwhelming as first thought because of the enormous Somali casualties and the brave stand made by the British. The defeat might have been total, but it did not result in a loss of prestige.[17] These images combined not only decorous language when reference was made to British casualties, but also qualifications and justifications which gave an overall impression that the defeat had not been so 'overwhelming', and through this perspective, hiding or denying the deaths.

A further way in which the dead and wounded were softly removed from the descriptions and discussions of warfare was to state that they were 'out of action', suggesting that they were temporarily and painlessly removed from the battlefield, away from the fighting, rather like unserviceable equipment. The term applied not only to the wounded, some of whom might indeed have returned to the fighting, but also to the dead who were, in actuality, more than just temporarily out of action. The term was also applied to large numbers of casualties. For the British in South Africa, casualties of 600–700 were unparalleled and shocking, yet the *Daily Mail* described the British casualties at Stromberg as about 600 who 'have been taken or put out of action'.[18] This image could easily be used to describe the death and wounding of several times that number of casualties. The *Daily Mirror* put the Japanese casualties at Liaoyang as more than 10,000 'put out of action', this being 'in proportion to the vast numbers of soldiers engaged'. Here, not only were the dead and wounded simply removed from the field of battle, but their extreme numbers were merely 'proportional', and therefore less devastating.[19]

A more frequently used variation of 'out of action' was the phrase '*hors de combat*' which also referred to both the dead and the wounded. The effect of using a foreign phrase further enhanced the gentle, civilized removal of casualties. For, like the phrase 'out of action', it was not applied to the uncivilized Imperial enemy, such as the Tibetans, Somalis or Arabs, although the Boers, as ambiguously semi-civilized, were an exception.[20] Moreover, European and Japanese casualties were more gently and discreetly 'placed' '*hors de combat*', just as they were 'taken' or 'put' 'out of action', rather than savagely mauled by the effects of modern weaponry, or obliterated like an Imperial enemy. This suggests a hierarchy of death, where 'civilized', but especially British, combatants died in a dignified and gentle manner, compared to 'non-civilized' combatants who were 'exterminated', an image applied in particular to the Arabs at the Oasis massacre and later battles.[21]

The theme of the removal of casualties from the psychological land-scape of readers was enhanced by a language of suppression which limited the discussion of death by invoking images which stifled realis-tic depictions of casualties and, instead, utilized terms and phrases which hid them. In this way, Lord Brooke could describe the Japanese as having 'crumbled like sand castles before the advancing tide', and *The Times* could see the same troops 'melt away from the glacis like solder before the flame of a blow pipe'.[22] Here, the remains of the Japanese were removed like sand in the water, or soft metal in a hot flame, transforming them from solid, recognized and real, into something unstructured and unrecognizable.

Indeed, the terms 'fallen', 'fell', or 'lying' were used frequently before the First World War to describe casualties, and were applied regardless of the scale of death and the 'civilized' status of the combatants. The *Daily Mail* described how Lieutenant-Colonel W. Aldworth, the Commanding Officer of the Duke of Cornwall's Light Infantry, 'fell with a bullet in his head while leading his regiment' at Paardeburg.[23] The impression conveyed here was that the Colonel simply fell down and that the bullet was almost incidental to his 'falling', for there was no description of the effect of the bullet or how long it took him to die. In addition, the scale of death did not seem to matter, as these terms were used to describe casualty figures of 1000, 15,000, 25,000, and even 50,000. The *Daily News* believed that the Battle of Mukden would prove to be the Russian Sedan, stating that 'it is estimated that already 100,000 men have fallen in the battle'.[24]

The 'civilized' status of combatants does not seem to have been a factor in the use of this particular image. The officers who died with Colonel Plunkett at Gumburu symbolized the intensity of the fighting, for 'within 15 minutes of the commencement of hostilities, three British officers had fallen'. Even the casualties of native troops fighting for the British were treated in a similar manner, for it was reported that 'the men [were] falling where they stood until no more remained to fill the gap'. Yet the casualties of those very Somalis whom the British and their native African troops were fighting were also described in a passive voice, as at Jidbali towards the end of the Fourth Expedition, where over 1000 of the Mullah's followers were killed, 'most of them falling in the pursuit'.[25] Once again, this image conveyed the impression of killed and wounded as merely having fallen down, suppressing the nature of casualties and avoiding a realistic discussion of death, while simultaneously removing the dead and wounded from the psycho-logical landscape of readers. This image was reinforced by others, such as those where the dead and wounded 'lie' on the battlefield,[26] where 'men dropped thickly' or were 'dropping in bunches',[27] or where they were simply 'down'.[28]

These terms and images, in addition to being 'decorous', are, as Daniel Pick has pointed out, both 'numbing and exonerating'. They are numbing in the sense that the scale of death in the modern era had been almost inconceivable, owing to the increased mechanization of warfare, and exonerating in that language was used to avoid realistic portrayals.[29] Pick examines this phenomenon and links it to the killing of animals for the consumption of meat. He sees the influences of technology, factory production and the increasing calculation of death as factors which were present both in the slaughterhouse and on the battlefield. Here, too, were trends regarding the removal of images of death which were present in Victorian attitudes towards the removal of the dead to suburban cemeteries and the destruction of the body through cremation. Pick examines how the slaughter of animals became 'less socially visible', as the function of the butcher became separated from the slaughterer, and, like the cemeteries, as the slaughterhouse moved from the inner cities. According to Pick, it was the 1860s which initiated a new 'systematic mechanization of death' in both warfare and meat production, as both areas were subject to the influence of technology, operated on a previously inconceivable scale, and were removed and distanced from everyday life. So similar were these two functions of systematic and calculated death that Pick has concluded that it was 'not by chance that the metaphor of the slaughterhouse [was] to become so inextricably intertwined with the language of modern war'.[30]

This was indeed the case in the Edwardian depictions of warfare in the press. The use of the emotive terms 'abattoir', 'slaughterhouse' and 'slaughter' in attempting to convey the scale and vastness of death on the modern battlefield merely served to distance readers from death, just as they were separated from the process of meat production while acting as consumers.[31] The image of the slaughterhouse as a bloody, messy space remained, but the actual slaughter of animals, with the accompanying sights, sounds and smells, was distant and hidden. In this way, events such as the massacre of Arabs in the Oasis near Tripoli could be described in both *The Times* and the *News of the World* as 'a human abattoir', giving the impression of graphic portrayals, but simply reinforcing the distance between the impressions of readers and the experience of those caught up in the war.[32]

The use of the term 'slaughter', and the associated image of 'butchery', were used extensively to describe death on a mass scale. These images were applied to British victories, but also, on occasion as at Twefontein, to their defeats.[33] They were used to describe the totality and one-sided nature of an enemy's defeat, such as the battles at Guru and Gyantse,[34] but also to the sheer scale of casualties, as those inflicted by both sides during the Russo-Japanese War.[35] Thus, while seemingly emotive and 'graphic', these descriptions were, in effect, removing the proximity of death from the psychological landscape of readers, just as the realities of the slaughterhouse were sanitized and removed from public view.

Related to the image of 'slaughter' and also utilized to describe vast numbers of casualties was the traditional image of 'the harvest', with death personified as 'the reaper'. Michael Wheeler has noted the strength of this image as a part of the 'cult of death' in Victorian literature, where 'Death' as 'reaper' was usually depicted with harvesting tools, such as a 'scythe', representative of an obsolete, pastoral past.[36] This image was present in the newspaper reports of war, especially in discussions of battles with large-scale casualties, such as the Boer War and, in particular, the Russo-Japanese War. The personification of death as 'reaper' was present, such as in the description of the battle at Green Hill in the *Morning Post*, which indicated that 'it was there that death had reaped the great harvest'.[37] It was, indeed, a strong image, as the war correspondents present at battles in the Russo-Japanese War utilized them in their books published after the war. Bennett Burleigh, for example, felt that 'Death was mowing savagely with both hands' at Liaoyang.[38]

Yet it was the ancillary images of 'the harvest' and 'death as reaper' which were used more frequently. For example, the *Daily Mail* described the effects of shrapnel on the retreating Turks as 'sowing its deadly seed over the whole area occupied by the Turks strewing the road and hill side with dead bodies'.[39] But the most frequently used of these ancillary 'harvesting' images was that of 'mowing'. This was an image which applied to large-scale British casualties as well as those of others, particularly the Japanese and the Russian. With this image, whole detachments, regiments and brigades were described as being 'mowed down'. Reports of Warren's withdrawal at Spion Kop depicted the British infantry as having 'gone down as before the scythe', while the Japanese at the Yalu met a 'withering fire ... from rifles and machine-guns' which 'mowed them down in heaps, but failed to stay their advance'.[40] These images were dependent upon a combination of the effects of modern weaponry on massed troops, either in attack or retreat, and the particular perspective of the war correspondent, who, observing from a distance, would perceive the far away bodies of men being 'cut down' in large numbers, an effect heightened if an attack was in large numbers and of particular persistence.[41]

The second dominant theme that reinforced the image of 'removal' was that of 'denial'. This theme contained many aspects of the discussion of casualties, such as an avoidance of the horrific effects of weapons, emphasis on the 'humane' nature of warfare, the depersonalization of casualties, and a manner of discussing casualties as an 'expenditure', thereby avoiding realistic depictions of death and wounding.

From 1866 to 1906, those reporting from the battlefield did not totally ignore the horrors of war, but rather their descriptions were not detailed or specific.[42] There were several instances where the Edwardian press stressed that their articles contained 'graphic descriptions' of battle, and indeed the images were often evocative and emotive. The use of the terms 'agony', 'suffering', 'carnage' and 'horrors' showed that reporters and readers were not completely isolated from the nature of war. Yet, the way in which those realities were discussed not only reinforces the assertion that casualties were down-played and minimized, but also suggests that the worst aspects of warfare were unimaginable and indescribable, and therefore not adequately or fully discussed. All combatants were said to have 'suffered' or 'suffered severely', but these terms referred more to the numbers of casualties absorbed by an army than to the experiences of individuals, who in many cases, did indeed suffer great pain in long and lingering deaths.[43] Reports only hinted at the amount and degree of carnage produced by warfare, with one Liberal newspaper even invoking a licentious and festive atmosphere by suggesting that the aftermath of the Oasis Massacre was 'a veritable carnival of carnage'.[44]

Indeed, many correspondents refused to delve into detailed descriptions of death, preferring to avoid them by 'drawing a veil' over them or settling for passing allusions to the horrific aspects they witnessed, concentrating instead on what were seen as the more positive aspects of war. These allusions and treatments were techniques understood and acceptable to audiences who did not see the 'unsavoury' elements of warfare. In its first leading article, the *News of the World* described Liaoyang as the 'Manchurian Field of Slaughter', where the wounded must have been 'gasping away their lives', an image which 'conjures up the very grimmest horrors of war'. But the editorial moved quickly from this perspective, stating that 'one gladly turns from this harrowing phase of the struggle to the unexampled gallantry and patriotism of the contending armies'. The same issue printed a story under the headline 'Horrors of Battle', promising 'graphic details of fighting', yet casualties were seen as 'the thick trail of prostrate khaki [which] told a tale that no pen can describe'.[45] In this way, a realistic image of death and wounding was avoided, though the details were said to be 'graphic'.

This inability or unwillingness to describe the realities of casualties adequately was also present in post-conflict publications of war correspondents and other military observers. David James, war correspondent for the *Daily Telegraph* at Port Arthur, wrote of casualties where maggots were present in decayed wounds, 'and scenes more horrible – but I refrain from further reference to the awful condition of the Japanese wounded'.[46] Even a professional soldier like Ian Hamilton felt constrained in describing the killed and wounded, preferring not to pile up the horrors of war 'beyond reasonable measure', to avoid giving the world the 'wrong impression' of warfare. His observations of 203 Metre Hill contained images of bodies and portions of bodies struck by artillery shell fragments, but after a brief mention of heads, arms, legs and bodies 'lying about', he ended abruptly, stating 'I have said much; perhaps too much', giving no further details.[47]

A further way in which written imagery denied the reality of death and wounding was to stress the humane nature of modern warfare, both in terms of the effects of weapons, primarily rifles, and also in comparison to the number of casualties inflicted in past wars. It was recognized in *Daily Mail* reports that while artillery fire resulted in frightful wounds, lyddite, the British secret weapon, was a 'humane explosive'. The paper explained that a 4.5 pound charge in a 50 pound howitzer shell produced an explosion so violent that projectiles scattered widely, thus 'thoroughly searching the ground'. The result was that 'everyone near the place of explosion was killed, those who are not struck by fragments dying painlessly by shock. There is less cruelty with lyddite than in using powder shells, which mangle terribly, but do not always kill'.[48] A small book, or *vade-mecum*, entitled *How to Read War News*, published in 1900 to guide readers on how to interpret newspaper reports from South Africa, explained the effects of lyddite in a similar manner. It stated that

> the magnitude of its explosive force is absolutely incredible. In order to be killed, it is not necessary that a man should be struck by even a fragment of the shell itself; the mere concussion of the displaced air particles suffices to destroy all life within a radius of 50 yards.[49]

The supposedly humane nature of lyddite, while not explicitly expressed, was apparent in this entry as readers were told that it was merely air particles that 'destroy all life' in an almost painless fashion; the effects on individual soldiers were essentially glossed over.

While lyddite was seen as a humane weapon because it was so efficient at killing, the Mauser rifle bullet was considered so because it was not an efficient 'man-stopper', being too aerodynamic; it was the 'merciful Mauser'. *Daily Mail* readers were reassured that the wounded soldiers at Wynberg hospital were 'happy and contented, not a few bearing the impression of excellent health'. The reason for their excellent condition was that 'modern bullet wounds' were clean, well defined and no larger than a 'good-sized goose-quill'. Mauser bullets were said to cut 'through flesh and bone as neatly as an Archimedean drill' producing little 'local disturbance or bad after-effect', meaning that men could be shot in the abdomen, head or legs and have little or no damage inflicted upon them.[50]

While these reports might have been intended to reassure home-front readers whose relatives were serving in South Africa, their overall effect was to de-emphasize and to deny the pain and suffering of those killed and wounded in battle. This certainly was one of the impressions found in a book written by George Lynch, war correspondent for the *Daily Chronicle*. He explained that, while the dead were unable to express an opinion, the lack of agonizing shrieks, the sudden staggers and drunken-sleepy demeanour displayed by those killed, indicated that 'death from a Mauser bullet is less painful than the drawing of a tooth'. Mourning mothers, he counselled, should therefore not think of their sons as 'drowning out of the world racked with the red torture from the bullet's track, but just as dropping off dully to sleep'. For, unlike shells which 'go in' an 'uncouth and butchering way', the Mauser produced a 'gentlemanly puncture'.[51]

Similarly, war was seen as 'humane' in comparison to battles conducted throughout the eighteenth and nineteenth centuries. In an article entitled 'Why War Is Becoming More Humane', the *Daily Mail* suggested that, statistically, loss of life in warfare was steadily decreasing, from 23.5 per cent of those engaged at Breslau, to 15 per cent at Inkerman and 12.5 per cent at Sedan. The paper proposed that the reason for this decrease was not only the aerodynamics of bullets, but their lower trajectory, the art of warfare adapting to technology, and medical advances which meant that surgical and microbiological techniques mitigated the fatal nature of weapons and disease. From the Snider rifle to the Lee-Metford, the 'stopping power' of rifle-fire moved from certain to unlikely. Indeed, the paper felt that only a clear shot from a Lee-Metford piercing the head or heart would be sufficient to kill an enemy. Even this was not always enough, as the *Mail* announced without irony that 'several men shot through the brain in China and South Africa are serving in the army to-day'.[52]

A further way in which casualties were denied was the tendency to depersonalize the dead, in effect, to remove their humanity and therefore de-emphasize the emotive reality of battlefield casualties. A wounded Turkish soldier lying in the distance could thus easily be described as 'a shapeless green khaki lump on the bare hill side', while a small group of Japanese soldiers could be seen as 'khaki-clad figures' who mysteriously vanished.[53] This image of the depersonalized was more powerful when newspapers described large-scale casualties, in particular of the Somalis, Japanese and Russians. The Somalis, for example, were said to have been 'piled in heaps in front of the maxims' where up to 2000 died in an attack on Major Gough's column at Daratoleh.[54]

No instances were found in the press reports of British casualties 'piled in heaps'. This was partly because their troops were not killed in numbers comparable to the Japanese and Russians, nor were they attacking machine-gun emplacements in the same manner as the Somalis. However, the main reason for this omission was that this depersonalization did not happen to British troops, particularly in Imperial settings like Somaliland where officers were the only white troops. After Plunkett's defeat, for example, the *Illustrated London News* published a list of all nine officers killed with short biographies, in addition to a head-and-shoulders photo-montage of them in uniform placed around a photograph of an anonymous group of black troops from the King's African Rifles. This tendency was enhanced in the discussions of British casualties in Tibet where officers were listed by name, rank and unit, with a short biography, white other ranks were listed by unit only, and native casualties mentioned only as an approximate number.[55] This suggests a sense of value with a distinct hierarchy within discussions of British casualties, which could not have been compatible with wholesale depersonalization suggested by masses of soldiers lying in 'heaps'.

It was this sense of value which pervaded discussions of casualties in the press. Soldiers' lives were depicted as 'buying' positions and victories in a way which denied their actual fate, and made them appear as a necessary expenditure to be expected and budgeted. Images of casualties as a 'cost' or a 'loss', a 'purchase price' or a 'toll', were the most frequently used to describe death and wounding on the battlefield. Thus, soldiers were seen as tokens or specie to be invested in order to purchase territory or to effect the destruction of an enemy. The best example of this ubiquitous image concerned the capture of Port Arthur, the fall of which instigated several reviews of 'What Port Arthur Has Cost', with money and materiel often receiving the same or a stronger emphasis than the number of casualties. The *Daily Mirror* was one of a number of newspapers that gave much attention to this aspect of the Russo-Japanese War. In a feature article published early in January 1905, the paper discussed the 'Port Arthur Bill', setting it at £150,000,000, listing the major costs, apparently in order of importance, as the money spent for construction of the fortress over a ten-year period, the money invested in battleships destroyed in the harbour, and, lastly, the soldiers' lives of both belligerents. The last of these was set at approximately 135,000 killed, wounded and taken prisoner, which the paper stated was 'a truly appalling figure upon which all humane eyes will not care to dwell'.[56] Indeed, it was easier to discuss enormous casualties in the same manner as the destruction of equipment and weapons, such as battleships, in order to convey the significance of mass casualties. The terms 'loss' and 'cost' were used to refer to both casualties and materiel, and acted as a means of comparison. In order to determine the value of the 'price' the Japanese 'paid' for Port Arthur in terms of casualties, an intricate formula was suggested based on the monetary value of the Russian battleships and ancillary ships sunk in the harbour. The battle-ships were said to have been worth £8 million, while the cruisers, destroyers, gun boats and other ships were estimated at £4 million. Moreover, one battleship was said to have a 'military value' of an army division containing 20,000 men. Thus, the seven battleships alone 'lost' by the Russians equalled 140,000 men 'placed *hors de combat*'. With Japanese casualties in the assault estimated at 80,000, the clear inference was that the Japanese 'purchase' of Port Arthur was a good investment, a perspective which was emphasized in a table of losses comparing the 'expenses' of both sides in terms of men, ships (numerically and monet-arily), and guns.[57] The consequences of these images of casualties as expenditure was that the dead and wounded, particularly those killed on a large unimaginable scale, were reduced to mere calculations of value and cost analyses. They became the exchangeable goods or 'toll' to be paid in order to achieve an objective, whether a material purchase such as that at Port Arthur, or something less tangible but equally valuable, such as the maintenance of prestige in Somaliland or a dem-onstration of power against an intransigent Tibetan enemy.

Other impressions related to these images of casualties as expense included a suggestion that the dead and wounded were 'lost' almost through carelessness or by accident, rather than through intentional and rational design. In this way, the Tibetans were said to have 'lost' about 200 men on the hills around the Karo La as if by accident rather than their being killed by the British. Similarly, at Liaoyang, one Russian regiment was reported to have 'lost 1500 men in the tall millet', conveying an impression that the soldiers had been misplaced rather than killed or wounded.[58] This form of imagery corresponds to the concept of 'decorous language' and similarly acts as a method of denying death by suggesting that soldiers merely lose their way, a variation of 'passed on'. It also suggests that by emphasizing the large scale of casualties through ever increasing numbers, newspapers conveyed the 'numbing' effect that Pick suggests was prevalent in the rationalization of death during the latter stages of the nineteenth-century.

Several commentators saw the 'expense' of warfare not just in terms of 'treasure', but also of 'blood'. The *Daily Express* saw the final Japanese victory at the end of the war as having been won with a 'vast expenditure of blood and treasure', a sentiment echoed by Winston Churchill early in the Boer War when he predicted that the necessity of retaining South Africa would be worth the 'blood and money' expended.[59]

Blood imagery was, indeed, a further means to represent the violence and deadly nature of warfare and avoid direct discussions of casualties. Battles which produced large numbers of dead and wounded were described as 'bloody' or 'sanguinary' in attempts to convey the intensity of fighting and the scale of casualties. Although Liaoyang was described as a conflict 'in which occurred some of the bloodiest fighting of the campaign' because of the sheer scale of the battle, smaller engagements, such as at Spion Kop, were seen as 'short, but bloody' and 'a bitter, bloody struggle'.[60] The shedding of blood, a symbol of life in Christian theology and Victorian literature, was a way in which death could be depicted indirectly, that is, without graphic depictions. Even the opposition press used the image of 'blood' to denote the loss of life in battle, as *Justice* described the South African War as a 'frightful and bloody muddle' after 'Black Week', and the *Daily News* referred to 'the parched plain of Somaliland, now watered only too well with the blood of our fellow-citizens' after Gumburu.[61] Thus, discussions of death and wounding even on a large scale were reduced to images of blood and bloodshed, representing the loss of life, rather than detailed, realistic descriptions. Yet reports of fighting which did purport to be 'graphic' descriptions of battle, distanced readers from complete and realistic portrayals of war. In attempting to convey the 'Titanic Struggle' around Liaoyang, the Japanese bombardment of a Russian artillery battery was described, with the casualties among the gunners represented by an image of the batteries being 'bespattered with blood', rather than by detailed descriptions of what effect the counter-battery shelling actually had on the men.[62] Attention here was focused on the guns and the blood sprayed upon them, not the pain and suffering of the gunners. These were images understood by readers, allowing them to maintain their positive impressions of warfare without having to address its deadly and agonizing realities.

'War as it is': visual images of death and wounding

In written images of casualties, descriptions of death on the battlefield utilized 'decorous language' and euphemistic expressions, but with visual imagery there was the possibility of more realistic presentations of death and wounding in the Edwardian press. This was the case with photographs in particular, for they were seen as representations of 'truth' and 'reality' untainted by an artist's interpretation, imagination or manipulation. An analysis of the way in which visual imagery conveyed casualties in war must include a number of aspects, such as a discussion of what 'moment' was captured in the image, how the physical state of the dead and wounded was presented, the manner in which the wounded were seen to be treated and how they were affected by their experiences, how the increased scale of mass casualties was portrayed, and what kind of symbolism was used to convey the idea of casualties. Visual imagery can be found in several media, including illustrations and drawings, photographs, cartoons, and advertisements.

It is important to examine the moment captured in illustrations in order to ascertain what images were consumed by readers, as the impression derived from the visual depiction could change significantly. Drawings that presented the moment just before or just as a soldier was struck by a weapon would show less detail in terms of pain and suffering compared to those illustrations which showed the moment after wounds had been inflicted, and would convey the image of death indirectly. Almost all of the illustrations examined captured the moment before wounding or just at the very moment that bullet or shell fragment made contact. Of those that varied from this tendency, the majority of illustrations depicted after-battle scenes reminiscent of Royal Academy battle paintings, such as Lady Butler's 'Roll Call' and Richard Caton Woodville's 'All That Was Left of Them', where the horrors of battle were depicted by the number of those missing or 'removed' from visual portrayals of the ranks.

In both British victories and defeats, the moment captured was generally that prior to their killing or being killed by the enemy. The *Illustrated
Mail* demonstrated this tendency in a front page illustration entitled,
'Fighting In Tibet – Great British Victory', where it showed a close-up of
two British Mounted Infantry officers in pursuit of the Tibetans retreating after the first battle at Guru. Here, the British forces were depicted
just as they were using their weapons, one brandishing a sword and the
other firing a revolver. There was no sense of the scale of Tibetan
casualties or of the effects of the expedition's weaponry.[63]

Similarly, the *Illustrated London News* chose to depict the moment
before serious casualties were inflicted by the Boers in a drawing showing General Hart's 'storming' of Sugar Loaf Hill. This attack failed,
causing 28 British killed and 280 wounded, and was later described as
a 'purposeless preparatory attack'. Yet the illustration showed only three
apparently wounded soldiers, with one in the middle distance stum-
bling among the rock-strewn slope, making it unclear whether he was
wounded or not.[64] Those illustrations that depicted after-battle scenes
gave the impression of casualties through the removal of soldiers from
the picture. However, these types of illustration, such as the full-page
photogravure copy of another Caton Woodville illustration of the Highland Brigade after Magersfontein, or the depiction of a depleted Russian
regiment after Liaoyang, also avoided the moment where death and
wounding occurred, depending upon the imagination of the viewer to
accept and conceptualize the mass scale of casualties.[65]

The moment captured in photographs reinforced the images found in
illustrations by avoiding the actual depiction of death and wounding,
relying instead on pre-battle and post-battle pictures. Technical limitations influenced this, as the field of vision in camera equipment was
such that photographers would have to be very close to subjects in order
to obtain a clear image. The moments conveyed were therefore invariably before or after battle, giving the impression of an empty, sanitized
and 'safe' battlefield. Photographs published in the *Daily Mirror* showed
the landscape of the Tuna Plain, devoid of soldiers from either side, but
described as 'Photographs of the Spot Where Tibetans Attacked the
British Mission to Tibet'. Here, the photograph showed the location of
battle before fighting began, without images of the post-battle dead
and dying, or the long trail of wounded Tibetans that so impressed
eye-witnesses.[66]

The way in which those casualties, both killed and wounded, were
portrayed, moreover, emphasized the twin themes of 'removal' and
'denial'. J. W. M. Hichberger has examined images present in Royal

Academy battle paintings of the period and has suggested that artists portrayed British casualties by following a 'polite formula', where the wounded displayed bandaged heads or shoulder wounds, and the dead lay in composed positions behind bushes, half-hidden from view. She contrasts this depiction with the treatment afforded to the Imperial enemy by comparing two paintings by G. D. Giles, 'An Incident at the Battle of Tamai, East Soudan, 19 March, 1884' and 'Battle of Tamai', where the Dervishes 'died with less dignity' in awkward positions, showing pain and a great deal of blood.[67]

While some of Hichberger's interpretations can be challenged, her 'polite formula' can be seen as the visual equivalent of Jennifer Leaney's 'decorous language' in the depiction of casualties.[68] It was, in addition, applied to both 'civilized' and 'uncivilized' belligerents. Casualties were frequently partially hidden behind bushes, rocks or by smoke from the battlefield, removing them from the direct vision of the viewer. Death and wounding were conveyed by various techniques, such as in a drawing made from the perspective of inside Major Gough's defensive zariba during the Third Expedition to Somaliland which showed a pair of prostrate legs protruding into the frame, merely alluding to casualties inflicted upon the British, half-hiding the effects of battle, and depending on the audience to 'read' the significance of the image. The Somalis were seen to display either panic or a certain amount of 'savagery', but they died no less 'politely', neither shedding large amounts of blood, nor displaying horrible disfiguring wounds.[69] Physical remains were also totally removed from visual depictions of casualties, further emphasizing the image of removal. The *Illustrated London News* accomplished this in a pair of full-page illustrations that showed two families, one in 'the Cottage' and the other in 'the Hall', receiving letters informing them of the death of a husband or son in South Africa.[70] In this way, death was portrayed without showing any overt signs of wounds, pain or physical suffering, once again, depending on the viewer to 'read' the message conveyed by the illustration.

As in the written images of death and wounding, symbolic representations were prevalent in the visual depictions of casualties. Like them, visual imagery conveyed the idea of casualties, but avoided their true nature. Hichberger has discussed the symbolic image of the horse, suggesting that artists such as John Charlton and T. J. Barker depended upon their audiences to grasp the significance of the 'riderless horse' in their after-battle scenes because of the 'mythologies surrounding the relation of horses to humans'.[71] In a double-page drawing in the *Illustrated London News* entitled 'The Transvaal War: The Loss of Our Guns at the Tugela River', Caton Woodville used the image of the horse to portray British casualties. The wounded soldiers were hidden from view, either by the horses, the guns or by having their backs turned to the viewer, but the horses had a central position in the picture. They showed not only the panic and fear of battle, but also the wounds, as blood poured from their mouths and the bullet wounds they incurred. The soldiers themselves were calm and ordered, with no visible wounds and no signs of blood. The wounded horses acted as a means to convey an image of British casualties without expressly showing them, an image unacceptable to viewers.[72]

Photographs operated in a similar manner, using dead horses as way of conveying the idea of dead soldiers without actually recording any on film. An example in the *Illustrated London News* highlighted this in announcing that Turkish 'drivers and dead horses had been killed by Bulgarian shrapnel' after the Battle of Kumanovo, but the accompanying photograph showed only the dead horses as they remained, still harnessed to the guns. The viewer was left to read into the scene the impression of dead Turkish soldiers, their wounded, and their suffering as a result of the shellfire.[73] In a similar manner, photographs produced images of casualties which showed, not the dead and the wounded, but the inanimate debris produced in battle. Indeed, photographs showed results of bombardment, but from a perspective sanitized by not containing images of the dead and wounded; they were taken after casualties had been removed. These photographs give the impression of the destructive nature of an artillery bombardment, but without the human element, allowing the scattered debris to represent casualties for readers.[74]

Yet, even those illustrations that showed casualties minimized and down-played them. Wounds were not seen as particularly debilitating, almost all being slight, concentrating on the head, shoulder or arm. These wounds produced little blood, for, unlike the written depictions of casualties, blood imagery was minimal in illustrations; small amounts of blood were sufficient to convey to readers an impression of death and wounding. The dead were almost invariably bodily intact, with no dismembered limbs or shattered arms, even if soldiers were depicted right next to an exploding shell or mine. In addition, the dead were characteristically portrayed with a peaceful, sleepy demeanour, reminiscent of Lynch's descriptions of Mauser bullet victims.

An example which combined these elements was a depiction of the Japanese assault on Wolf Hill, published in *Black and White* and covering two full-pages. The centre of the illustrations showed an artillery shell exploding among a group of Japanese soldiers and horses with great force. The soldiers were shown being lifted out and towards the top of the illustration, emphasizing the effect of the blast. Yet these figures, those most affected by the blast, were bodily intact, with even their uniforms unshredded by the shell fragments. The wounded soldiers in the foreground displayed only minor head wounds, with merely a trickle of blood shown through bandages. Others in the foreground appeared to be dead, but displayed a calm, peaceful look, as if sleeping. Thus, the force of the blast was made obvious, but the effect it had on the soldiers, in terms of wounds and cause of death, was avoided.[75]

The only example found of an illustration that showed the dismembered bodies of those killed in warfare was a rough sketch by Frederick Villiers of the Japanese attempting to blow up the electrified wire entanglements around Port Arthur. The sketch was incomplete, and published with the artist's instructions as to colours, tones and other explanations. There were only two figures in the sketch, both of whom were indistinct, but obviously dead. Both were lying in small pools of blood, one with at least a single limb separated from his body, accompanied by a short note by Villiers explaining that 'these men are shattered by shell'. Despite this display of realism in showing the results of artillery fire, the effect was blunted by the crudity of the sketch, published without being made up by a London-based artist, and the indistinct depiction of the men; the perspective was from a distance, their faces were hidden, and the wounds were not detailed.[76]

Photographs presented the images of casualties in a similar manner, following the example of illustrations and using the same 'polite formula' in their depictions. While photographs were limited in their range of subjects in that they could not show explosions or situate the viewer in close proximity to the battlefield as illustrations could, they still hid the images of casualties, showed the dead as bodily intact with little or no blood, and conveyed no visible signs of discomfort or pain.

The most emotive event depicted in photographs was perhaps the aftermath of the Oasis Massacre, where photographers took pictures of dead and wounded Arabs. The *Illustrated London News* published several photographs showing these scenes, including a collection of four photographs entitled 'War As It Is: Dead Arabs in Heaps in Tripoli', which utilized the belief in the ability of the camera to eschew manipulation and show the realities of war: war 'as it is'. These photographs are not in close-up, are indistinct and the wounds inflicted upon the Arabs are not shown, nor is there much indication of blood on their bodies. They were seen, as the title suggests, as 'heaps' of bodies, looking more like piles of clothing than distinct individual soldiers (Plates 4–6).[77] Thus the dead and wounded were not shown clearly and distinctly in photographs, despite their unique suitability as subjects that did not move and could be easily approached.

Cartoons for their part presented wounds in ways which, while obvious, reinforced the impression that the battlefield was not necessarily such a deadly environment. 'Civilized' belligerents were represented by allegorical figures, either soldiers or national animals in uniform, while 'uncivilized' belligerents tended not to be soldiers and were out of uniform. These figures represented countries or armies and could therefore never die, but could only be dishevelled or bruised and battered, for to show these allegorical figures as dead would indicate the elimination of belligerent countries. A *News of the World* cartoon illustrated this in a depiction of the Yalu crossing, entitled 'A River of No Importance', where the Russian army was depicted as a Russian officer retreating from the Japanese with dishevelled hair and torn uniform and missing one boot. Yet even in the latter stages of the war, casualties were portrayed in a similar manner despite the increased number of killed and wounded. *Punch* published a cartoon during the Battle of Mukden, one that caused 20,000 Russian casualties, which portrayed the Russian army as a bear in uniform with a bandage over one eye and its left paw in a sling. The bear, representing the Russian army, was not seen to suffer greatly, thus the cartoon avoided the pain and horrors of war.[78] This is a significant point with regard to Marshall McLuhan's idea of 'low definition' or 'cool' medium, as the viewer must participate in the reading of cartoons by filling in information and understanding representations, more so than in drawings and photographs.[79] Thus, the Russians were represented by their national animal because this was understood by audiences, and, in the same way, wounds and deaths on the battlefield were represented by minor cuts and bruises because viewers did not see war as particularly painful, agonizing or deadly, but as something more positive and beneficial. Cartoons thus played upon the perception of readers that war was not horrific and that the likelihood of dying was minimal or, in the case of allegorical figures, impossible.

The illustrations in advertisements displayed a similar tendency to deny the reality of death and wounding, as these would naturally associate products with the negative and suppressed aspects of warfare. Yet advertisements often did utilize images of actual warfare, but ones in which the beneficial qualities of the product were presented. 'Dr. Tibbles' Vi-Cocoa' used the image of a Gordon Highlander charging forward with rifle and bayonet in South Africa as shells exploded directly above his head with absolutely no effect. Similarly, the first use of bombing from an airplane during the Turco-Italian War inspired the advertisement of 'Pergen – The Ideal Aperient'. The product was depicted as bombs being dropped from an aeroplane onto bell tents marked 'Constipation', 'Ill Health', and 'Loss of Appetite' in the same manner that the Italians dropped bombs on Turkish camps. The casualties suffered in these bombing raids, their negative effect, were hidden and denied, as the targets were not soldiers but tents representing disease rather than life, the destruction of which was a beneficial objective (Plate 7).[80]

The presentation of the treatment the wounded received, as portrayed in illustrations, was also important in contributing to the denial of a realistic depiction of casualties. Like Royal Academy battle paintings, British troops were seen to be caring and compassionate towards their wounded, and to return to pick up their dead, whereas the Imperial enemy was not.[81] On the battlefield, soldiers were depicted as supporting those wounded around them, as in the *Penny Illustrated Paper*'s rendering of the assault on Gyantse Jong, where a sergeant was shown stopping to aid a wounded young bugler in the centre of the picture. Even after death, the British still cared for the remains of their comrades, as indicated by a photograph of a party returning to Gumburu almost a year later to collect the bones of Plunkett's soldiers.[82] Other combatants were depicted caring for their wounded in similar ways, as both the Japanese and the Russians were shown to have clean, orderly hospitals at the front, where the wounded were neither in pain nor suffering serious bloody wounds, and where the dead were covered over or not present.[83] The image conveyed in these illustrations was that in the unlikely event of soldiers getting wounded, they would be treated compassionately on the battlefield and in the hospital. If they were killed, their mortal remains would be collected for a decent burial. This essentially denied the agony suffered by soldiers, not only when originally wounded, but also when transported to field dressing stations for medical care.

These portrayals were reinforced by those found in photographs, contributing to the sense of denial with regard to the pain of casualties. Soldiers who were wounded were shown to be well looked after, carried in dhoolies, examined in field dressing stations and eventually recovering in clean, orderly hospitals behind the lines. In showing the British casualties at Elandslaagte, photographs in the *Illustrated London News* emphasized that all wounded soldiers were cared for and carefully carried to be treated. The pain of being wounded and then of being transported over rough ground was ignored by hiding the wounded, even when ostensibly showing them being picked up from the battle-field. Once at either field dressing stations or hospitals, the wounded appeared well looked after in comfortable surroundings, with none of the blood and clutter characteristic of military hospitals after battle. Indeed, a group of patients depicted in a photograph showed happy, cheerful, wounded men, lying in wicker cots under a tree, smoking and enjoying themselves as if on holiday.[84] The image of well-cared-for casualties – who were never more than slightly wounded – cheerful, and not too badly hurt, combined with photographs showing smiling British and native soldiers posing with local inhabitants, conveyed the idea that the consequences of war, horrific wounds and lingering death were unimportant and relatively insignificant.[85]

Advertisements played upon this idea by associating their products with regenerative qualities which aided in the recovery of the wounded. Bovril, for example, ran a half-page advertisement in the *Illustrated London News*, which claimed that: 'Bovril gives life to the soldier faint from loss of blood.' It showed a wounded soldier with one arm in a sling, signifying a minor wound, looking healthy, strong and in no pain while drinking a cup of Bovril. The illustration was accompanied by a testimonial from Sir William MacCormac after the 'Battle of Tugela', who stated that

> on the field of battle, Bovril is playing a conspicuous part in uphold-ing the British Flag, and contributing to the success of British valour by assisting in the recovery of the wounded soldiers.

Here, the advertisement implied that wounds inflicted in war were minor and painless, and that because they were so, they could be treated through simply consuming 'liquid life' Bovril (Plate 8).[86]

The increased scale of mass casualties was presented in a manner which also did not express the realities of war. In conveying the impression of more deadly battles with larger numbers of casualties, illustrations merely contained more bodies within the visual plane of viewers. These added bodies followed the 'polite formula' convention and did not depict battles with high casualties as any more horrific than less deadly encoun-ters. The successful crossing of the Yalu River by the Japanese was the first major contact between land forces in the Russo-Japanese War, resulting in casualties of 3000 for the Russians and 1000 for the Japanese. The visual depictions of the crossing showed either very few or no casualties at all. Yet, the way in which mass casualties were depicted later in the conflict at the forts around Port Arthur showed hundreds of Japanese casualties, an increasing number having 'fallen' as they approached the Russian fort. However, the intensity of the assault was not conveyed in realistic portrayals of wounding or death; the 'polite formula' was maintained. A similar approach to scale can be seen in photographs, as the size of the 'heaps' of bodies grew, but the horrors were still avoided. In this way, it was the increased scale of dead and wounded which was conveyed, while the horrors of war, with its pain and lingering death, continued to be down-played and denied.[87]

Conclusion: 'merciful soft focus'

The denial of death was very much in place well before 1914, but histories of death must examine war and casualties in order to understand fully attitudes towards death. There was a change in the perception of death from the decline of the 'celebration' of civilian death in the 1880s, to an increasing 'glorification' of death on the battlefield. This change can be seen as one which arose from a combination of international tensions, the influence of Social Darwinist thought and the impact of the public school athletic ethos, all of which combined to associate war with sports and games where defeat was not equated with death. Indeed, death on the battlefield was seen as 'something noble, heroic, splendid, romantic – and unlikely'.[88]

Both Michael C. Kearl and Paul Fussell have discovered the application of Leaney's 'decorous language' to military experience, extending what she saw as a form of denial of death. Kearl shows how modern soldiers use words such as 'eliminate', 'neutralize', and 'zapping' as replacements for the word 'kill'.[89] Similarly, Fussell shows how soldiers on the Western Front relied on a range of euphemisms for both getting killed, such as 'to be knocked out', 'going out of it', or 'going under', and for killing, where men 'melted away' or 'fell'. Here Fussell suggests that the 'passive voice' was used to create a distance between action and result and to 'throw a scene into merciful soft focus, as in the cinema'.[90] Yet, this form of 'decorous language' was not only employed during the First World War, but existed before 1914 to describe battlefield casualties in earlier conflicts, as newspapers utilized the 'passive voice' in reports concerning death and wounding for readers.

There is a further dimension to this discussion on representations of the corpse during the First World War. While the soldiers at the front occupied a world of corpses, the civilians at home experienced the death of their soldiers as 'pure corpselessness'. As bodies were not repatriated, if indeed they could be found, civilians focused on newspaper reports and casualty lists, creating a distance between the representation and reality of corpses. Those at home occupied a psychological space 'wiped clean of corpses'.[91]

However, this was also the experience of those who read war reports before 1914 – able to speak about war and death without ever seeing the dead. Both written and visual imagery in the pre-1914 press effectively removed the dead and the wounded, and suppressed the horrific nature of warfare from the vicarious experience of readers. Newspaper depictions of actual warfare did not contradict the essentially positive perspective of war present in Edwardian society through full and realistic representations of war casualties. The consequences of battle were not ignored, but the written and illustrative images down-played and minimized their realities.

The denial of death in newspaper reports played upon readers' vicarious experiences of warfare which were romantic, idealized, painless and beneficial. Death in these circumstances was noble, honourable, a price to be paid and, ultimately, infrequent. Images essentially and necessarily depicted casualties in this way, partly because that was the way in which the creators of images, as products of their times, perceived warfare, but mostly it coincided with the experience of war possessed by readers.

It was also partly due to the limitations of language: image 'makers' used the language and visual imagery which was available to them and intelligible to the 'consumers 'of those images. To convey the idea of death adequately, either on an 'unimaginably' massive scale or, indeed, individual deaths, was impossible. As Sigmund Freud professed when attempting to internalize the mass deaths on the Western Front in 1915, 'your own death is unimaginable, and whenever we make the attempt to imagine it we can perceive that we survive as spectators.'[92]

Thus, death is the ultimate fiction, one which, as for the war correspondent George Lynch, has to be speculated upon since it cannot be written about once experienced. In this way, illustrations and writings constructed ways of conveying death which could not be based upon experience, but used imagery that would be obvious to viewers and readers. This imagery, firmly rooted in the emerging death-denying culture, masked the reality of casualties through suppression and denial, and did not effectively counter the pervasive image of war as beneficial, sporting, entertaining and adventurous.

7
Conclusion: 'The Blessings of War'

In examining the Edwardian press and the way in which it presented warfare before 1914, it is possible to determine the perceptions of war possessed by readers. It is clear that these perceptions were for the most part positive and were not challenged or contradicted by images of the horrific and brutal aspects of warfare. These images were not only conveyed in the reporting of *actual* warfare in the news columns and leading articles, but were also evident in other areas of the newspaper, such as cartoons, advertisements, illustrations, drawings and photographs.

Examined, as they must be, in the context of the Edwardian age, these images take on a resonance and importance which helps to explain the enthusiasm for war in 1914 and gives flesh to the dry bones of the more conventional explanations offered hitherto. We cannot assume that the recruiting rush of 1914 was due to people being told to join up, either by the Government or by the press. Military activity before 1914 was seen to offer solutions to the many problems, fears and anxieties of modernism which plagued the Edwardians. It was felt that war countered the gnawing ravages of physical and racial deterioration, and facilitated the development of an ordered and efficient nation. Martial development also signalled the degree to which a nation had climbed the ladder of civilization, while success on the battlefield indicated that the nation, or 'race', was not only an efficient one, but also a *just* one.

In addition, those images of warfare were presented in a context of new communication technologies giving much wider scope to an equally new self-improving lower-middle class and a increasingly empowered working class; the very groups which were to dominate the volunteer armies. All this occurred in an increasingly 'militaristic', or 'martial', society where there was a marked surge of interest in things

134

military, and where volunteering for individual wars, as opposed to a fixed term in the army, was becoming more acceptable.

In examinations of war imagery found in the pages of the press, the dual ideas of distance and denial interweave and connect the various themes discussed in each chapter. The notion of distance can be detected in the positive image of the soldier/warrior as a result of the changing role of the army in society over the course of the nineteenth century. Not only were soldiers no longer seen as agents of domestic suppression, having been replaced by a newly created civilian police force, but they were also seen to be more remote by conducting their activities in the distant Empire. This perception of distance from the activities of the military was augmented by a sense of denial of what those activities entailed, enabling the image of the soldier to be representative of civilization, both in the 'dark' corners of the Empire and at home. Soldiers who had been feared and despised were, by the Edwardian period, models of desirable virtue and advertising icons.

This sense of denial concerning the image of the soldier can be seen in further positive discussions relating to the activities of the military. The use of force was presented and perceived as a natural mode of behaviour, part of life and a method of defining masculinity. It was also seen as beneficial for the 'race', as a means to avoid physical degeneration and prevent over-civilization, and as medicinal. In addition, the use of force was seen as desirable in that it was an acceptable method of arbitration between states and a test of a nation's morality and virtue. The negative nature of military force was essentially denied by equating it with the worthy activities of the police and schools, both desirable agents of socialization. The connection between warfare and the positive conceptions of 'work' and the means by which 'history is made' also add to the perception of the desirability of military activity.

These same themes can be seen in descriptions of war which used images of sport, games, and hunting. Readers were distanced from warfare as non-participants, just as they were in the burgeoning reporting of sporting activities. Games created a distance between the reader and the nature of warfare in that pastimes like chess are strategic games which have a high-level perspective, a point of view augmented by the use of maps and 'bird's-eye-view' drawings. Hunting also created an image of distance, as it was usually associated with Imperial frontier warfare where participants were seen to cross from civilization into barbarism. Similarly, these images denied the reality of warfare in that sporting representations implied fitness and the countering of physical deterioration. In seeing war and sport as similar activities, it was implied that they would have similar positive effects. Games also acted as a form of denial as concentrations on strategy avoided discussions of what was actually happening 'on the ground'. Hunting was also an image which denied the realities of warfare, presenting it as an exciting and ecstatic form of combat, but with no feelings of guilt attached to the actual killing.

The themes of distance and denial can be seen to apply to the images of war as theatre and spectacle. In suggesting that warfare was an entertaining theatrical event, newspapers presented it to readers as an activity to be watched from a distance, through the 'fourth wall' and from seats in an auditorium. Similarly, the idea that warfare was a spectacle to be watched like a 'pyrodrama' from a safe physical distance, gave the impression of picturesque and pretty warfare. In addition, late-nineteenth-century developments in the theatre, where 'naturalism' in acting and 'realism' in stage design became prevalent, paralleled the presentations of war as not representing 'reality', but rather as more 'realistic' illusions, and the falsification of life and war. These illusions were also displayed in the image of war as spectacle in that the impression conveyed to readers was that weapons were like fireworks: pretty and loud, but entertaining and safe.

These essentially positive views of warfare were not countered or contradicted by discussions of the negative consequences of battle, as images of death and wounding also corresponded to the themes of distance and denial. Written images did not convey specific descriptions of the graphic details, while visual images removed the physical remains of the dead from the visual landscape of readers, just as burial grounds and slaughterhouses removed death from urban areas. Death was denied through use of the language of suppression which 'swept away' or 'pushed down' descriptions of casualties from the reader's eye. Casualties were also depersonalized as a loss or a cost, while their bodies were portrayed visually following a 'polite formula'.

The ideas of distance and denial, as presented in the various images of war, represented the 'reality' of war which the Edwardians possessed. Their experience and knowledge of real warfare was limited to these descriptions, reinforced by other sources of imagery, such as those presented in schools, youth movements and literature. They ensured that those Edwardians about to feel the ravages of the First World War were woefully unprepared for what they were to experience. These images also help to explain the longevity of the perceptions of war as the war progressed.

Furthermore, the presence of these images in a wide variety of newspapers representing a range of political hues and socio-economic positions in British society indicates that those who participated or encouraged others to participate in the First World War imagined warfare in similar ways. This goes far to explain the united war commitment and the lack of significant class conflict in 1914 after the war began, as well as the longevity and intensity of support for the war.

It must be stressed that an examination of Edwardian 'realities' of war is not a condemnation nor a harsh judgement of a society possessing 'obsolete' patriotism. It is an attempt to understand their motivations and world view, in the hope that it might help us to see our own modern vision of warfare as contributing to the use of military violence. For if the years leading up to more contemporary wars, such as the Falklands, the Gulf War, Kosovo, and Afghanistan were to be studied in a similar manner, there surely would be no doubt that we too possess a woefully unrealistic image of warfare. As a letter in the opposition paper *Mother Jones* pointed out in reflecting upon the attitudes to war before the outbreak of hostilities in the Gulf, war was cast not 'in terms of death and destruction', but rather 'in terms of adventure. War as if it were a football game', where the important consideration was that 'our boys go in there and kick some ass'.[1]

If we can become more conscious of the realties of war, we also might be less willing to resort to military conflict as a knee-jerk reaction to terrorism, and perhaps attempt to seek alternatives to our aggressive, self-serving foreign policies. If this study can contribute to a debate about creating a new moral paradigm in any small way, then it will have done its job.

Notes

Chapter 1   Introduction: 'They Had Been Taught to Howl'

1. Michael Howard, 'Reflections on the First World War', in Michael Howard, ed., *Studies in War and Peace* (London, 1970), pp. 101–2.
2. Ibid., p. 102.
3. James Joll, *The Origins of the First World War* (London, 1984), p. 194.
4. Peter Dewey, *War and Progress: Britain 1914–1945* (Harlow, 1997), p. 12.
5. J. M. Winter, *The Great War and the British People* (London, 1985), pp. 30, 35.
6. Zara Steiner, *Britain and the Origins of the First World War* (London, 1977), chapters 2, 3, 4, 7.
7. A. J. A. Morris, *The Scaremongers: The Advocacy of War and Rearmament 1896–1914* (London, 1984).
8. Steiner, pp. 167, 134.
9. Colin Nicolson, 'Edwardian England and the Coming of the First World War', in Alan O'Day, ed., *The Edwardian Age: Conflict and Stability 1900–1914* (London, 1979), pp. 167, 164, 163, 165.
10. Ibid., p. 165.
11. John Gooch, 'Attitudes to War in Late Victorian and Edwardian England', in John Gooch, ed., *The Prospects of War: Studies in British Defence Policy 1847–1942* (London, 1981), pp. 35–6.
12. W. J. Reader, *'At Duty's Call': A Study in Obsolete Patriotism* (Manchester, 1988), p. 15.
13. See: Kelly Boyd, 'Exemplars and Ingrates: Imperialism and the Boys' Story Paper, 1880–1930', in *Historical Research* 1994, 67 (163), pp. 143–55.
14. Reader, pp. 27, 30.
15. F. Lauriston Bullard, *Famous War Correspondents* (Boston, 1914).
16. See: R. J. Wilkinson-Latham *From Our Special Correspondent: Victorian War Correspondents and their Campaigns* (London, 1979): Phillip Knightley, *The First Casualty From the Crimea to Vietnam: The War Correspondent as Hero, Propagandist and Myth Maker* (London, 1982); Trevor Royle, *War Report: The War Correspondents' View of Battle from the Crimea to the Falklands* (London, 1989).
17. Roger Thomas Stearn, 'War Images and Image Makers in the Victorian Era: Aspects of the British Visual and Written Portrayal of War and Defence *c.*1866–1906', unpublished PhD thesis, University of London, 1987; R. T. Stearn, 'War and the Media in the Nineteenth Century: Victorian Military Artists and the Image of War, 1870–1914', *Journal of the Royal United Service Institution*, 131, September 1986, pp. 55–62; Roger T. Stearn, 'War Correspondents and Colonial War, *c.*1870–1900', in John M. MacKenzie, ed., *Popular Imperialism and the Military, 1850–1950* (Manchester, 1992), pp. 139–61.
18. John M. MacKenzie, 'Postscript', in MacKenzie, ed., *Popular Imperialism*, p. 221.
19. J. W. M. Hichberger, *Images of the Army: The Military in British Art, 1815–1914* (Manchester, 1988), p. 118.

20. Ibid., pp. 111–14.
21. John Springhall ' "Up Guards and at Them!": British Imperialism and Popular Art, 1880–1914', in John M. MacKenzie, ed., *Imperialism and Popular Culture* (Manchester, 1986), pp. 50–1, 68–9.
22. Robin Prior and Trevor Wilson, 'Paul Fussell at War', *War in History*, 1, 1994, pp. 63–80.
23. Samuel Hynes, *The Edwardian Turn of Mind* (Princeton, 1968), p. 7, chapter 2; Paul Thompson, *The Edwardians: The Making of British Society* (London, 1992).
24. Modris Eksteins, *Rites of Spring: The Great War and the Birth of the Modern Age* (London, 2000), pp. xiv–xv.
25. Alfred Vagts, *A History of Militarism: Civilian and Military* (London, 1959), pp. 15, 41, 156. For feudal links, see: Mark Girouard, *The Return to Camelot: Chivalry and the English Gentleman* (New Haven, 1981).
26. Anne Summers, 'Militarism in Britain before the Great War', *History Workshop Journal*, 2, 1976, pp. 105, 111.
27. Geoffrey Best, 'Militarism and the Victorian Public School', in Brian Simon and Ian Bradley, eds, *The Victorian Public School* (Dublin, 1975), pp. 129–46. See also Norman Vance 'The Ideal of Manliness', pp. 115–28.
28. Peter Parker, *The Old Lie: The Great War and the Public School Ethos* (London, 1987). See also: John Springhall, *Youth, Empire and Society: British Youth Groups 1883–1940* (London, 1977); Jeffrey Richards, ed., *Imperialism and Juvenile Literature* (Manchester, 1989); J. S. Bratton 'Of England, Home and Duty: The Image of England in Victorian and Edwardian Juvenile Fiction', in MacKenzie, ed., *Imperialism and Popular Culture*, pp. 73–93.
29. H. J. Perkin, 'The Origins of the Popular Press' *History Today*, 7, 1957, pp. 425–35; Ken Ward, *Mass Communication and the Modern World* (London, 1989), p. 39; Lucy Brown, *Victorian News and Newspapers* (Oxford, 1985), pp. 3–4, chapter 1.
30. Stephen Koss, *The Rise and Fall of the Political Press in Britain* (London, 1981), vol. I, chapters 6, 8 and 9.
31. The idea of late-nineteenth-century readers as their own editors has been suggested by Nicholas Hiley in a series of lectures in the History of Journalism course at City University, London, January–February, 1994.
32. Laurel Brake, *Subjugated Knowledges: Journalism, Gender and Literature in the Nineteenth Century* (New York, 1994), p. 83.
33. Robert W. Desmond, *Windows on the World: The Information Process in a Changing Society 1900–1920* (Iowa City, 1980), p. 165.
34. Donald Read, *Edwardian England 1901–15: Society and Politics* (London, 1972), p. 60.
35. Koss, *Political Press*, vol. I, p. 9.
36. Marshall McLuhan, *Understanding Media* (London, 1987), pp. 22–3.
37. Terence Nevett, 'Advertising', in J. Don Vann and Rosemary T. Van Arsdel, eds, *Victorian Periodicals and Victorian Culture* (Toronto, 1995), p. 219.
38. Jennifer Wicke, *Advertising Fictions: Literature, Advertisements and Social Reading* (Ithaca, 1988), p. 2; Judith Waters and George Ellis, 'The Selling of Gender Identity', in Mary Cross, ed., *Advertising and Culture: Theoretical Perspectives* (Westport CT, 1996), pp. 91 and 96.
39. Waters and Ellis, p. 101; Jib Fowles, *Advertising and Popular Culture* (London, 1996), pp. 13–14.

40. E. S. Turner, *The Shocking History of Advertising!* (London, 1952), pp. 15 and 160; Blanche Beatrice Elliott, *A History of English Advertising* (London, 1962), pp. 171–2, 174. See also Lori Loeb, *Consuming Angels* (Oxford, 1994), p. 9.

41. Loeb, *Consuming Angels, Advertising and Victorian Women*, p. 7.

42. Correlli Barnett, *Britain and Her Army 1509–1970* (London, 1970), p. 313; Turner, *Shocking History*, pp. 111–12, 178.

43. For further discussions of newspapers as a source, see Jerry W. Knudson, 'Late to the Feast: Newspapers as Historical Sources', *Perspectives*, 31, October 1993, pp. 9–11; Glenn R. Wilkinson 'Sources: Newspapers', *Modern History Review*, 3, November 1991.

44. Gerard J. DeGroot, *Blighty: British Society in the Era of the Great War* (London, 1996), p. 15.

45. Ralph Blumenfeld, *The Press in My Time* (London, 1933), p. 45.

46. Stearn, 'War Correspondents and Colonial War', p. 141.

47. Frederick Arthur McKenzie, *From Tokyo to Tiflis: Uncensored Letters From the War* (London, 1905), p. 271.

48. Francis Younghusband to his wife, 7 November 1904, India Office Library, Mss/Eur/F197/175; Younghusband to his sister, 25 April 1904, India Office Library, Mss/Eur/F197/158.

49. Reuters Telegraphic Company Ltd., *Annual Report 1904*, Reuters' Archives.

50. Philip Towle 'The Debate on Wartime Censorship in Britain, 1902–1914', in Brian Bond and Ian Roy, eds, *War and Society* (London, 1975), pp. 103–16; Colin Lovelace, 'British Press Censorship During the First World War', in George Boyce, James Curran and Pauline Wingate, eds, *Newspaper History from the Seventeenth Century to the Present* (London, 1978), pp. 307–19; Alasdair Palmer, 'The History of the D-Notice Committee', in Christopher Andrew and David Dilks, eds, *The Missing Dimension: Governments and Intelligence Communities* (London, 1984), pp. 227–49.

51. Nicholas Hiley, 'The British News Media and Government Control 1914–1916', unpublished PhD thesis, Open University, 1984, pp. 10–11, 23–78.

52. Bullard, *Famous War Correspondents*, p. 27.

Chapter 2 'Uncouth, Unkempt Barbarians'

1. Victor Bonham-Carter, *Soldier True: The Life and Times of Field-Marshal Sir William Robertson* (London, 1963), p. 5.

2. Ibid., p. 1.

3. Edward M. Spiers, *The Army and Society 1815–1914* (London, 1980), pp. 280–1.

4. W. J. Reader, *'At Duty's Call': A Study in Obsolete Patriotism* (Manchester, 1988), p. 2.

5. The events of 1857–58 have been traditionally known as the 'Indian Mutiny', but are now being recognized as the 'Sepoy Rebellion', the 'Indian Rebellion', or even the 'Great Revolt of 1857', in, for example, Mrinalini Sinha's *Colonial Masculinity: The 'Manly Englishman' and the 'Effeminate Bengali' in the late Nineteenth Century* (Manchester, 1995), p. 4.

6. John MacKenzie, 'Introduction: Popular Imperialism and the Military', in John MacKenzie, ed., *Popular Imperialism and the Military, 1850–1950* (Manchester, 1992), pp. 1, 4.
7. G. R. Searle, *The Quest for National Efficiency* (Oxford, 1971), pp. 2, 4.
8. Samuel Hynes, *Edwardian Turn of Mind* (London, 1991), pp. 24–7; [Elliott E. Mills] *The Decline and Fall of the British Empire* (Oxford, n.d.); Michael Howard, 'Empire, Race and War', in Michael Howard, *The Lessons of History* (Oxford, 1991), p. 69.
9. Hynes, *Edwardian Turn of Mind*, p. 23; Daniel Pick, *Faces of Degeneration: A European Disorder, c.1848–c.1919* (Cambridge, 1989), pp. 185–6; Searle, *National Efficiency*, p. 60.
10. Searle, *National Efficiency*, pp. 65, 56; Ian F. W. Beckett, 'The Nation in Arms', in Ian F. W. Beckett and Keith Simpson, eds, *A Nation in Arms: A Social History of the British Army in the First World War* (Manchester, 1985), p. 3.
11. Howard, 'Empire, Race and War', p. 78; Beckett, 'The Nation in Arms', p. 6.
12. Anne Summers, 'Militarism in Britain before the Great War', *History Workshop*, 2, Autumn 1976, p. 105.
13. J. R. Seeley *The Expansion of England*, pp. 302, 291.
14. C. E. Callwell, *Small Wars: Their Principles and Practice*, p. 26.
15. *The Clarion*, 8 April 1904, p. 4.
16. *Daily Express*, 8 August 1904, p. 4. See also: *News of the World*, 22 November 1903, p. 6.
17. Howard, 'Empire, Race and War', p. 72.
18. *Daily Mail*, 20 October 1902, p. 4: 22 October 1902, p. 5.
19. *Illustrated London News*, 23 May 1903, p. 790.
20. Ray Beachey, *The Warrior Mullah: The Horn Aflame, 1892–1920* (London, 1990), p. 38; *Daily Mail*, 20 October 1902, pp. 4, 5.
21. *Justice*, 25 October 1902, p. 1.
22. The battle at Erigo occurred in 1902, not in 1901 as stated by Lawrence James in *The Savage Wars: British Campaigns in Africa 1870–1920* (London, 1985), p. 152. Similarly, the battle at Gumburu occurred in 1903 rather than 1902. See also *Official History of the Operations in Somaliland 1901–04* (London, 1907), Map Number 2 with battle sites.
23. *Daily Mail*, 29 October 1902, pp. 4, 5; 24 April 1903, p. 4. For the Boers as insane/foolish, see *Daily Mail*, 13 October 1899, p. 4 and 14 October 1899, p. 7.
24. *Daily News*, 20 October 1902, p. 6; 25 October 1902, p. 7.
25. *Illustrated London News*, 30 September 1899, p. 453.
26. *Daily Mail*, 11 October 1899, p. 4.
27. Searle, *National Efficiency*, pp. 9–10.
28. *Daily Mail*, 25 January 1900, p. 7: *Punch*, 13 December 1899, p. 295. See also: *Illustrated London News*, 17 March 1900, p. 356 and *Lloyd's Weekly News*, 4 February 1900, p. 4. This attitude contrasts with the sober and reflective attitude of *The Times History of the War in South Africa 1899–1902*, published after the war, where Amery dismisses the furore over the abuse of the white flag as 'much nonsense' and an 'unnecessary outcry raised against the Boers', p. 268.
29. *Daily Mail*, 8 August 1900, p. 5; 19 February 1902, p. 5; *Lloyd's Weekly News*, 17 December 1899, p. 1.

30. Mark Girouard, *The Return to Camelot: Chivalry and the English Gentleman* (New Haven, 1981), p. 7.
31. *Daily Mail*, 2 January 1900, p. 4.
32. See Christine Bolt, *Victorian Attitudes to Race* (London, 1971), p. 209 for a hierarchy of cultures. Tibet, like India, had a recognized civilization and therefore they were more civilized than the Africans, who did not.
33. *The Times*, 8 April 1904, p. 7. See also *Illustrated London News*, 14 May 1904, p. 736. For a similar perspective on the Somalis, see *Daily Mail*, 24 April 1903, p. 4.
34. *The Times*, 6 February 1904, p. 11; *Clarion*, 6 January 1905, p. 4; *Penny Illustrated Paper*, 30 January 1904, p. 73.
35. *Penny Illustrated Paper*, 17 September 1904, p. 179; *News of the World*, 11 September 1904, p. 1 (while on the front page, this report of looting consisted of only four lines of close print at the bottom left of the page); *Illustrated London News*, 3 September 1904, p. 330; *Lloyd's Weekly News*, 28 August, 1904, p. 6; *Daily Express*, 3 January 1905, p. 4; 16 February 1904, p. 4; *Penny Illustrated Paper*, 14 January 1905, p. 25.
36. *Black and White*, 9 January 1904, p. 46; *The Times*, 6 February 1904, p. 11.
37. *Daily Express*, 16 February 1904, pp. 1, 4. See also: *Clarion*, 23 December 1904, p. 4; *Lloyd's Weekly News*, 28 August 1904, p. 6; *Morning Post*, 7 March 1905, p. 7.
38. *Lloyd's Weekly News*, 1 October 1911, pp. 4, 5. Particularly the German press. See Sir James Rennell Rodd, *Social and Diplomatic Memories* (London, 1925), vol. III, pp. 146–7.
39. *The Times*, 31 October 1911, p. 8.
40. *Daily Mail*, 1 November 1911, p. 4; *Daily News*, 31 October 1911, p. 1; 1 November 1911, p. 6; 3 November 1911, p. 1. See also: *Justice*, 7 October 1911, p. 1. For a graphic description of an Italian soldier shooting an Arab prisoner, see: Francis McCullagh, *Italy's War for a Desert* (London, 1912), pp. 143, 12.
41. *Illustrated London News*, 4 November 1911, pp. 705, 711; Francis McCullagh, *Italy's War for a Desert*, p. 63. See also: *Lloyd's Weekly News*, 5 November 1911, p. 5 for photographs of two elderly Arabs being executed by Italian soldiers.
42. *Illustrated London News*, 11 November 1911, p. 753.
43. *Illustrated London News*, 27 July 1901, p. 128. See also 25 October 1902, p. 603, for a visual comparison between drawings of the native Somalis and a group photograph of the 2nd Battalion King's African Rifles. The Somalis were seen to have no organization, whereas both the battalion and the regiment of the African troops were mentioned. The KAR were photographed (photography itself being a modern medium) in uniform, well turned out, and on different levelled rows, but the Somalis were drawn in small groups or as individual subjects in 'savage' clothing.
44. Pick, *Faces of Degeneration*, pp. 203, 223.
45. Gustave Le Bon, *The Crowd: A Study of the Popular Mind* (London, 1896).
46. War Office, *Military Notes on the Dutch Republics in South Africa*, June 1899, pp. 50–1, 13.
47. *Daily Mail*, 10 October 1899, pp. 4, 5; *The Times*, 12 October 1899, p. 9; *News of the World*, 8 October 1899, p. 7. This contrasted with Kitchener's perceived 'scientific organization', *Lloyd's Weekly News*, 4 February 1900, p. 1.

48. *Daily Mail*, 15 December 1899, p. 7; *Daily News*, 24 December 1900, p. 5.
49. *Daily Express*, 19 November 1903, p. 6.
50. Preman Addy, *Tibet on the Imperial Chessboard: The Making of British Policy Towards Lhasa 1899–1925* (Calcutta, 1984) pp. 12–13.
51. *Manchester Guardian*, 8 July 1904, p. 4.
52. *Illustrated London News*, 7 May 1904, p. 693. The perspective was emphasized and reinforced by the accompanying text, which described the Tibetans as 'little better than a mob, armed with swords, leather cannon and long Oriental matchlocks'. For a similar example of the Somalis, see War Office, *Official History of the Operations in Somaliland*, p. 306; *News of the World*, 17 January 1903, p. 6. For an illustration showing the Somali lack of coordination during an attack, see *Illustrated London News*, 8 November 1902, p. 703, where trappings of barbarism such as animal skins and amulets combined with no clear indication of leadership.
53. *Lloyd's Weekly News*, 12 June 1904, p. 5. See also *Daily News*, 10 June 1904, p. 7.
54. *The Times*, 6 September 1904 p. 4. Lieutenant William Glencross was serving with the 2nd Battalion XXth (East Devonshire) Regiment of Foot, and was transferred from India, where the regiment was stationed, to Japan.
55. Sir Ernest Satow, *A Diplomat in Japan*, p. 391.
56. W. A. Beasley, *The Modern History of Japan*, pp. 136–7.
57. *Illustrated London News*, 16 January 1904, supplement VII, and for a similar view of the Japanese navy see supplement VI. See also *Daily Express*, 13 February 1904, p. 4.
58. Ibid., supplements II and III.
59. *Morning Post*, 6 May 1904, p. 4.
60. *Daily Mail*, 10 May 1904, p. 4. See also: *Daily Express*, 16 February 1904, p. 4 and *Official History of the Russo-Japanese War*, vol I, 1910, p. 15.
61. By the time of the Sino-Japanese War in 1894, the Japanese were equipped with modern rifles and artillery of Japanese manufacture. See W. G. Beasley, *The Rise of Modern Japan* (London, 1990), pp. 64–5.
62. Michael Adas, *Machines as the Measure of Men: Science, Technology and Ideologies of Western Dominance* (Ithaca, 1987), pp. 357–65.
63. *Daily News*, 7 May 1904, p. 6; *Lloyd's Weekly News*, 8 May 1904, p. 6; 15 January 1905, p. 12; *Illustrated London News*, 21 May 1904, p. 753.
64. Searle, *National Efficiency*, p. 57.
65. *The Times*, 12 May 1904, p. 9; 7 January 1905, p. 9. See also *Morning Post*, 10 February 1904, p. 6.
66. *Black and White*, 9 January 1904, p. 46; Ellis Ashmead-Bartlett, *Port Arthur: the Siege and Capitulation*, p. 481; *The Times*, 2 September 1904, p. 12.
67. Field-Marshall Viscount Wolseley, *The Story of a Soldier's Life* (London, 1903), p. 20.
68. Hynes, *Edwardian Turn of Mind*, p. 307–8. See also Suzanne Nalbantian, *Seeds of Decadence in the Late Nineteenth Century Novel: a Crisis in Values* (London, 1988).
69. *Daily Express*, 16 February 1904, p. 4; 30 August 1904, p. 1.
70. *Punch*, 12 June 1901, p. 439.
71. *Daily News*, 24 December 1900, p. 5; *Lloyd's Weekly News*, 4 February 1900, p. 5; *Daily Mail*, 30 December 1899, p. 7; Rudyard Kipling, 'The Parting of the Columns' in M. M. Kaye, ed., *Rudyard Kipling: The Complete Verse*, pp. 379–80.

72.   See: Peter Parker, *The Old Lie: the Great War and the Public School Ethos* (London, 1987); W. J. Reader, *'At Duty's Call': A Study in Obsolete Patriotism* (Manchester, 1988); Geoffrey Best, 'Militarism and the Victorian Public School' in Brian Simon and Ian Bradley, eds, *The Victorian Public School* (Dublin, 1975), pp. 126–46; Mark Girouard, *Return to Camelot: Chivalry and the English Gentleman* (New Haven, 1981); John Springhall, *Youth, Empire and Society: British Youth Movements 1883–1940* (London, 1977).

73.   Howard, 'Empire, Race and War', p. 63.

74.   *Glasgow Herald*, 7 July 1904, p. 7.

75.   *Penny Illustrated Paper*, 16 July 1904, p. 7; *Illustrated Mail*, 16 July 1904, p. 1; *News of the World*, 8 August 1904, p. 8. For reports on Gyantse see: *Daily Express*, 7 July 1904, p. 1; *Daily Mail*, 7 July 1904, p. 5; *Daily News*, 7 July 1904, p. 7; *Manchester Guardian*, 7 July 1904, p. 6; *News of the World*, 10 July 1904, p. 10; *Daily Mirror*, 7 July 1904, p. 3; *Illustrated London News*, 16 July 1904, p. 82.

76.   *News of the World*, 17 December 1899, p. 9; *Lloyd's Weekly News*, 17 December 1899, p. 4. Further examples in the same journals see *News of the World*, 4 February 1900, p. 6; *Lloyd's Weekly News*, 24 December 1899, p. 7.

77.   For more, see Thomas Pakenham, *The Boer War* (London, 1982), pp. 201–6, where he states that most of the 'brigade died with their backs to the enemy', and Edward M. Spiers, 'The Scottish Soldier in the Boer War', in John Gooch, ed., *The Boer War: Direction, Experience and Image* (London, 2000), p. 154, where he relates that 'many [soldiers] would panic in a wide-spread retreat that cost even more lives'. Denis Judd and Keith Surridge, in their book *The Boer War* (London, 2002), p. 124, suggest that the soldiers from the Highland Brigade 'escaped as best they could'.

78.   *Justice*, 22 December 1900, p. 1.

79.   John MacKenzie, 'Heroic Myths of Empire' in John MacKenzie, ed., *Popular Imperialism and the Military, 1850–1950* (Manchester, 1992).

80.   Correlli Barnet, *Britain and Her Army 1509–1970*, p. 313; E. S. Turner, *The Shocking History of Advertising!* (London, 1952), pp. 111–12, 178.

81.   Blanche Beatrice Elliott, *A History of English Advertising* (London, 1962), p. 174. For more on the connection between cigarettes, masculinity, modernity, and the Boer War see Glenn R. Wilkinson, ' "To The Front": British Newspaper Advertising and the Boer War', in John Gooch, ed., *The Boer War: Direction, Experience and Image* (London, 2000).

82.   *Illustrated London News*, 7 April 1900, p. 491; 5 January 1901, p. 20; 29 April 1900, p. 557; 29 September 1900, p. 465; 10 November 1900, p. 705.

83.   *Daily Mail*, 19 July 1900, p. 8.

84.   *Lloyd's Weekly News*, 28 January 1900, p. 16; 28 February 1900, p. 16.

85.   *Daily News*, 3 January 1905, p. 11.

86.   *Comic Cuts*, 23 July 1904, p. 7. See also 9 July 1904, p. 7; 6 August 1904, p. 15; 20 August 1904, p. 7.

87.   *Lloyd's Weekly News*, 4 March 1900, p. 12; *Daily News*, 26 February 1900, p. 7; 28 February 1900, p. 4.

88.   See for example: Lionel Caplan, ' "Bravest of the Brave": Representations of "The Gurkha" in British Military Writings', *Modern Asian Studies*, vol. 25, July 1991, pp. 571–97; David Omissi, ' "Martial Races": Ethnicity and Security in Colonial India 1859–1939', *War and Society*, vol. 9, May 1991, pp. 1–27;

Mrinalini Sinha, *Colonial Masculinity: the 'Manly Englishman' and the 'Effeminate Bengali' in the Late Nineteenth Century* (Manchester, 1995).

89. *Penny Illustrated Paper*, 18 June 1904, pp. 388, 392; *Lloyd's Weekly News*, 12 June 1904, p. 5; *Daily News*, 10 June 1904, p. 7; *Daily Mirror*, 4 April 1904, p. 5; 5 April 1904, p. 3. See also: Philip Mason, *A Matter of Honour: an Account of the Indian Army, Its Officers and Men* (London, 1974), pp. 315, 365.
90. *Daily Mail*, 10 October 1899, pp. 4, 5.
91. *Daily News*, 15 December 1899, p. 7; 30 December 1899, p. 4; 28 February 1900, pp. 3–4. For a similar image of the Boers as 'shabbily dressed', see *Punch*, 4 October 1899, p. 166.
92. *Justice*, 9 December 1899, p. 1; 23 December 1899, p. 2; *Daily Mail*, 29 January 1900, p. 4.
93. *The Times*, 19 December 1903, p. 7; *Daily Express*, 26 June 1903, p. 1; 19 November 1903, p. 6.
94. *Lloyd's Weekly News*, 3 April 1904, p. 5; *Daily Express*, 2 April 1904, p. 1; *Daily Mail*, 4 April 1904, p. 4; *Glasgow Herald*, 4 April 1904, p. 7; *Manchester Guardian*, 4 April 1904, p. 5; *News of the World*, 3 April 1904, p. 1; *Daily Mirror*, 4 April 1904, p. 1.
95. *Daily Express*, 29 June 1904, p. 4; *The Times*, 11 June 1904, p. 11.
96. *Daily Mail*, 31 May 1904, pp. 4–5; *Daily Mirror*, 10 July 1904, p. 1.
97. See for example: *Daily Express*, 8 February 1904, p. 4; 2 May 1904, pp. 1, 4.
98. *Morning Post*, 28 December 1904, p. 6; 10 February 1904, p. 7.
99. *The Times*, 5 January 1905, p. 7; 3 January 1905, p. 4.
100. *News of the World*, 8 January 1905, pp. 8, 9; *Penny Illustrated Paper*, 7 January 1905, p. 2.
101. Howard, 'Empire, Race and War', p. 73.
102. See: Gustave Le Bon, *The Crowd: A Study of the Popular Mind* (London, 1896).
103. Reader, *'At Duty's Call'*, pp. 58–9.
104. *Daily Express*, 3 January 1905, p. 4. 'Bobs' was the popular and familiar nickname of Field-Marshal Roberts.
105. *Daily Express*, 16 February 1904, p. 4; Bennett Burleigh, *Empire of the East or Japan and Russia at War 1904–5* (London, 1905), p. 166; Ellis Ashmead-Bartlett, *Port Arthur: the Seige and Capitulation* (London, 1906), p. 75; David H. James, *Siege of Port Arthur: Records of an Eye-Witness* (London, 1905), pp. 82, 136, 141, 167, 175; F. A. McKenzie, *From Tokyo to Tiflis: Uncensored Letters from the War* (London, 1905), p 177. For 'Turkish Tommies' see G. F. Abbott, *Holy War in Tripoli* (London, 1912), p. 13.

Chapter 3   'The Woof and Warp of the Web of Life'

1. Samuel Hynes, *A War Imagined: the First World War and English Culture* (London, 1990), p. 12.
2. Ibid., pp. 13, 18.
3. Rupert Brooke, '1914', in Rupert Brooke, *The Collected Poems of Rupert Brooke* (London, 1918), p. 5.
4. John Gooch, 'Attitudes to War in Late Victorian and Edwardian England', in John Gooch, *The Prospects of War: Studies in British Defence Policy 1847–1942* (London, 1981), pp. 41–3.

5. W. J. Reader, *'At Duty's Call': A Study in Obsolete Patriotism* (Manchester, 1988), pp. 27–8.
6. Sandi E. Cooper, *Patriotic Pacifism: Waging War on War in Europe 1815–1914* (New York, 1991), p. 10.
7. Gooch, 'Attitudes to War', p. 40.
8. *Illustrated London News*, 13 February 1904, p. 216.
9. *Punch*, 4 October 1899, p. 163. See also *News of the World*, 24 September 1899, p. 1.
10. *Daily Mirror*, 8 February 1904, p. 1; *Lancaster Guardian*, 13 February 1904, p. 5.
11. *Clarion*, 12 February 1904, p. 4; *The Times*, 6 September 1904, p. 8; *Justice*, 17 January 1911, p. 1; 4 November 1912, p. 4; 19 July 1913, p. 1. See also [Charles à Court Repington] *The War in the Far East 1904–1905* (London, 1905), pp. 17, 300; Bennett Burleigh, *Empire of the Sun or Japan and Russia at War, 1904–5* (London, 1905), p. 9.
12. *Punch*, 11 October 1899, p. 175; 21 March 1900, p. 209. See also: *Daily Mail*, 13 October 1899, p. 3. For other wars see: *Daily Mirror*, 9 September 1904, p. 7; 8 December 1904, p. 4; *News of the World*, 8 October 1911, p. 1; *Punch*, 11 October 1911, p. 261.
13. *Penny Illustrated Paper*, 23 January 1904, pp. 50–1.
14. Edmund Candler, *The Unveiling of Lhasa* (London, 1905), pp. 17, 257.
15. *Daily Mail*, 30 September 1911, p. 4; *Daily Mirror*, 9 December 1904, p. 3; R. M. Connaughton, *The War of the Rising Sun and the Tumbling Bear: A Military History of the Russo-Japanese War 1904–5* (London, 1988), pp. 195, 204.
16. *Illustrated London News*, 3 February 1900, p. 142.
17. *Lloyd's Weekly Newspaper*, 17 November 1913, p. 16; 13 July 1913, p. 14.
18. Burleigh, *Empire of the Sun*, p. 2.
19. Maurice Baring, *With the Russians in Manchuria* (London, 1905), p. 133.
20. For an interesting examination of the 'procreative' role of soldiers, see Marilyn Lake, 'Mission Impossible: How Men Gave Birth to the Australian Nation – Nationalism, Gender and Other Seminal Acts', *Gender and History*, IV, Autumn 1992, pp. 305–22.
21. Margaret Randolph Higonnet et al., *Behind the Lines: Gender and the Two World Wars* (New Haven, 1987), p. 4.
22. Field-Marshal Viscount Wolseley, *The Story of a Soldier's Life* (London, 1903), p. 20. For a similar perspective from war correspondents, see: Chevalier Tullio Irace, *With the Italians In Tripoli: The Authentic History of the Turco-Italian War* (London, 1912), p. 208; Francis McCullagh, *Italy's War for a Desert: Being Some Experiences of a War Correspondent With the Italians in Tripoli* (London, 1912), p. 4.
23. Laurel Brake, *Subjugated Knowledges: Journalism, Gender and Literature in the Nineteenth Century* (New York, 1994), p. 148.
24. Samuel Hynes, *A War Imagined: The First World War and English Culture* (London, 1992), p. 16; Philip Hoare, *Wilde's Last Stand: Decadence, Conspiracy and the First World War* (London, 1997), chapter 1.
25. I am grateful to Geraldine Blare for pointing this out to me.
26. *Daily Mail*, 12 October 1912, p. 6.
27. Samuel Hynes, *The Edwardian Turn of Mind* (Princeton, 1991), pp. 199–200. See also: Paul Thompson, *The Edwardians: The Remaking of British Society* (London, 1992), p. 228.

28. Gerard DeGroot, in his revisionist work *Blighty: British Society and the Era of the Great War*, erroneously places the First Conference in 1901.
29. *Daily Mail*, 24 October 1912, p. 7.
30. Anne-Marie Käppeli, 'Feminist Scenes', in Geneviève Fraisse and Michelle Perrot, eds, *A History of Women in the West: Emerging Feminism from Revolution to World War*, vol 4 (Cambridge, 1993), pp. 493–4.
31. 'Introduction', in Margaret Randolph Higonnet, Jane Jenson, Sonya Michel and Margaret Collins Weitz, eds, *Behind the Lines: Gender and the Two World Wars* (New Haven, 1987), p. 4.
32. Richard Holmes, *Firing Line* (Harmondsworth, 1989), p. 161.
33. *Daily Mail*, 25 September 1911, p. 4; *Black and White*, 6 February 1904, p. 197; *Daily News*, 10 February 1904, p. 8; *The Times*, 1 September 1905, p. 5.
34. *Daily News*, 26 February 1900, p. 7.
35. *Illustrated London News*, 13 February 1904, pp. 232–3; 7 January 1905, p. 3; *News of the World*, 13 January 1901. p. 1; *Punch*, 2 January 1901, p. 1; 5 February 1902, p. 101; 14 May 1902, p. 353; 4 June 1902 Supplement; 11 January 1905, p. 29.
36. *Daily Mail*, 30 January 1900, p. 5.
37. *Penny Illustrated Paper*, 17 September 1904, p. 179; *Daily News*, 31 August 1904, p. 7; *News of the World*, 4 September, p. 9.
38. Michael Howard, 'Reflections on the First World War', in Michael Howard, *Studies in War and Peace* (London, 1970), pp. 103–4.
39. Benjamin Kidd, *Social Evolution* (London, 1894), p. 39.
40. Zara Steiner, *Britain and the Origins of the First World War* (London, 1977), p. 155; James Joll, *The Origins of the First World War* (London, 1984), p. 184.
41. See, for example: Gooch, 'Attitudes to War', p. 46; Reader, '*At Duty's Call*', p. 21.
42. H. F. Wyatt, *God's Test By War* (London, 1912), pp. 3, 17.
43. Hynes, *The Edwardian Turn of Mind*, pp. 21–3.
44. *Daily News*, 1 September 1904, pp. 6, 7; 10 March 1905, p. 6.
45. *Daily Mail*, 1 January 1900, p. 4; 24 January 1900, p. 4.
46. *Lloyd's Weekly Newspaper*, 28 January 1900, p. 12.
47. *News of the World*, 1 June 1902, p. 6; 8 June 1902, p. 6.
48. Bernard Semmel, *Imperialism and Social Reform: English Social-Imperialist Thought 1895–1914* (London, 1960), pp. 40–1; Howard, 'Empire, Race and War', p. 75.
49. *Daily Mirror*, 5 April 1904, p. 5.
50. Paul Crook, *Darwinism, War and History* (Cambridge, 1994), p. 98.
51. Paul Crook, 'War as Genetic Disaster? The First World War Debate over the Eugenics of Warfare', *War and Society*, 8, May 1990, p. 47.
52. *Daily News*, 29 August 1904, p. 6.
53. Wyatt, *God's Test By War*, pp. 9, 17, 24.
54. *Justice*, 13 February 1904, p. 1.
55. *Daily Mail*, 26 February 1900, p. 4.
56. *News of the World*, 1 October 1899, p. 1.
57. Burleigh, *Empire of the East*, p. 64. See also: Howard, 'Empire, Race and War', p. 75.
58. *Daily Mail*, 24 October 1912, p. 7.
59. *Daily Express*, 11 February 1904, p. 3. See also 16 February 1904, p. 7 for a similar advertisement by Oxo.

60. Peter Paret, 'Clausewitz and the Nineteenth Century' in Michael Howard, ed., *The Theory and Practice of War* (London, 1965), pp. 26–7.
61. Reader, '*At Duty's Call*', p. 20.
62. *Daily Mail*, 11 October 1899, p. 4.
63. *Illustrated London Newspaper*, 14 October 1899, p. 524; 16 November 1912, pp. 720–1; 23 November 1912, supplements IV, V. See also: *Daily Mirror*, 8 February 1904, p. 1; *Daily News*, 10 March 1905, p. 6; *Justice*, 13 February 1904, p. 1; *Lloyd's Weekly News*, 3 September 1905, p. 14.
64. Wyatt, *God's Test By War*, p. 10.
65. *Illustrated London News*, 29 September 1900, p. 445; 10 November 1900, p. 676. See also: *Daily Mail*, 11 October 1899, p. 4; 21 May 1904, p. 5; *Lancaster Guardian*, 17 July 1904, p. 8; *News of the World*, 28 January 1900, p. 7; 17 January 1904, p. 8; *The Times*, 5 September 1904, p. 7.
66. *The Times*, 2 April 1904, p. 3; *Manchester Guardian*, 2 April 1904, p. 4.
67. *Glasgow Herald*, 8 August 1904, p. 6.
68. *Daily Mail*, 1 November 1911, pp. 4,5; *Daily Express*, 2 April 1904, p. 1.
69. Gooch, 'Attitudes to War', p. 40.
70. *Daily News*, 13 October 1899, p. 4; *Daily Mail*, 26 February 1900, p. 5. See also Edgar Wallace, *Unofficial Dispatches* (London, 1901), p. 12.
71. *Daily Express*, 2 April 1904, p. 4; *Daily Mail*, 7 April 1904, p. 4. For Boers as burglars, see *Lloyd's Weekly Newspaper*, 17 December 1899, p. 12.
72. *Daily News*, 16 October 1899, p. 4.
73. *Daily Mail*, 14 December 1899, p. 5; *Lloyd's Weekly Newspaper*, 21 January 1900, p. 4. See also: *Daily Mail*, 19 December 1899, p. 5; *Daily News*, 30 January 1900, p. 5; *Lloyd's Weekly News*, 17 December 1899, p. 4; 10 March 1912, p. 8; *News of the World*, 28 August 1904, p. 6; *The Times*, 5 September 1904, p. 7; Ellis Ashmead-Bartlett, *Port Arthur: The Siege and Capitulation* (London, 1906), pp. 77–8; Irace, *With the Italians in Tripoli*, p. 119.
74. *Morning Post*, 6 May 1904, p. 6.
75. Cooper, *Patriotic Pacifism*, p. 113.
76. Ibid., pp. 152–3.
77. Gillian Sutherland, 'Education', in F. M. L. Thompson, ed., *Cambridge Social History of Britain 1750–1950* (Cambridge, 1990), vol. III, p. 119.
78. Geoffrey Best, 'Militarism and the Victorian Public School' in Brian Simon and Ian Bradley, eds, *The Victorian Public School* (Dublin, 1975), pp. 129, 131–6; M. D. Blanch, 'British Society and the War', in Peter Warwick, ed., *The South African War 1899–1902* (Harlow, 1980), p. 211. For the Canadian equivalent see David W. Brown, 'Social Darwinism, Public Schooling and Sport in Victorian and Edwardian Canada', in J. A. Mangan, ed., *Pleasure, Profit, and Proselytism: British Culture and Sport at Home and Abroad 1700–1914* (London, 1988), pp. 216–17.
79. Blanch, 'British Society and the War', p. 211.
80. *Glasgow Herald*, 2 April 1904, p. 4; 8 August 1904, p. 6.
81. *Daily Express*, 2 April 1904, p. 4. For other Tibetan examples, see *Daily Express*, 8 August 1904, p. 1; *Daily Mail*, 4 April 1904, p. 4; 7 April 1904, p. 4; 30 June 1904, p. 4; *Illustrated London News*, 21 May 1904, p. 756; *Lloyd's Weekly Newspaper*, 15 May 1904, p. 12; *The Times*, 1 April 1904, p. 7; Perceval Landon, *Lhasa* (London, 1905), I, p. 154; Edmund Candler, *The Unveiling of Lhasa* (London, 1905), pp. 147, 148, 255.

82. *Manchester Guardian*, 9 May 1904, p. 4.
83. Alistair Lamb, *British India and Tibet 1766–1910* (London, 1986), p. 244.
84. *Clarion*, 23 September 1904, p. 4; *Lancaster Guardian*, 17 September 1904, p. 5.
85. *News of the World*, 17 June 1900, p. 1. For a similar example, see 22 April 1900, p. 1.
86. *Daily Mail*, 3 November 1911, p. 4; *Illustrated London News*, 4 November 1911, p. 709.
87. *Daily Mail*, 10 October 1899, p. 4; 20 October 1902, p. 4.
88. Walter E. Houghton, *The Victorian Frame of Mind 1830–1870* (New Haven, 1957), pp. 242, 248, 249.
89. *Daily Mail*, 26 February 1900, p. 5. See also: 11 December 1899, p. 5; 10 March 1903, p. 5; 31 October 1911, p. 5; *Daily News*, 14 October 1899, p. 7; 20 February 1900, p. 5; 24 April 1903, p. 7; 31 October 1911, p. 1; *Illustrated London News*, 4 November 1911, p. 715; *Lloyd's Weekly Newspaper*, 15 October 1911, p. 2; 27 October 1912, p. 2; *Manchester Guardian*, 2 April 1905, p. 5; 8 July 1904, p. 4; *News of the World*, 5 April 1903, p. 1; 8 October 1911, p. 8.
90. *News of the World*, 17 November 1901, p. 1; 30 December 1900, p. 1; 19 May 1901, p. 1; 18 August 1901, p. 1. See also: *Daily Mail*, 30 October 1912, p. 3.
91. *News of the World*, 19 October 1902, p. 1.
92. *Morning Post*, 6 May 1904, p. 1.
93. *Punch*, 21 August 1901, p. 136; 29 October 1902, p. 299.
94. *The Times*, 6 December 1904, p. 5.
95. *Daily News*, 30 August 1904, p. 6; *News of the World*, 4 September 1904, p. 8. See also: *Daily News*, 10 March 1905, p. 6; *Lloyd's Weekly Newspaper*, 3 September 1905, p. 14; *News of the World*, 14 February 1904, p. 6; 11 September 1904, p. 8; *The Times*, 1 September 1905, p. 5; Committee of Imperial Defence Historical Section *Official History, Naval and Military, of the Russo-Japanese War* (London, 1912), vol. II, pp. 694–5.
96. *Daily News*, 24 April 1903, pp. 6,7.

Chapter 4   'The Great Game of War'

1. Paul Thompson, *The Edwardians: the Remaking of British Society* (London, 1992), p. 184.
2. Juliet R. V. Barker, *The Tournament in England 1100–1400* (Woodridge, 1986), pp. 17, 19.
3. See for example: Mark Girouard, *Return to Camelot: Chivalry and the English Gentleman* (New Haven, 1981).
4. John MacKenzie, *The Empire of Nature: Hunting, Conservation and British Imperialism* (Manchester, 1988), pp. 44, 46, 47, 194, 186.
5. For further discussion of these issues see: Tony Mason, *Sport in Britain* (London, 1988), p. 46; Wray Vamplew, 'Sport and Industrialization: an Economic Interpretation of the Changes in Popular Sport in Nineteenth Century England', pp. 12–13, 17; and R. J. Holt, 'Football and the Urban Way of Life in Nineteenth Century Britain', pp. 71–2, both in J. A. Mangan, *Pleasure, Profit and Proselytism: British Culture and Sport At Home and Abroad 1700–1914* (London, 1988).
6. Mason, *Sport in Britain*, pp. 47–9.

7. See Samuel Hynes, *The Edwardian Turn of Mind* (Princeton, 1968), p. 23.
8. Richard Holt, *Sport and the British: a Modern History* (Oxford, 1990), p. 88. See also: John Springhall *Youth, Empire and Society: British Youth Movements* (London, 1977), pp. 14–16.
9. John Gooch, 'Attitudes to War in Late Victorian and Edwardian England', in John Gooch, ed., *The Prospects of War: Studies in British Defence Policy 1847–1942* (London, 1981), pp. 41–2.
10. Paul Crook, 'War as Genetic Disaster? The First World War Debate Over the Eugenics of Warfare', in *War and Society*, 8, May 1990, p. 51.
11. Holt, *Sport and the British*, p. 346.
12. Geoffrey Best, 'Militarism and the Victorian Public School', in Brian Simon and Ian Bradley, eds, *The Victorian Public School* (Dublin, 1975), pp. 140–1.
13. Peter Parker, *The Old Lie: The Great War and the Public School Ethos* (London, 1987), p. 17 and chapter 3.
14. Holt, 'Football and the Urban Way of Life', p. 71.
15. Patric Dickinson, ed., *Selected Poems of Henry Newbolt* (London, 1981), pp. 38–9.
16. *Daily Mirror*, 3 May 1904, p. 1; *Lloyd's Weekly News*, 17 November 1912, p. 16; *Comic Cuts*, 26 November 1904, p. 2; 24 December 1904, p. 7; 18 February 1904, p. 7. See also: *Daily Mirror*, 4 May 1904, pp. 6 and 7; *Illustrated London News*, 21 May 1904, p. 769; *Punch*, 7 March 1900, p. 169.
17. *Daily Mail*, 2 September 1904, p. 5; *Daily News*, 7 March 1905, p. 7; *The Times*, 2 September 1904, p. 3.
18. *Daily Mail*, 21 August 1900, p. 4.
19. Lt.-Col. R. S. S. Baden-Powell, *Aids to Scouting for N.-C.O.s and Men* (London, 1899), p. 124. For another soldier's view of war as a game, see Sir Francis Younghusband, *India and Tibet* (London, 1910), p. 193.
20. *Daily News*, 13 December 1899, p. 6; 27 January 1900, p. 5. For an image of 'playing possum', see: 13 February 1900, p. 6.
21. Best, 'Militarism and the Victorian Public School', pp. 129, 135–6, 141.
22. *Daily Mail*, 10 March 1903, p. 5. For further examples see *Daily Express*, 30 August 1904, p. 1; *Lloyd's Weekly News*, 28 August 1904, p. 12; 4 September 1904, p. 12.
23. *Daily Mail*, 8 January 1902, p. 5.
24. *Black and White*, 7 May 1904, p. 688; 14 May 1904, p. 716; *Clarion*, 6 January 1905, p. 6; 1 September 1905, p. 4; *Daily Mail*, 6 September 1904, p. 4; 2 January 1905, p. 5; *Daily Mirror*, 4 January 1905, p. 3; *Daily News*, 3 January 1905, p. 6; *Lloyd's Weekly News*, 4 December 1904, p. 12; *Morning Post*, 1 March 1905, p. 7; *News of the World*, 4 September 1904, p. 8; *The Times*, 2 September 1904, p. 4. See also for example: Charles à Court Repington, *The War in the Far East 1904–1905* (London, 1905), p. 20.
25. Alan J. Lee, *The Origins of the Popular Press in England 1855–1914* (London, 1976), p. 121; Donald Read, *Edwardian England 1901–1915: Society and Politics* (London, 1972), pp. 58–9; H. J. Perkin, 'The Origin of the Popular Press', in *History Today*, 7, 1957, p. 434.
26. *Daily Mail*, 28 October 1912, p. 6. For further examples of war as a 'duel', see *Daily Mail*, 20 November 1912, p. 7; *Daily News*, 8 February 1904, p. 8; 1 September 1904, p. 7; 2 December 1904, p. 6; *The Times*, 1 September 1904, p. 3; 2 December 1904, p. 6. For 'fencing' imagery see *Illustrated*

London News, 16 November 1912, supplement VI, VII; *The Times*, 3 May 1904, p. 6; 31 August 1904, p. 7.

27. *News of the World*, 17 January 1904, p. 6.
28. John Lowerson, 'Brothers of the Angle: Coarse Fishing and English Working-Class Culture 1850–1914' in Mangan, *Pleasure, Profit and Proselytism*, pp. 105–6, 109. The middle classes tended to seek 'game fish' such as salmon, trout and grayling; 'coarse fishing' included every other type of fish.
29. *News of the World*, 9 June 1901, p. 1; 13 October 1901, p. 1; 18 September 1904, p. 1.
30. Holt, *Sport and the British*, p. 301.
31. *Daily News*, 7 May 1904, p. 6; *Penny Illustrated Paper*, 20 February 1904, p. 114. For further examples of boxing imagery see: *Black and White*, 7 May 1904, p. 688; *Daily Mail*, 31 October 1912, p. 7; 1 November 1912, p. 7; *Daily News*, 14 October 1899, p. 5; 18 December 1899, p. 5; *News of the World*, 17 December 1899, p. 1; 28 August 1904, p. 6; *Penny Illustrated Paper*, 16 January 1904, p. 35. For images of fighting as 'blows' see: *Daily News*, 11 February 1904, p. 8; *Morning Post*, 5 May 1904, p. 6; 31 December 1904, p. 5; 13 March 1905, p. 8; *News of the World*, 4 September 1904, p. 9; *The Times*, 2 September 1904, p. 7; 2 December 1904, p. 7. For images of wrestling see *News of the World*, 14 February 1904, p. 1; *Punch*, 17 February 1904, p. 119.
32. Holt, *Sport and the British*, p. 179.
33. *Punch*, 15 May 1901, p. 359; *Lloyd's Weekly News*, 3 November 1912, p. 16. For examples of direct cricket imagery and associated terminology such as 'stroke', see: *Black and White*, 14 May 1904, p. 716; *Daily Mail*, 1 November 1912, p. 7; *Daily News*, 15 December 1899, p. 5; *Illustrated London News*, 23 December 1899, p. 912; *Punch*, 24 February 1904, p. 128; *The Times*, 31 August 1904, p. 7; 2 September 1904, p. 4; 6 September 1904, p. 8. For football images and allusions see *Daily Mail*, 18 December 1899, p. 7; 30 January 1900, p. 7; *Daily News*, 11 December 1899, p. 8; *Illustrated London News*, 11 November 1911, p. 733.
34. *Daily Mail*, 2 January 1900, p. 4; *Daily News*, 1 September 1904, p. 6.
35. *News of the World*, 18 February 1900, p. 1; *Punch*, 1 June 1904, p. 389.
36. Ellis Ashmead-Bartlett, *Port Arthur: The Siege and Capitulation* (London, 1906), p. 289.
37. Holt, *Sport and the British*, p. 179; Mark Clapson, *A Bit of a Flutter: Popular Gambling and English Society c.1823–1961* (Manchester, 1992), p. 115. Off-course betting was made legal in 1961.
38. *Morning Post*, 4 March 1905, p. 7; *Daily News*, 29 August 1904, p. 6.
39. Ashmead-Bartlett, *Port Arthur*, p. 300; Repington, *The War in the Far East*, p. 391.
40. Repington, p. 133; *Daily News*, 24 October 1912, p. 3.
41. *Punch*, 30 April 1902, p. 317.
42. H. J. R. Murray, *A History of Chess* (Oxford, 1962), p. 25.
43. *Daily Mail*, 25 October 1912, p. 7.
44. *Black and White*, 10 September 1904, p. 688; *Daily News*, 7 March 1905, p. 7. See also *Daily News*, 30 August 1904, p. 7.
45. *News of the World*, 10 September 1904, p. 8. For other contemporary references to war as a chess 'game of strategy' where 'men are pawns', see

Repington, p. 230; Frederick Arthur McKenzie, *From Tokyo to Tiflis: Uncensored Letters from the War* (London, 1905), p. 198.

46. *Daily News*, 18 December 1899, p. 5.

47. Preman Addy, *Tibet on the Imperial Chessboard: The Making of British Policy Towards Lhasa 1899–1925* (Calcutta, 1984), p. 82.

48. *Daily Mail*, 10 February 1904, p. 5. See also 9 February 1904, p. 2; *Daily News*, 10 February 1904 pp. 5, 16; *News of the World*, 14 February 1904, p. 8; *Illustrated London News*, 2 January 1904, p. 17; 16 January 1904, supplement IV, V; *The Times*, 3 January 1905, p. 10.

49. *Lloyd's Weekly News*, 27 October 1912, p. 3; *Daily Mail*, 8 February 1904, p. 5; *The Times*, 3 September 1904, p. 10.

50. Kenneth and Marguerite Fawdry, *Pollock's History of English Dolls and Toys* (London, 1979), pp. 139–40; Bethnal Green Museum of Childhood, Display Case G13/57; Pollock's Toy Museum, *Soldiers and Miniatures* (London, n.d.); H. G. Wells, *Little Wars: A Game for Boys* (London, 1913), p. 97. Wells also suggested that his game could be played by junior officers and girls 'of the better sort'.

51. *Daily Mail*, 12 October 1899, pp. 3, 7 for an advertisement for 'The *Illustrated Mail* Transvaal Game'; *Daily Mirror*, 11 February 1904, pp. 8–9.

52. *Daily News*, 27 January 1900, p. 6.

53. *Illustrated London News*, 16 December 1899, p. 869; *Punch*, 16 March 1904, p. 187; 20 April 1904, p. 285.

54. *Daily Mirror*, 12 February 1904, p. 5; Phil Shaw, *Collecting Football Programmes* (London, 1980), p. 8.

55. *Penny Illustrated Paper*, 24 September 1904, p. 193; 12 November 1904, p. 305.

56. Ian F. W. Beckett, *Johnny Gough V. C.: A Biography of Brigadier-General Sir John Edmond Gough V. C., K. C. B.* (London, 1989), p. 90.

57. General Staff, War Office, *Military Report on Somaliland* (London, 1907), Appendix H, p. 272. See also: Malcolm McNeil, *In Pursuit of the 'Mad' Mullah: Service and Sport in Somali Protectorate* (London, 1902), where the author concentrates more on 'sport' than on 'service', and in which he included a copy of the Somaliland Game Regulations for 1901.

58. *Illustrated London News*, 8 November 1902, p. 707. See also *Daily Express*, 26 December 1903, p. 1, where the paper similarly outlined the hunting possibilities before the Tibet Expedition.

59. Lt.-General Sir Robert Baden-Powell, *Indian Memories: Recollections of Soldiering Sport, etc.* (London, 1915), p. 30.

60. *Daily Mail*, 5 September 1904, p. 4.

61. Baden-Powell, *Indian Memories*, p. 205.

62. *Daily Mirror*, 5 April 1904, p. 5.

63. *Daily Express*, 26 June 1903, p. 1; 19 November 1903, p. 6; 26 December 1903, p. 1; 31 December 1903, p. 1; 18 January 1904, p. 1.

64. MacKenzie, *Empire of Nature*, pp. 34, 47.

65. *Punch*, 7 March 1900, p. 165; *News of the World*, 6 October 1901, p. 1.

66. *Daily Mail*, 18 December 1899 p. 7; *Illustrated London News*, 27 June 1903 p. 982. For 'ecstasy' see MacKenzie, *Empire of Nature*, p. 42.

67. Baden-Powell, *Aids to Scouting*, p. 37. For quotes found in newspapers from Baden-Powell's book, see for example *Daily Mail*, 30 January 1900, p. 7; *Daily News*, 11 December 1899, p. 8.

68. *News of the World*, 6 January 1901, p. 1. See also 19 November 1899, p. 1, for a similar image of Buller and White as dogs chasing Kruger, a rabbit.
69. *Lloyd's Weekly News*, 9 December 1900, pp. 1, 9.
70. Baden-Powell, *Indian Memories*, pp. 37–9, 55.
71. *Daily Mail*, 22 January 1902, p. 4; *Daily News*, 14 October 1902, p. 3.
72. MacKenzie, *Empire of Nature*, p. 186.
73. Thompson, *The Edwardians*, pp. 184–5; Mason, *Sport in Britain*, p. 1.

Chapter 5   'This Wonderfully Lovely Theatre of War'

1. David Blackbourn, 'Politics as Theatre: Metaphors of the Stage in German History, 1848–1933', *Transactions of the Royal Historical Society*, 37, 1987, p. 149.
2. Paul Fussell, *The Great War and Modern Memory* (Oxford, 1977), pp. 191–2.
3. John Gooch, 'Attitudes to War in Late Victorian and Edwardian England', in Brian Bond and Ian Roy, eds, *War and Society* (London, 1975), p. 91.
4. Lieutenant-General Sir Ian Hamilton, *A Staff Officer's Scrapbook During the Russo-Japanese War* (London, 1905), vol. I, p. 2.
5. James Woodfield, *English Theatre in Transition: 1889–1914* (London, 1984), p. 1; Michael Booth, *Theatre in the Victorian Age* (Cambridge, 1991), p. 120; Russell Jackson, *Victorian Theatre* (London, 1989), p. 153.
6. Woodfield, *English Theatre*, pp. 12, 16; Jackson, *Victorian Theatre*, pp. 3, 11.
7. Jackson, *Victorian Theatre*, p. 153.
8. Woodfield, *English Theatre*, pp. 16, 3, 18, 19; J. C. Trewin, *The Edwardian Theatre* (Oxford, 1976), p. 3.
9. Jackson, *Victorian Theatre*, pp. 3–4.
10. Penny Summerfield, 'Patriotism and Empire: Music Hall Entertainment 1870–1914', in John MacKenzie, ed., *Imperialism and Popular Culture* (Manchester, 1986), pp. 22, 24; Dave Russell, ' "We Carved Our Way To Glory": The British Soldier in Music Hall Song and Sketch, *c.* 1880–1914', in John MacKenzie, ed., *Popular Imperialism and the Military 1850–1950* (Manchester, 1992), pp. 51–3.
11. Summerfield, 'Patriotism and Empire', pp. 32–3, 35.
12. Russell, ' "We Carved Our Way To Glory" ', pp. 50–1, 54.
13. Hamilton, *A Staff Officer's Scrapbook*, vol. II, p. v.
14. Fussell, *The Great War and Modern Memory*, p. 196.
15. *Daily Mirror*, 10 February 1904, p. 1; 3 September 1904, p. 7.
16. *Black and White*, 3 September 1904, p. 310; *Daily News*, 13 June 1904, p. 6; Committee of Imperial Defence Historical Section, *Official History, Naval and Military, of the Russo-Japanese War* (London, 1912) vol. 2, pp 694–5; *Daily Express*, 2 January 1905, p. 1.
17. *Daily Mail*, 1 January 1900, p. 4; *News of the World*, 5 November 1911, p. 6; *Daily News*, 24 April 1903, p. 6.
18. *Daily News*, 1 September 1904, p. 7; *News of the World*, 11 September 1904, p. 9.
19. Hamilton, *A Staff Officer's Scrapbook*, vol. II, p. v.
20. Ellis Ashmead-Bartlett, *Port Arthur: The Siege and Capitulation* (London, 1906), pp. 303–4, 325.
21. *Black and White*, 10 September 1904, p. 358.

22. For example see *Daily Express*, 2 January 1905, p. 4; *Daily Mail*, 3 January 1905, p. 4; 13 February 1904, p. 4; *The Times*, 2 September 1904, p. 4. See also Charles à Court Repington, *The War in the Far East 1904–1905* (London, 1905), pp. 27, 79.

23. *Daily Mail*, 28 October 1912, p. 6. A 'super' is a supernumerary or stage extra.

24. *Illustrated London News*, 3 February 1900, p. 3.

25. *The Times*, 3 September 1904, p. 3.

26. George Lynch, *Impressions of a War Correspondent* (London, 1903), p. xi.

27. *Daily Mail*, 26 February 1900, p. 5. See also *Daily Express*, 4 May 1904, p. 1; 5 September 1904, p. 4; *Daily Mail*, 20 October 1902, p. 5; *Daily Mirror*, 4 April 1904, p. 2; 23 November 1904, p. 8; *Glasgow Herald*, 4 April 1904, p. 7; *Manchester Guardian*, 4 April 1904, p. 5; *Illustrated London News*, 30 July 1904, p. 164.

28. *News of the World*, 8 January 1905, p. 5; *Daily Express*, 2 January 1905, p. 1. See also *Black and White*, 10 September 1904, p. 358; *Daily Mail*, 24 October 1912, p. 4; 30 October 1912, p. 6; *Daily News*, 3 January 1905, p. 8; *Lloyd's Weekly News*, 5 November 1911, p. 5; 1 December 1912, p. 1. For further examples of both forms of 'scene' imagery see Henry Newman, *A Roving Commission* (London, 1937), p. 147; Repington, *The War in the Far East*, pp. 79, 397, 419; Ashmead-Bartlett, *Port Arthur*, pp. 147–8; David H. James, *The Siege of Port Arthur: Records of An Eye-Witness* (London, 1905), pp. 78, 97.

29. *Daily News*, 8 February 1904, p. 8; 5 May 1904, p. 6. See also for example: *Daily Mail*, 13 February 1904, p. 4; 3 September 1904, p. 4; Bennett Burleigh, *Empire of the East or Japan and Russia at War 1904–5* (London, 1905), p. 284; Repington, *The War in the Far East*, pp. 79–80, 419.

30. *Morning Post*, 27 October 1904, p. 4. See also *Daily Express*, 7 July 1904, p. 1.

31. *Daily Mail*, 3 September 1904, p. 4. See also *Black and White*, 27 August 1904, p. 278.

32. Jackson, *Victorian Theatre*, p. 219.

33. *Black and White*, 10 September 1904, p. 358; Ashmead-Bartlett, *Port Arthur*, p. vii.

34. Lynch, *Impressions of a War Correspondent*, p. 34; *Punch*, 6 February 1901, p. 117. See also: *Daily Mirror*, 4 June 1905, p. 7; *News of the World*, 20 November 1904, p. 1; *Punch*, 4 October 1905, p. 237; 25 May 1904, p. 371.

35. *News of the World*, 1 October 1911, p. 1; *Justice*, 14 October 1911, p. 1; Francis McCullagh, *Italy's War for a Desert* (London, 1912), p. 108.

36. Dave Russell 'Popular Musical Culture and Popular Politics in the Yorkshire Textile District 1880–1914', in John K. Walton and James Walvin, eds, *Leisure in Britain 1780–1939* (Manchester, 1983), p. 100.

37. *Black and White*, 10 September 1904, p. 358; *Daily Mail*, 29 January 1900, p. 4; 13 February 1904, p. 4; *Daily Mirror*, 5 May 1904, p. 4.

38. Repington, *The War in the Far East*, p. 543. For weapons 'singing' see *Black and White*, 10 September 1904, p. 348; *Daily Mail*, 1 November 1911, p. 5; *Morning Post*, 27 October 1904, p. 4; 28 October 1904, p. 3; Lynch, *Impressions of a War Correspondent*, p. 55.

39. See Jeffrey Richards, ed., *Imperialism and Juvenile Fiction* (Manchester, 1989).

40. See for example *Illustrated London News*, 3 February 1900, p. 142; *Lloyd's Weekly News*, 4 February 1900, p. 4; *News of the World*, 4 February 1900, p. 6; 26 April 1903, p. 1; 3 May 1903, p. 7.

41. See *Daily Express*, 7 July 1904, p. 1; *Daily News*, 7 July 1904, p. 7; *Glasgow Herald*, 7 July 1904, p. 7; *Manchester Guardian*, 7 July 1904, p. 6; *News of the World*, 10 July 1904, p. 10.

42. *Daily Express*, 4 April 1904, p. 1; *Daily Mirror*, 4 April 1904, p. 9; *Daily News*, 4 April 1904, p. 7; *Glasgow Herald*, 4 April 1904, p. 5; *Lloyd's Weekly News*, 10 April 1904, p. 5; *News of the World*, 10 April 1904, p. 9.

43. *Daily Mail*, 4 April 1904, p. 5; 24 October 1912, p. 12.

44. Scott Hughes Myerly, ' "The Eye Must Entrap the Mind": Army Spectacle and Paradigm in Nineteenth Century Britain', *Journal of Social History*, 26, Fall 1992, pp. 108–11.

45. Ibid., p. 106.

46. *Lloyd's Weekly News*, 4 March 1900, p. 4; *Illustrated London News*, 23 November 1912, pp. 754–5.

47. *Daily News*, 25 October 1902, p. 7; 24 April 1903, p. 7. For the picturesque descriptions of a Turkish camp see 27 December 1911, p. 2.

48. *Manchester Guardian*, 30 March 1904, p. 5; *Lloyd's Weekly News*, 9 December 1900, p. 1. See also *Daily Mail*, 5 January 1905, p. 4; *Daily Mirror*, 30 August 1904, p. 3; *Lloyd's Weekly News*, 23 December 1900, p. 4; 8 January 1905, p. 6; *The Times*, 30 August 1904, p. 3; Burleigh, *Empire of the East*, pp. 321–2.

49. Lynch, *Impressions of a War Correspondent*, pp. 51, 53.

50. *Daily Mail*, 25 January 1900, p. 4; *Lloyd's Weekly News*, 11 March 1900, p. 4.

51. *Daily News*, 1 September 1904, p. 6.

52. *Black and White*, 10 August 1904, p. 358. See also for example: Burleigh, *Empire of the East*, p. 325.

53. David Mayer 'The World on Fire...: Pyrodramas at Belle Vue Gardens, Manchester, *c*.1850–1950', in MacKenzie, ed., *Popular Imperialism and the Military*, p. 179.

54. *Daily News*, 31 August 1904, p. 7; *Morning Post*, 28 October 1904, p. 3.

55. *Penny Illustrated Paper*, 12 November 1904, p. 307. See also: *Lloyd's Weekly Paper*, 25 February 1900, p. 4; Ashmead-Bartlett, *Port Arthur*, p. 277; Lord Brooke, *An Eye-Witness in Manchuria* (London, 1905), p. 133; James, *The Seige of Port Arthur*, p. 188; G. F. Abbott, *The Holy War in Tripoli* (London, 1912), p. 129.

56. *Morning Post*, 29 April 1904, p. 4. See also: *News of the World*, 26 October 1902, p. 7, where the Somaliland Expeditions were described as 'military promenades'.

57. Edmund Candler, *The Unveiling of Lhasa* (London, 1905), p. 267. See also: H. C. Seppings-Wright, *Two Years under the Crescent* (London, 1913), pp. 253, 260.

58. *Daily Express*, 7 July 1904, p. 1; *Daily Mail*, 7 July 1904, p. 5; *Daily Mirror*, 7 July 1904, p. 3; *Daily News*, 7 July 1904, p. 7; *Glasgow Herald*, 7 July 1904, p. 7; *Illustrated London News*, 16 July 1904, pp. 82, 87; *Illustrated Mail*, 16 July 1904, pp. 1–2; *Manchester Guardian*, 7 July 1904, p. 6; *News of the World*, 10 July 1904, p. 10; *Penny Illustrated Paper*, 16 July 1904, p. 41.

59. Francis Younghusband, *India and Tibet*, (London, 1910), p. 219.

60. Seppings-Wright, *Two Years under the Crescent*, pp. 262–3.

61. Ashmead-Bartlett, *Port Arthur*, p. 472.

Chapter 6   'A Withering Fire that Mowed Them Down in Heaps'

1. Garrett Stewart, *Death Sentences: Styles of Dying in British Fiction* (Cambridge, 1984), pp. 4–5.
2. James Stevens Curl, *The Victorian Celebration of Death* (Newton Abbot, 1972).
3. Jennifer Leaney, 'Ashes to Ashes: Cremation and the Celebration of Death in Nineteenth Century Britain', in Ralph Houlbrooke, ed., *Death, Ritual and Bereavement* (London, 1989), p. 134.
4. Philippe Aries, *The Hour of Our Death* (London, 1981), pp. 579, 611.
5. Ruth Richardson, 'Why was Death So Big in Victorian Britain?', in Houlbrooke, *Death, Ritual and Bereavement*, p. 114. See also: Ruth Richardson, *Death, Dissection and the Destitute* (London, 1987).
6. John Morley, *Death, Heaven and the Victorians* (Pittsburg, 1971); Michael Wheeler *Death and the Future Life in Victorian Literature* (Cambridge, 1991), especially chapter 1; Curl, *Victorian Celebration of Death*.
7. Leaney, 'Ashes to Ashes', p. 118; David Cannadine, 'War and Death, Grief and Mourning in Modern Britain', in Joachim Whaley, ed., *Mirrors of Mortality: Studies in the Social History of Death* (London, 1981), p. 192.
8. Ralph Houlbrooke, 'Introduction', in Houlbrooke, ed., *Death, Ritual and Bereavement*, p. 13. See also: Sylvia M. Barnard, *'To Prove I'm Not Forgot': Living and Dying in a Victorian City* (Manchester, 1990).
9. Leaney, 'Ashes to Ashes', pp. 118, 129.
10. Ibid., p. 131.
11. Martha McMakin Garland, 'Victorian Unbelief and Bereavement', in Houlbrooke, ed., *Death, Ritual and Bereavement*, pp. 160–2.
12. Cannadine, 'War and Death', p. 227. In 1919, there were 309 and by 1938 there were 530.
13. *Lloyd's Weekly News*, 29 October 1911, p. 6. See also: *Daily Express*, 4 January 1905, p. 4; *Daily Mail*, 4 April 1904, p. 4; *Daily News*, 25 October 1912, p. 1; 26 October 1912, p. 1; *Lloyd's Weekly News*, 27 October 1912, p. 2; *Morning Post*, 27 October 1904, p. 4; *News of the World*, 8 May 1904, p. 6.
14. Ellis Ashmead-Bartlett, *Port Arthur: The Seige and Capitulation* (London, 1906), pp. 75, 195.
15. *Daily Mail*, 31 October 1911, p. 5; *Lloyd' Weekly News*, 17 January 1904, p. 5; *News of the World*, 17 January 1904, p. 8. See also: *Daily Mirror*, 7 July 1904, p. 3.
16. *Penny Illustrated Paper*, 16 July 1904, p. 8. See also: *Lloyd's Weekly News*, 8 January 1905, p. 35; *Morning Post*, 3 January 1905, p. 8; *The Times*, 1 April 1904, p. 7; Lieutenant-Colonel H. A. Iggulden, 'To Lhasa with the Tibet Expedition 1903–1904', *Royal United Service Institution*, 49, 1905, January–June, p. 674; Major W. J. Ottley *With Mounted Infantry In Tibet* (London, 1906), p. 62; Francis Younghusband *India and Tibet*, (London, 1910), p. 189.
17. *Daily News*, 24 April 1903, p. 7; *Lloyd's Weekly News*, 26 April 1903, p. 12. See also *Daily Mail*, 14 December 1899, p. 5; 31 October 1911, p. 5; *Daily Mirror*, 3 January 1905, p. 11; *News of the World*, 5 November 1911, p. 6; *Punch*, 7 September 1904, p. 172.
18. *Daily Mail*, 12 December 1899, p. 5.
19. *Daily Mirror*, 31 August 1904, p. 3.

20.   See for example *Daily Mail*, 10 February 1902, p. 4.

21.   *Daily Mail*, 31 October 1905, p. 5; *Daily News*, 31 October 1911, p. 1; *News of the World*, 5 May 1911, p. 6. See also: W. K. McClure, *Italy in North Africa: An Account of the Tripoli Enterprise* (London, 1913), p. 205.

22.   Lord Brooke, *An Eye-Witness in Manchuria* (London, 1905), p. 106; *The Times*, quoted in R. M. Connaughton, *The War of the Rising Sun and the Tumbling Bear: A Military History of the Russo-Japanese War 1904–05* (London, 1988), p. 75. For a similar image of the Turks melting away 'like snow before the Summer sun', see *Lloyd's Weekly News*, 10 November 1912, p. 8.

23.   *Daily Mail*, 26 February 1900, p. 5. For a full account of the whole attack, see Thomas Pakenham, *The Boer War* (London, 1982), pp. 337–8.

24.   *Daily News*, 10 March 1905, p. 7. See also *Lloyd's Weekly News*, 25 December 1904, p. 6; *News of the World*, 11 September 1904, p. 1; *Daily News*, 3 September 1904, p. 7; *Daily Mirror*, 5 May 1904, p. 2.

25.   *News of the World*, 3 May 1903, p. 7; *Daily News*, 30 April 1903, p. 7; 12 January 1904, p. 9. An interesting variation of this image is to be found in Chevalier Tullio Irace's *With The Italians In Tripoli: The Authentic History of the Turco-Italian War* (London, 1912), dedication and p. 15, where the book was dedicated to 'the Italian martyrs who fell', while the Arabs were seen as the 'fallen barbarians'.

26.   *Daily Mail*, 26 February 1900, p. 5; 25 August 1900, p. 4; 2 November 1912, p. 5; *Morning Post*, 10 March 1905, p. 7; Francis McCullagh, *Italy's War for a Desert* (London, 1912), p. 127.

27.   *Morning Post*, 27 October 1904, p. 4; Percival Landon, *Lhasa* (London, 1905), p. 150; Edmund Candler, *The Unveiling of Lhasa* (London, 1905), p. 220; Bennett Burleigh, *Empire of the East* (London, 1905), pp. 242, 321; McClure, *Italy in North Africa*, p. 205.

28.   *Daily Mail*, 2 November 1912, p. 5; *Lloyd's Weekly News*, 10 November 1912, pp. 8 and 9; *News of the World*, 3 May 1903, p. 7; 11 December 1904, p. 9; Candler, *The Unveiling of Lhasa*, p. 227. For images of casualties as 'shot down', see *Daily Mail*, 13 February 1902, p. 5; *Daily News*, 15 December 1899, p. 6; 29 January 1900, p. 5; *Manchester Guardian*, 5 April 1904, p. 4; *The Times*, 29 June 1904, p. 3; Peter Fleming, *Bayonets to Lhasa: The First Full Account of the British Invasion of Tibet in 1904* (London, 1961), p. 151.

29.   Daniel Pick, *War Machine: The Rationalisation of Slaughter in the Modern Age* (New Haven, 1993), p. 11.

30.   Ibid., pp. 178, 180, 185.

31.   In addition, battles were depicted as resembling a 'shambles', an archaic term but one which neatly combined the impression of devastation and disorder on the battlefield with the image of a meat market or slaughter-house. See: *Daily Mail*, 20 November 1912, p. 7; *News of the World*, 3 May 1904, p. 6; David H. James, *The Seige of Port Arthur: Records of An Eye-Witness* (London, 1905), p. 200.

32.   *The Times*, 31 October 1911, p. 8; *News of the World*, 5 November 1911, p. 6.

33.   *Daily Mail*, 19 February 1902, p. 5.

34.   *Clarion*, 8 April 1904, p. 4; *Daily Express*, 4 April 1904, p. 1; *Glasgow Herald*, 7 July 1904, p. 6. See also Candler, *The Unveiling of Lhasa*, pp. 146, 272; Iggulden, 'To Lhasa With the Tibet Expedition', p. 668.

35. *Daily Mail*, 5 May 1904, p. 5; 6 September 1904, p. 5; *Daily Mirror*, 3 September 1904, p. 3; 30 August 1904, p. 7; *Lloyd's Weekly News*, 25 December 1904, p. 6; *News of the World*, 11 September 1904, pp. 1, 8, 9; 11 December 1904, p. 9; *The Times*, 1 September 1904, p. 3; 5 September 1904, p. 7; 7 January 1905, p. 12. See also James, *The Siege of Port Arthur*, pp. 49, 98.

36. Wheeler, *Death and the Future Life*, p. 25.

37. *Morning Post*, 28 October 1904, p. 3. See also 2 November 1904, p. 5; *Illustrated London News*, 25 February 1905, p. 257.

38. Bennett Burleigh, *Empire of the East: Or Japan and Russia at War 1904–5* (London, 1905), p. 309. See also p. 302; Brooke, *An Eye-Witness in Manchuria*, p. 145; David H. James, *The Siege of Port Arthur*, p. 187; Frederick Arthur McKenzie, *From Tiflis to Tokyo: Uncensored Letters from the War* (London, 1905), pp. 150, 246, 259.

39. *Daily Mail*, 30 October 1912, p. 7. See also *Daily News*, 25 October 1912, p. 1; *Illustrated London News*, 22 October 1904, pp. 586–7; *Lloyd's Weekly News*, 8 May 1905, p. 12; 8 January 1905, p. 12; *Manchester Guardian*, 5 April 1904, p. 4; *News of the World*, 29 October 1911, p. 8; *The Times*, 31 December 1904, p. 7.

40. *Daily News*, 29 January 1900, p. 5; *Lloyd's Weekly News*, 8 May 1904, p. 6.

41. A similar image was one where groups and individuals were depicted as being 'cut up', 'cut to pieces', or 'cut down'.

42. Roger T. Stearn, 'War Images and Image Makers in the Victorian Era: Aspects of the British Visual and Written Portrayal of War and Defence *c.*1866–1906', unpublished PhD thesis, University of London, 1987, p. 162.

43. See, for example, *Glasgow Herald*, 2 April 1904, p. 5; *Illustrated Mail*, 16 July 1904, p. 162.

44. *Daily News*, 3 November 1911, p. 1.

45. *News of the World*, 11 September 1904, pp. 8,9.

46. David H. James, *The Siege of Port Arthur*, p. 90. See also: Ashmead-Bartlett, *Port Arthur*, p. 104; McKenzie, *From Tiflis to Tokyo*, p. 154; G. F. Abbott, *The Holy War in Tripoli* (London, 1913), p. vii; A. G. Hales, *My Life of Adventure* (London, 1918), p. 215.

47. Lieutenant-General Sir Ian Hamilton, *A Staff Officer's Scrapbook During the Russo-Japanese War* (London, 1905), vol. II, pp. 308–9.

48. *Daily Mail*, 2 June 1904, p. 4; 4 January 1905, p. 5; 15 December 1899, p. 5.

49. *How to Read War News*, (London, 1900), pp. 78–9.

50. *Daily Mail*, 18 December 1899, p. 4. See also *Daily News*, 26 January 1900, p. 7.

51. George Lynch, *Impressions of a War Correspondent* (London, 1903), pp. 1–2, 11.

52. *Daily Mail*, 2 November 1912, p. 5. See also: *Daily Express*, 2 September 1904, p. 7; *Daily Mirror*, 1 September 1904, p. 3.

53. *Daily Mail*, 2 November 1912, p. 5; Ashmead-Bartlett, *Port Arthur*, p. 75.

54. *The Times*, 27 April 1903, pp. 5, 9. See also 5 May 1904, p. 5; 30 August 1904, p. 3; *Daily Mail*, 27 April 1903, p. 5; 2 December 1904, p. 5; *Daily Mirror*, 2 April 1904, p. 2; 5 May 1904, p. 2; *Daily News*, 27 April 1903, p. 7; 30 April 1904, p. 7; 2 December 1904, p. 7; *Illustrated London News*, 7 April 1904, p. 693; 30 November 1912, pp. 802–3; *Lloyd's Weekly News*, 3 May 1903, p. 5; 3 April 1904, p. 5; 8 May 1904, p. 6; 4 December 1904, p. 6; 27 October 1912, p. 1; *News of the World*, 3 May 1903, p. 7; Ashmead-Bartlett, *Port Arthur*, p. 221; David H. James, *The Siege of Port Arthur*, pp. 195, 200; H. C. Seppings-Wright, *Two Years under the Crescent* (London, 1913), p. 235; McCullagh, *Italy's War for a Desert*, p. 127.

55. *Illustrated London News*, 2 May 1903, pp. 656–7; *Daily Express*, 8 July 1904, p. 1.
56. *Daily Mirror*, 4 January 1905, p. 11.
57. Ibid., 3 January 1905, p. 5.
58. *Daily News*, 9 May 1904, p. 7; *The Times*, 5 September 1904, p. 3.
59. *Daily Express*, 30 August 1905, p. 4; *Daily Mail*, 3 December 1899, p. 5. See also *Daily News*, 8 February 1904, p. 9; *News of the World*, 2 February 1902, p. 6.
60. *Lloyd's Weekly News*, 4 September 1904, p. 1; *News of the World*, 4 February 1900, p. 6.
61. *Justice*, 23 December 1899, p. 1; *Daily News*, 24 April 1903, p. 6.
62. *Daily News*, 1 September 1904, p. 7. See also: *News of the World*, 4 September 1904, p. 9.
63. *Illustrated Mail*, 9 April 1904, p. 1.
64. *Illustrated London News*, 24 February 1900, supplement IV; Leo Amery, *The Times History of the War in South Africa* (London, 1905), vol. 3, pp. 231–3.
65. *Illustrated London News*, 20 January 1900, p. 102; *Penny Illustrated Paper*, 29 October 1904, p. 281.
66. *Daily Mirror*, 11 April 1904, pp. 8,9.
67. J. W. M. Hichberger, *Images of the Army: The Military in British Art 1815–1914* (Manchester, 1988), pp. 112–13.
68. Jennifer Leaney, 'Ashes to Ashes: Cremation and the Celebration of Death in Nineteenth Century Britain', in Ralph Houlbrooke, *Death, Ritual and Bereavement* (London, 1989), p. 131.
69. *Illustrated London News*, 30 May 1903, p. 829.
70. Ibid., 23 December 1899, pp. 910–11.
71. Hichberger, *Images of the Army*, pp. 90–1.
72. *Illustrated London News*, 6 January 1900, pp. 18–19.
73. Ibid., 16 November 1912, p. 724.
74. Ibid., 2 November 1912, pp. 640–1.
75. *Black and White*, 27 August 1904, pp. 292–3.
76. *Illustrated London News*, 26 November 1904, p. 781.
77. *Illustrated London News*, 11 November 1911, pp. 770–1. For an example from the Russo-Japanese War, see 25 February 1905, p. 257.
78. *News of the World*, 8 May 1904, p. 1; *Punch* 1 March 1905, p. 147. See also: *Punch*, 17 August 1904, p. 111, where the Dalai Lama and the British forces were depicted as a llama in native dress and a lion in an officer's uniform.
79. Marshall McLuhan, *Understanding Media* (London, 1987), pp. 22–3.
80. *News of the World*, 28 January 1900, p. 11; *Illustrated London News*, 17 February 1912, p. 268.
81. Hichberger, *Images of the Army*, p. 113.
82. *Penny Illustrated Paper*, 16 July 1904, p. 41; *Illustrated London News*, 2 April 1904, supplement I.
83. *Daily Mirror*, 4 May 1904, p. 1; *Penny Illustrated Paper*, 24 September 1904, p. 193. For a British example from the Boer War, see *Illustrated London News*, 13 January 1900, p. 37.
84. *Illustrated London News*, 25 November 1899, supplement VI; 13 January 1900, p. 37; 10 March 1900, supplement VIII; 25 February 1905, p. 257.
85. See, for example *Daily Mirror*, 11 April 1904, pp. 8, 9; 12 April 1904, pp. 1, 9; *Illustrated Mail*, 2 July 1904, p. 11.

86. *Illustrated London News*, 24 February 1900, p. 275. For an example of an Oxo advertisement, 'The Healer', see 19 March 1904, p. 437. See also *Daily Mail*, 3 January 1900, p. 8.
87. *Illustrated London News*, 7 May 1904, pp. 678–9; *Penny Illustrated Paper*, 14 May 1904, pp. 1, 312–13; *Illustrated London News*, 10 September 1904, supplement I.
88. Cannadine, 'War and Death', pp. 195–6.
89. Michael C. Kearl, *Endings: A Sociology of Death and Dying* (New York, 1989), p. 348.
90. Paul Fussell, *The Great War And Modern Memory* (Oxford, 1977), pp. 177–8.
91. Allyson Booth, 'Figuring the Absent Corpse: Strategies of Representation in World War 1', *Mosaic*, 26, Winter 1993, pp. 69–72.
92. Sigmund Freud, 'Thoughts for the Times on War and Death' (1915), in John Rickman, ed., *Civilisation, War and Death: Selections from Three Works by Sigmund Freud* (London, 1939), p. 15.

Chapter 7   Conclusion 'The Blessings of War'

1. *Mother Jones*, May/June 1991, p. 6. See also p. 8.

Bibliography

Primary sources

Newspapers
Black and White
Black and White Budget
Bon Accord
Bristol Evening News
Clarion
Comic Cuts
Daily Express
Daily Graphic
Daily Mail
Daily Mirror
Daily News
Daily Telegraph
Funny Cuts
Glasgow Herald
The Globe
Illustrated London News
Illustrated Mail
Justice
Lancaster Guardian
Lloyd's Weekly News
Manchester Guardian
Morning Post
News of the World
Northern Echo
Penny Illustrated Paper
Picture Politics
Porcupine
Punch
Reynolds's Newspaper
Scotsman
The Star
The Times

Directories
The Newspaper Press Directory and Printers' Guide
Sell's Directory of the World's Press

Official documents and manuscripts
India Office Library:

Younghusband Papers (MSS/EUR/F197)
National Army Museum:
Tibet Military Operations (1706–1907)
Public Record Office:
Royal Commission on the Press, 1949 and 1964 (HO 251 and 252)
Directorate of Military Operations and Intelligence (WO 106)
South African War Papers (WO 108)
Reuters Archives:
Account Books

Books

Abbott, G. F., *The Holy War in Tripoli* (London, 1912)
Alderson, E. A. H., *Lessons from 100 Notes Made in Peace and War* (Aldershot, 1908)
Amery, Leo, *The Times History of the War in South Africa*, 7 vols (London, 1900–9)
Angell, Norman, *The Great Illusion* (London, 1910)
Ashmead-Bartlett, Ellis, *Port Arthur: The Siege and Capitulation* (London, 1906)
Baden-Powell, Lieutenant-Colonel R. S. S., *Aids to Scouting for N.-C.O.s and Men* (London, 1899)
Baden-Powell, Lieutenant-General Sir Robert, *Indian Memories: Recollections of Soldiering, Sport Etc.* (London, 1915)
Baldwin, Herbert, *A War Photographer in Thrace* (London, 1913)
Baring, Maurice, *With the Russians in Manchuria* (London, 1905)
Battersby, H. F. Prevost, *Richard Corfield of Somaliland* (London, 1914)
[Brander, H. R.], *32nd Sikh Pioneers: Regimental History*, 2 vols (Calcutta, 1905–6)
Brooke, Lord Greville L., *An Eye-Witness in Manchuria* (London, 1905)
Brooke, Rupert, *The Collected Poems of Rupert Brooke* (London, 1918)
Bullard, F. Lauriston, *Famous War Correspondents* (Boston, Mass., 1914)
Burleigh, Bennett, *Empire of the East or Japan and Russia at War 1904–5* (London, 1905)
Callwell, Colonel C. E., *Small Wars: Their Principles and Practice* 3rd edn (London, 1906)
Candler, Edmund, *The Unveiling of Lhasa* (London, 1905)
Committee of Imperial Defence Historical Section *Official History, Naval and Military, of the Russo-Japanese War*, 3 vols (London, 1910, 1912, 1920)
Cowen, T., *The Russo-Japanese War* (London, 1904)
Curzon, George N., *Russia in Central Asia in 1889 and the Anglo-Russian Question* (London, 1889)
Dyson, Will, *Cartoons* (London, 1913)
——, *Will Dyson's War Cartoons* (London, 1916)
Forbes, Nevill, *The Balkans* (Oxford, 1915)
Fraser, David, *A Modern Campaign: Or War and Wireless Telegraphy in the Far East* (London, 1905)
——, *Persia and Turkey in Revolt* (Edinburgh, 1910)
Furniss, Harry, *The Confessional of a Caricaturist* (London, 1901)
Gibbs, Philip and Bernard Grant, *Adventures of War with Cross and Crescent* (London, 1912)
Gould, Sir Francis Carruthers, *Political Caricatures* (London, 1903)
Great Britain, *Further Papers Relating to Tibet* (London, 1904)

——, *Further Papers Relating to Tibet No. 2* (London, 1905)

——, *Papers Relating to Tibet* (London, 1904)

——, *Return of the Military Operations Undertaken by the Government of India on the North-West Frontier, the North-East Frontier and Beyond India, in the Period 1899–1908 inclusive* (London, 1908)

Gugliemo, Ferrero, *Militarism* (London, 1902)

Hales, A. G., *My Life of Adventures* (London, 1918)

Hamilton, Angus, *Somaliland* (London, 1911)

Hamilton, Lieutenant-General Sir Ian, *A Staff Officer's Scrapbook during the Russo-Japanese War* (London, 1905)

——, 'National Life and National Training', in *Political Tracts 1867–1913* (London, 1918)

Haselden, W. K., *Daily Mirror Reflections* (London, 1908)

How to Read War News A Vade-Mecum of Notes and Hints to Readers of Despatches and Intelligence from the Seat of War with a Coloured War Map and A Glossary of Military Technical Terms, Local, African and Dutch Phrases, etc. (London, 1900)

Irace, Chevalier Tullio, *With the Italians in Tripoli: the Authentic History of the Turco-Italian War* (London, 1912)

Jackson, Mason, *The Pictorial Press: Its Origin and Progress* (London, 1885)

James, David H., *The Siege of Port Arthur: Records of an Eye-Witness* (London, 1905)

James, Colonel Lionel, *With the Conquered Turk* (London, 1913)

Jennings, James Willes, *With the Abyssinians in Somaliland* (London, 1905)

Kidd, Benjamin, *Social Evolution* (London, 1894)

Landon, Perceval, *Lhasa: An Account of the Country and People of Central Tibet and of the Progress of the Mission sent there by the English Government 1903–4* (London, 1905)

Le Bon, Gustave, *The Crowd: A Study of the Popular Mind* (London, 1896)

'Linesman', *Words by an Eye-Witness: The Struggle in Natal* (Edinburgh, 1903)

Lynch, George, *Impressions of a War Correspondent* (London, 1903)

McClure, William Kidstone, *Italy in North Africa: An Account of the Tripoli Enterprise* (London, 1913)

McCullagh, Francis, *Italy's War for a Desert: Being Some Experiences of a War Correspondent with the Italians in Tripoli* (London, 1912)

McKenzie, Frederick Arthur, *From Tokyo to Tiflis: Uncensored Letters from the War* (London, 1905)

McNeil, Captain Malcolm, *In Pursuit of the 'Mad' Mullah: Service and Sport in the Somali Protectorate* (London, 1902)

Maude, Colonel F. N., *War and the World's Life* (London, 1907)

Maxwell, William, *From the Yalu to Port Arthur* (London, 1906)

May, Phil, *The Phil May Folio of Caricature Drawings and Sketches* (London, 1904)

Miller, Margaret and Helen Miller, eds, *A Captain of the Gordons: Service Experience* (London, 1914)

[Mills, Elliott], *The Decline and Fall of the British Empire* (Oxford, n.d.)

Murray, H. J. R., *A History of Chess* (Oxford, 1913)

Newbolt, Henry, *The Book of the Happy Warrior* (London, 1917)

Ostler, Alan, *The Arabs in Tripoli* (London, 1912)

Ottley, W. J., *With Mounted Infantry in Tibet* (London, 1906)

Prior, Melton, *Campaigns of a War Correspondent* (London, 1912)

Ramaciotti, Lieutenant-Colonel G., *Tripoli: A Narrative of the Principal Engagements of the Italian-Turkish War, 23 October 1911–15 June 1912* (London, 1912)

[Repington, Charles à Court], *The War in the Far East 1904–5* (London, 1905)

Richmond-Smith, W., *The Siege and Fall of Port Arthur* (London, 1905)

Sakurai, Lieutenant T., *Human Bullets* (London, 1907)

Seeley, J. R., *The Expansion of England* (London, 1909 ed.) (1883)

Seppings-Wright, H. C., *Two Years Under the Crescent* (London, 1913)

Sinclair, Alexander, *Fifty Years of Newspaper Life 1845–1895* (Glasgow, 1895)

Stark, Malcolm, *The Pulse of the World: Fleet Street Memories* (London, 1915)

Story, Douglas, *The Campaign with Kuropatkin* (London, 1904)

Waddell, L. A., *Lhasa and Its Mysteries, with a Record of the Expedition of 1903–4)* (London, 1905)

Wallace, Edgar, *Unofficial Dispatches* (London, 1901)

War Office, The Militant Forces of British Colonies and Protectorates (London, 1902 and 1905)

——, *Military Notes on the Dutch Republics of South Africa* (York, revised June 1899)

——, *Military Report on Somaliland* (London, 1907)

——, *Official History of the Operations in Somaliland, 1901–5* (London, 1907)

——, *Regulations for Intelligence Duties in the Field* (London, 1904)

——, *Somaliland Despatches etc. Regarding Military Operations from 18 January 1902 to 31 May 1904*, (London, 1904)

——, *War Game on a Map* (London, 1897)

Wells, H. G., *Little Wars: A Game for Boys* (London, 1913)

White, Arnold, *Efficiency and Empire* (London, 1901)

Wolseley, Field-Marshal Viscount, *The Story of a Soldier's Life*, 2 vols (London, 1903)

Wyatt, H. F., *God's Test By War* (London, 1912)

Younghusband, F. E., *India and Tibet; A History of the Relations which have Subsisted between the Two Countries from the Time of Warren Hastings to 1910; With a Particular Account of the Mission to Lhasa of 1904* (London, 1910), pp. 24–5

Articles

Aldridge, A. R., 'With the Tibet Force', *Journal of the Royal Army Medical Corps*, 3, 1905, pp. 272–3; 4, 1905, pp. 235–40

Bennett, E. N., 'Press Censors and War Correspondents: Some Experiences in Turkey', *Nineteenth Century and After*, 73, 1913, pp. 28–40

Cunliffe Owen, Major F., 'The Somaliland Operations June 1903, to May 1904', *Journal of the Royal United Service Institution*, 49, 1905, pp. 169–82

Dillon, E. J., 'The Mission to Tibet', *Contemporary Review*, 85, 1904, pp. 123–6

Iggulden, H. A., 'To Lhasa with the Tibet Expedition 1903–4', *Journal of the Royal United Service Institution*, 49, 1905, pp. 659–79

Kirton, W., 'With the Japanese on the Yalu', *Journal of the Royal United Service Institution*, 49, 1905, pp. 269–86

'Kuropatkin Special Service Message: The Russo-Japanese War', *Reuters Journal*, 14 February 1904, pp. 1–4

Landon, Perceval, 'War Correspondents and the Censorship', *Nineteenth Century and After*, 52, 1902, pp. 327–37

Maxwell, William, 'Old Lamps for New: Some Reflections on Recent Changes in Journalism', *Nineteenth Century and After*, 75, 1914, pp. 1085–96

'The War Correspondent in Sunshine and Eclipse', *Nineteenth Century and After*, 73, 1913, pp. 608–23

Wylly, H. C., 'Lhasa and its Armed Rabble', *United Services Magazine*, 30, 1904–5, pp. 31–8

Secondary Sources

Books

Adams, Michael C. C., *The Great Adventure: Male Desire and the Coming of World War One* (Bloomington, 1990)

Adas, Michael, *Machines as the Measure of Men: Science, Technology and Ideologies of Western Dominance* (Ithaca, 1987)

Addy, Preman, *Tibet on the Imperial Chessboard: The Making of British Policy Towards Lhasa, 1899–1925* (Calcutta, 1984)

Albertini, Luigi, *The Origins of the War of 1914*, 3 vols (London, 1952, 1953 and 1957)

Allen, Robert, *Voice of Britain: The Inside Story of the Daily Express* (Cambridge, 1983)

Amery, Leo, *The Leo Amery Diaries: Volume 1, 1896–1929*, (London, 1980); *My Political Life: Volume 1 – England Before the Storm 1896–1914* (London, 1953)

Andrews, Sir Linton, *Lords and Labourers of the Press* (Carbondale, Ill. 1970)

Aries, Philippe, *The Hour of Our Death* (London, 1981)

Askew, W., *Europe and Italy's Acquisition of Libya* (Durham, NC, 1942)

Ayerst, David George Ogilvy, *The Guardian: Biography of a Newspaper* (London, 1971)

——, ed., *The Guardian Omnibus 1821–1971* (London, 1973)

Bailey, Peter, *Music Hall: The Business of Pleasure* (Milton Keynes, 1986)

Barker, Juliet R. V., *The Tournament in England 1100–1400* (Woodbridge, 1986)

Barnard, Sylvia M., *"To Prove I'm Not Forgot": Living and Dying in a Victorian City* (Manchester, 1990)

Barnett, Correlli, *Britain and Her Army 1509–1970* (London, 1970)

Beachey, Ray, *The Warrior Mullah: The Horn Aflame, 1892–1920* (London, 1990)

Beasley, W. G., *The Modern History of Japan* (London, 1978)

——, *The Rise of Modern Japan* (London, 1990)

Beckett, Ian F. W., *Johnny Gough V. C.* (London, 1989)

——, *Riflemen Form: A Study of the Rifle Volunteers Movement, 1859–1908* (Aldershot, 1982)

——, *The War Correspondents: The American Civil War* (Dover, NH, 1993)

Beckett, Ian F. W. and Keith Simpson, eds, *A Nation in Arms: A Social History of the British Army in the First World War* (Manchester, 1985)

Belich, James, *The New Zealand Wars and the Victorian Interpretation of Racial Conflict* (Harmondsworth, 1988)

Berrey, R. Power, *The Romance of a Great Paper* (London, 1933)

Blatchford, Robert, *My Eighty Years* (London, 1931)

Blumenfeld, Ralph David, *All in a Lifetime* (London, 1931)

——, *The Press in My Time* (London, 1953)

——, *Ralph David Blumenfeld's Diary 1887–1914* (London, 1930)

Bolt, Christine, *Victorian Attitudes to Race* (London, 1971)

Bonham-Carter, Victor, *Soldier True: The Life and Times of Field-Marshal Sir William Robertson 1860–1933* (London, 1963)

Booth, Michael R., *Theatre in the Victorian Age*, (Cambridge, 1991)
——, *Victorian Spectacular Theatre 1850–1910* (Boston, MA, 1981)
Bosworth, R. J. B., *Italy and the Approach of the First World War* (London, 1983)
——, *Italy, the Least of the Great Foreign Powers: Italian Foreign Policy Before World War I* (Cambridge, 1979)
Bourke, Joanna, *Dismembering the Male: Men's Bodies, Britain and the Great War* (Chicago, 1996)
Boyce, George, James Curran and Pauline Wingate, eds, *Newspaper History from the Seventeenth Century to the Present Day* (London, 1978)
Brake, Laurel, *Subjugated Knowledges: Journalism, Gender and Literature in the Nineteenth Century* (New York, 1994)
Brake, Laurel, Aled Jones and Lionel Madden, eds, *Investigating Victorian Journalism* (London, 1990)
Bratton, J. S., *Acts of Supremacy: The British Empire and the Stage 1790–1930* (Manchester, 1991)
Brendon, Piers, *Eminent Edwardians* (London, 1979)
Brown, Lucy, *Victorian News and Newspapers* (Oxford, 1985)
Buitenhuis, Peter, *The Great War of Words: Literature as Propaganda 1914–18 and After* (London, 1989)
Burrow, J. W., *Evolution and Society: A Study in Victorian Social Theory* (Cambridge, 1966)
Carpenter, K., *Penny Dreadfuls and Comics* (London, 1983)
Centre for the Study of Cartoons and Caricature, *Getting them In Line: An Exhibition of Caricature in Cartoons* (Canterbury, 1975)
Childs, Timothy W., *Italo-Turkish Diplomacy and the War Over Libya, 1911–1912* (Leiden, 1989)
Chirol, Sir Valentine, *Fifty Years in a Changing World* (London, 1927)
Clapson, Mark, *A Bit of a Flutter: Popular Gambling and English Society c. 1828–1961* (Manchester, 1992)
Clark, I. F., *Voices Prophesying War 1763–1984* (London, 1966)
Clausewitz, Carl von (edited and translated by Michael Howard and Peter Paret), *On War* (New Jersey, 1976)
Coglan, W. N., *The Readership of Newspapers and Periodicals in Great Britain* (London, 1936)
Collins, H. M., *From Pigeon Post to Wireless* (London, 1925)
Connaughton, R. M., *The War of the Rising Sun and the Tumbling Bear: A Military History of the Russo-Japanese War 1904–5* (London, 1988)
Cooper, Sandi E., *Patriotic Pacifism: Waging War on War in Europe 1815–1914* (New York, 1991)
Cranfield, G. A., *The Press and Society from Caxton to Northcliffe* (London, 1978)
Croce, Benedetto, *A History of Italy 1871–1915* (Oxford, 1929)
Crook, Paul, *Darwinism, War and History* (Cambridge, 1994)
Cunningham, Hugh, *The Volunteer Force: A Social and Political History 1859–1908* (London, 1975)
Curl, James Stevens, *The Victorian Celebration of Death* (Newton Abbot, 1972)
Dark, Sidney Ernest, *The Life of Sir Arthur Pearson, Bt., G.B.E* (London, 1922)
Dennis, Peter, *The Territorial Army 1906–1940* (Woodbridge, 1987)
de Saussure, F., *Course in General Linguistics* (London, 1983)

Desmond, Robert W., *Windows on the World: The Information Press in a Changing Society: 1900–1920* (Iowa City, 1980)

Dewey, Peter, *War and Progress: Britain 1914–1945* (Harlow, 1997)

Dickinson, Patric, ed., *Selected Poems of Henry Newbolt* (London, 1981)

Dilks, D., *Curzon in India* (London, 1970)

Douglas, Roy, *The World War 1939–1945: The Cartoonist's Vision* (London, 1990)

Eby, Cecil D., *Road to Armageddon: The Martial Spirit in English Popular Literature 1870–1914* (London, 1988)

Eco, Umberto, *The Role of the Reader: Exploration in the Semiotics of Texts* (London, 1981)

Edwardes, Michael, *High Noon of Empire: India under Curzon* (London, 1965)

Eksteins, Modris, *Rites of Spring: The Great War and the Birth of the Modern Age* (London, 2000)

Elbhloul, Theib Abdullah, *Italian Colonialism, the Young Turks and the Libyan Resistance* (Ann Arbor, MI, 1990)

Eldridge, C. C., *Victorian Imperialism* (London, 1978)

Ellegard, Alvar, *The Readership of the Imperial Press in Mid-Victorian Britain* (Göteborg, 1957)

Elliott, Blanche Beatrice, *A History of English Advertising* (London, 1962)

Emsley, Clive, *Crime and Society in England 1750–1900* (London, 1987)

Ensor, R. C. K., *England 1870–1914* (Oxford, 1952)

Etherington, Norman, *Theories of Imperialism* (London, 1984)

Evans, R. J. W. and Hartmut Pogge von Strandmann, *The Coming of the First World War* (Oxford, 1988)

Everdell, William F., *The First Moderns* (Chicago, 1997)

Farwell, Byron, *For Queen and Country: A Social History of the Victorian and Edwardian Army* (Harmondsworth, 1981)

——, *Queen Victoria's Little Wars* (London, 1973)

Fawdry, Kenneth and Margarite, *Pollock's History of English Dolls and Toys* (London, 1975)

Feest, Christian, *The Art of War* (London, 1980)

Fiske, John, *Introduction to Communications Studies* (London, 1990)

Fitzgibbon, Louis, *The Betrayal of the Somalis, 1866–1982* (London, 1982)

Fleming, Peter, *Bayonets to Lhasa: The First Full Account of the British Invasion of Tibet in 1904* (London, 1961)

Fletcher, Ian, ed., *Decadence and the 1890s* (London, 1979)

Foucault, Michel (translated by Alan Sheridan), *Discipline and Punish: The Birth of the Prison* (Harmondsworth, 1991)

Fowles, Jib *Advertising and Popular Culture* (London, 1996)

Freedbers, David, *Power of the Images: A Study in the History and Theory of Response* (Chicago, 1985)

Fuller, Major-General J. F. C., *The Last of the Gentlemen's Wars: A Subaltern's Journal of the War in South Africa 1899–1902* (London, 1937)

Fuller, J. G., *Troop Morale and Popular Culture in the British and Dominion Armies 1914–1918* (Oxford, 1990)

Furneaux, Rupert, *News of War: Stories and Adventures of the Great War* (London, 1964)

Fussell, Paul, *The Great War and Modern Memory* (Oxford, 1977)

Gewehr, Wesley, *The Rise of Nationalism in the Balkans 1800–1930* (Hamden, CT, 1967)

Gibbs, Philip, *Adventures in Journalism* (London, 1923)

Gilbert, Vivian, *The Romance of the Lost Crusades: With Allenby to Jerusalem* (New York, 1923)

Girouard, Mark, *The Return to Camelot: Chivalry and the English Gentleman* (New Haven, CT., 1981)

Gooch, John, *The Boer War: Direction, Experience and Image* (London, 2000)

——, *Army, State and Society in Italy 1870–1915* (Basingstoke, 1989)

——, ed., *The Prospects of War: Studies in British Defence Policy 1847–1942* (London, 1981)

Gorer, Geoffrey, *Death, Grief and Mourning in Contemporary Britain* (London, 1965)

Grainger, J. H., *Patriotisms: Britain 1900–1939* (London, 1986)

Grant, Bernard, *To the Four Corners: The Memoirs of a New Photographer* (London, 1933)

Green, Martin, *Children of the Sun: A Narrative of "Decadence" in England After 1918* (New York, 1976)

Gurevitch, Michael, Tony Bennett, James Curran, and Janet Woollacott, eds, *Culture, Society and the Media* (London, 1982)

Hale, Oron J., *The Great Illusion* (New York, 1971)

Hall, Stuart, ed., *Culture, Media and Language: Working Papers in Cultural Studies, 1972–79* (London, 1980)

Harris, Michael and Alan J. Lee, *The Press in English Society from the Seventeenth to the Nineteenth Centuries* (Rutherford, 1986)

Harrison, Stanley, *Poor Men's Guardians: A Record of the Struggles for a Democratic Newspaper Press, 1963–1973* (London, 1974)

Hart-Davis, Duff, *The House the Berrys Built: Inside the Telegraph 1928–1986* (London, 1990)

Headrick, Daniel R., *The Tools of Empire, Technology and European Imperialism in the Nineteenth Century* (Oxford, 1981)

Helmreich, E. C., *The Diplomacy of the Balkan Wars, 1912–13* (New York, 1969)

Henle, Paul, *Language, Thought and Culture* (Ann Arbor, MI, 1958)

Hess, Stephen, *The Government/Press Connection: Press Officers and their Offices* (Washington, DC, 1984)

Hichberger, J. W. M., *Images of the Army: The Military in British Art 1815–1914* (Manchester, 1988)

Higonnet, Margaret Randolph et al., eds, *Behind the Lines: Gender and the Two World Wars* (New Haven, CT, 1987)

Hiley, Michael, *Seeing through Photographs* (London, 1983)

Hinsley, Francis Harry, *British Foreign Policy under Sir Edward Grey* (Cambridge, 1977)

Hoare, Philip, *Wilde's Last Stand: Decadence, Conspiracy and the First World War* (London, 1997)

Hobsbawm, Eric and Terrance Ranger, eds, *The Invention of Tradition* (Cambridge, 1983)

Hodgson, Pat, *Early War Photographs* (Reading, 1974)

——, *The War Illustrators* (London, 1977)

Holloway, David, *Playing the Empire: The Acts of the Holloway Touring Theatre Company* (London, 1979)

Holmes, Richard, *Firing Line* (London, 1985)

Holt, Richard, *Sport and the British: A Modern History* (Oxford, 1989)

Houghton, Walter E., *The Victorian Frame of Mind 1830–1870* (New Haven, CT, 1957)

Houlbrooke, Ralph, ed., *Death, Ritual and Bereavement* (London, 1989)

Howard, Michael, *The Lessons of History* (Oxford, 1991)

—— , *Studies in War and Peace* (London, 1970)

—— , *The Theory and Practice of War* (London, 1965)

—— , *War and the Liberal Conscience* (New Brunswick, NJ, 1978)

Howard, Philip, *We Thundered Out: 200 Years of 'The Times' 1785–1985* (London, 1985)

Howarth, P., *Play Up and Play the Game: The Heroes of Popular Fiction* (London, 1973)

Hynes, Samuel, *The Edwardian Turn of Mind* (Princeton, NJ, 1968)

—— , *A War Imagined: The First World War in English Culture* (London, 1992)

Jackson, Ian, *The Provincial Press and the Community* (Manchester, 1971)

Jackson, Russell, *Victorian Theatre* (London, 1989)

James, Lawrence, *The Savage Wars: British Campaigns in Africa 1870–1920* (London, 1985)

James, Colonel Lionel, *High Pressure: Activities in the Service of The Times* (London, 1929)

—— , *Times of Stress* (London, 1929)

Jardine, Douglas J., *The Mad Mullah of Somaliland* (London, 1923)

Jelavich, Barbara, *History of the Balkans*, 2 vols (Cambridge, 1983)

—— , *The Establishment of the Balkan National States 1304–1920* (Seattle, WA, 1977)

Joll, James, *The Origins of the First World War* (London, 1984)

Jones, Leslie S. A., *Robert Blatchford and the Clarion* (London, 1986)

Joyce, Patrick, *Visions of the People: Industrial England and the Question of Class 1848–1914* (Cambridge, 1991)

Judd, Denis, *Empire: The British Imperial Experience, From 1765 to the Present* (London, 1996)

Judd, Denis, and Surridge, Keith, *The Boer War* (London, 2002)

Kaye, M. M., ed., *Rudyard Kipling: The Complete Verse* (London, 1990)

Kearle, Michael C., *Endings: A Sociology of Death and Dying* (New York, 1989)

Kent, Marian, ed., *The Great Powers and the End of the Ottoman Empire* (London, 1984)

Király, Béla K. and Dimitrise Djordsenic, *East Central European Society and the Balkan Wars* (Boulder, CO, 1987)

Klancher, Jon P., *The Making of English Reading Audiences 1790–1832* (Madison, WI, 1987)

Knightley, Philip, *The First Casualty: From the Crimea to Vietnam: The War Correspondent as Hero, Propagandist and Myth-Maker* (London, 1982)

Koch, H. W., *The Origins of the First World War* (London, 1972)

Koss, Stephen, *The Rise and Fall of the Political Press in Britain: The Nineteenth Century*, I (London, 1981)

—— , *The Rise and Fall of the Political Press in Britain: The Twentieth-Century*, II (London, 1984)

Lamb, Alistair, *British India and Tibet: 1766–1910* (London, 1986)

Lee, Alan J., *The Origins of the Popular Press in England: 1855–1914* (London, 1976)

Leed, Eric J., *No Man's Land: Combat and Identity in World War I* (Cambridge, 1979)

Lehmann, J. H., *The First Boer War* (London, 1972)

Lewinski, Jorge, *The Camera at War: A History of the War Photography from 1848 to the Present Day* (London, 1978)

Lewis, Ioan Myrddin, *A Modern History of Somalia: Nation and State in the Horn of Africa* (London, 1980)

Lloyd-Jones, W., *K. A. R. Being an Official Account of the Origin and Activities of the King's African Rifles* (London, 1926)

Loeb, Lori Anne, *Consuming Angels: Advertising and Victorian Women* (Oxford, 1994)

Lorimer, Douglas A., *Colour, Class and the Victorians: English Attitudes to the Negro in the mid-Nineteenth-Century*, (Leicester, 1978)

Lowe, Robson, *Indian Field Post Offices 1903–1904* (London, 1979)

Luvaas, Jay, *The Education of an Army: British Military Thought 1815–1940* (London, 1965)

McKenzie, Frederick Arthur, *The Mystery of the Daily Mail, 1896–1921* (London, 1921)

MacKenzie, John M., *The Empire of Nature: Hunting, Conservation and British Imperialism* (Manchester, 1988)

——, ed., *Imperialism and Popular Culture* (Manchester, 1986)

——, ed., *Popular Imperialism and the Military, 1850–1950* (Manchester, 1992)

——, *Propaganda and Empire: The Manipulation of British Public Opinion 1880–1960* (Manchester, 1984)

McLuhan, Marshall, *Understanding Media* (London, 1987)

Mangan, J. A., *Athleticism in the Victorian and Edwardian Public Schools: The Emergence and Consolidation of the Educational Ideology* (Cambridge, 1981)

——, *The Cultural Bond: Sport, Empire and Society* (London, 1993)

——, *The Games Ethic and Imperialism: Aspects of the Diffusion of an Idea* (Harmondsworth, 1986)

——, ed., *Making Imperial Mentalities: Socialization and British Imperialism* (Manchester, 1990)

——, *Pleasure, Profit and Proselytism: British Culture and Sport at Home and Abroad 1700–1914* (London, 1988)

Mansfield, Susan, *The Gestalt of War: An Inquiry into its Origins and Meanings as a Social Institution* (New York, 1982)

Marcuse, Herbert, *One Dimensional Man* (London, 1968)

Martin, Christopher, *The Russo-Japanese War* (London, 1867)

Mason, Philip, *A Matter of Honour: An Account of the Indian Army its Officers and Men* (London, 1974)

Mason, Tony, *Sport in Britain* (London, 1988)

——, *Sport in Britain: A Social History*, (Cambridge, 1989)

Mendilow, Jonathan, *The Romantic Tradition in British Political Thought* (London, 1986)

Middleton, Dorothy, *Victorian Lady Travellers* (London, 1965)

Morley, John, *Death, Heaven and the Victorians* (Pittsburgh, PA, 1971)

Morris, A. J. A., *The Scaremongers: The Advocacy of War and Rearmament 1896–1914* (London, 1984)

Morris, James, *Farewell the Trumpets* (Harmondsworth, 1980)

Moyse-Bartlett, Lieutenant-Colonel H., *The King's African Rifles* (Aldershot, 1956)

Nalbatian, Suzanne, *Seeds of Decadence in Late Nineteenth Century Novels* (London, 1988)

Nevett, Terry, *Advertising in Britain: A History* (London, 1982)

Newman, Henry, *A Roving Commission* (London, 1937)

Nish, Ian, *Britain and Japan 1600–1975* (London, 1975)

——, *Contemporary European Writing on Japan*, (Ashford, 1988)

O'Day, Alan, ed., *The Edwardian Age: Conflict and Stability 1900–1914* (London, 1979)

Opie, Robert, *The Art of the Label: Designs of the Times* (London, 1987)

——, *Rule Britannia: Trading on the British Image* (London, 1985)

Osborne, John Morton, *The Voluntary Recruitment Movement 1914–16* (New York, 1982)

Packard, Vance, *The Hidden Persuaders* (Harmondsworth, 1981)

Packenham, Thomas, *The Boer War* (London, 1982)

Parker, Peter, *The Old Lie: The Great War and the Public School Ethos* (London, 1987)

Perham, Margery, *Lugard: The Years of Adventure 1858–1898* (London, 1956)

Phillips, Alastair, *Glasgow's Herald: 1783–1983, 200 Years of a Newspaper* (Glasgow, 1982)

Phillips, Percival, *Far Vistas* (London, 1933)

Pick, Daniel, *Faces of Degeneration: A European Disorder c.1848–c.1918* (Cambridge, 1989)

——, *War Machine: The Rationalisation of Slaughter in the Modern Age* (New Haven, CT, 1993)

Pictorial Photography in Britain 1900–1920 (London, 1978)

Playne, Caroline E., *The Pre-War Mind in Britain: An Historical Review* (London, 1928)

Preston, Adrian, *In Relief of Gordon: Lord Wolseley's Campaign Journal of the Khartoum Relief Expedition, 1884–5* (London, 1967)

Price, Richard, *An Imperial War and the British Working Class: Working Class Attitudes and Relations to the Boer War, 1899–1902* (London, 1972)

Rayne, Henry, *Sun, Sand and Somalis: Leaves from the Notebook of a District Commissioner in British Somaliland* (London, 1921)

Read, Anthony and David Fischer, *Colonel Z: The Life and Times of a Master of Spies – A Military and Intelligence Career from 1900–1945)* (London, 1984)

Read, Donald, *Edwardian England 1901–15: Society and Politics* (London, 1972)

——, ed., *Edwardian England* (New Brunswick, NJ, 1982)

Reader, W. J., *At Duty's Call: A Study in Obsolete Patriotism* (Manchester, 1988)

Rich, Paul B., *Race and Empire in British Politics* (Cambridge, 1990)

Richards, Jeffrey, ed., *Imperialism and Juvenile Literature* (Manchester, 1989)

Richards, Thomas, *The Commodity Culture of Victorian England: Advertising and Spectacle 1851–1914* (Stanford, CA, 1990)

Richardson, Ruth, *Death, Dissection and the Destitute* (London, 1987)

Rickman, John, ed., *Civilization, War and Death: Selections from Three Works by Sigmund Freud* (London, 1939)

Riddell, George, *More Pages from My Diary: 1908–1914* (London, 1934)

Rodd, Sir James Rennell, *Social and Diplomatic Memories*, 3 vols (London, 1922, 1923, 1925)

Rose, Jonathan, *The Edwardian Temperament 1855–1919* (Athens, OH, 1986)

Rose, Lionel, *Drink and Drugs* (London, 1984)

Rowbotham, Judith, *Good Girls Make Good Wives: Guidance for Girls in Victorian Fiction* (Oxford, 1989)
Royle, Trevor, *War Report: The War Correspondent's View of Battle from the Crimea to the Falklands* (London, 1989)
Satow, Sir Ernest, *A Diplomat in Japan* (London, 1921)
Scottish Newspapers in the Making: The Outram Press (Glasgow, 1931)
Seaman, L. C. B., *Post-Victorian Britain, 1902–1951* (London, 1966)
Searle, G. R., *Eugenics and Politics in Britain 1900–1914* (Leyden, 1976)
——, *The Quest for National Efficiency*, (Oxford, 1971)
Semmel, Bernard, *Imperialism and Social Reform: English Social-Imperial Thought 1895–1914* (London, 1960)
Shaw, Phil, *Collecting Football Programmes* (London, 1980)
Shaw, Stanford and Ezel K. Shaw, *History of the Ottoman Empire and Modern Turkey*, 2 vols (Cambridge, 1977)
Simkins, Peter, *Kitchener's Army: The Raising of the New Armies 1914–16* (Manchester, 1988)
Simon, Brian and Ian Bradley, eds, *The Victorian Public School* (Dublin, 1975)
Sinha, Mrinalini, *Colonial Masculinity: The 'Manly Englishman' and the 'Effeminate Bengali'* (Manchester, 1995)
Sitwell, Osbert, *Great Morning: Being the Third Volume of Left Hand; Right Hand: An Autobiography* (London, 1948)
Sixsmith, Major-General, E. K. G., *British Generalship in the Twentieth-Century* (London, 1970)
Spiers, Edward M., *The Army and Society 1815–1914* (London, 1980)
——, *Haldane: An Army Reformer* (Edinburgh, 1980)
Springhall, John, *Youth, Empire and Society: British Youth Movements 1883–1940* (London, 1977)
Stavrianos, Leften Stauros, *The Balkans Since 1453* (New York, 1958)
Steed, H. Wickham, *The Making of a Newspaper* (London, 1924)
——, *The Press* (London, 1938)
——, *Through Thirty Years: 1892–1922* (London, 1924)
Steiner, Zara, *Britain and the Origins of the First World War* (London, 1977)
Stewart, Garrett, *Death Sentences: Styles of Dying in British Fiction* (Cambridge, Mass., 1984)
Tagg, John, *The Burden of Representation: Essays on Photographies and Histories* (Basingstoke, 1988)
Thompson, F. M. L., ed., *The Cambridge Social History of Britain 1750–1950* (Cambridge, 1990)
Thompson, Laurence, *Robert Blatchford: Portrait of an Englishman* (London, 1951)
Thompson, Paul, *The Edwardians: The Remaking of British Society* (London, 1992)
Travers, T. H. E., *The Killing Ground* (London, 1987)
Trewin, J. C., *The Edwardian Theatre* (Oxford, 1976)
Tucker, Frederick, *Private Tucker's Boer War Diary* (London, 1980)
Turner, E. S., *The Shocking History of Advertising!* (London, 1952)
Turner, John, *Britain and the First World War* (London, 1988)
Vagts, Alfred, *A History of Militarism: Civilian and Military* (London, 1959)
Villiers, Frederic, *Villiers: His Fine Decades of Adventure*, 2 vols (London, 1920)
Walder, David, *The Short Victorious War: The Russo-Japanese Conflict 1904–5* (London, 1973)

Walkowitz, Judith R., *City of Dreadful Delight: Narratives of Sexual Danger in Late-Victorian London* (London, 1992)

Walton, John and James Walvin, *Leisure in Britain 1780–1939* (Manchester, 1983)

Ward, Ken, *Mass Communication and the Modern World* (London, 1989)

Warner, Marina, *Monuments and Maidens: The Allegory of the Female Form* (London, 1985)

Warner, Philip, *The Best of British Pluck* (London, 1976)

——, *The Best of Chums* (London, 1978)

Warwick, Peter, ed., *The South African War 1899–1902* (Harlow, 1980)

Watson, Peter, *A Terrible Beauty: The People and Ideas that Shaped the Modern Mind* (London, 2000)

Westwood, J. N., *Russia against Japan 1904–5: A New Look at the Russo-Japanese War* (Basingstoke, 1986)

Whaley, Joachim, ed., *Mirrors of Mortality: Studies in the Social History of Death* (London, 1981)

Wheeler, Michael, *Death and the Future Life in Victorian Literature* (Cambridge, 1991)

Whittam, John, *The Politics of the Italian Army 1861–1918* (London, 1977)

Wicke, Jennifer *Advertising Fictions: Literature, Advertisements and Social Reading* (Columbia, NY, 1988)

Wiener, Joel H., ed., *Innovators and Preachers: The Role of the Editor in Victorian England* (Westport, CT, 1985)

——, *Papers for the Millions: The New Journalism in Britain 1850s to 1914* (New York, 1988)

Wilkinson-Latham, R. J., *From Our Special Correspondent: Victorian War Correspondents and their Campaigns* (London, 1979)

Williams, Francis, *Dangerous Estates: The Anatomy of Newspapers* (Cambridge, 1957)

Williams, Raymond, ed., *Contact: Human Communication* (London, 1981)

Williams, Rhodri, *Defending the Empire: The Conservative Party and British Defence* (New Haven, CT, 1991)

Wilson, Albert Edward, *Edwardian Theatre* (London, 1951)

Winter, J. M., *The Great War and the British People* (London, 1985)

Wohl, Robert, *The Generation of 1914* (London, 1979)

Wood, Stephen, *The Scottish Soldier* (Edinburgh, 1987)

Woodfield, James, *English Theatre in Transition 1889–1914* (London, 1984)

Woods, Oliver and James Bishop, *The Story of The Times* (London, 1983)

Articles and chapters

Alder, Garry, 'Big Game Hunting in Central Asia', *Journal of Imperial and Commonwealth History*, 9, 1981, pp. 318–30

Andrew, Eric, 'The Media and the Military: Australian War Correspondents and the Appointment of a Corps Commander, 1918 – A Case Study', *War and Society*, 8, 1990, pp. 83–103

Ashplant, T. G., 'Psychoanalysis in Historical Writing', *History Workshop Journal*, 26, 1988, pp. 102–19

Bailes, Howard, 'Patterns of Thought in the Late Victorian Army', *Journal of Strategic Studies*, 4, 1981, pp. 29–45

Bailey, Peter, 'Ally Sloper's Half-Holiday: Comic Art in the 1880s', *History Workshop Journal*, 16, 1983, pp. 4–31

Beardsworth, Alan, 'Analysing Press Content: Some Technical and Methodological Issues', in Harry Christian, ed., *The Sociology of Journalism and the Press* (Keele, 1980), pp. 371–95

Beckett, Ian F. W., 'H. O. Arnold-Foster and the Volunteers', in Ian F. W. Beckett and John Gooch, eds, *Politicians and Defence: Studies in the Formulation of British Defence Policy 1845–1970* (Manchester, 1981), pp. 47–68

——, 'The Nation in Arms', in Ian F. W. Beckett and Keith Simpson, eds, *A Nation in Arms: A Social History of the British Army in the First World War* (Manchester, 1985), pp. 1–35

——, 'The Territorial Force', in Ian F.W. Beckett and Keith Simpson, eds, *A Nation at Arms: A Social History of the British Army in the First World War* (Manchester, 1985), pp. 127–45

Belich, James, 'The Victorian Interpretation of Racial Conflict and the New Zealand Wars: an Approach to the Problem of One-Sided Evidence', *Journal of Imperial and Commonwealth History*, 15, January 1987, pp. 123–47

Bennett, Tony, 'Media, "Reality", and Signification', in Michael Gurewitch, Tony Bennett, James Curran, and Janet Woollacott, eds, *Culture, Society and the Media* (London, 1982), pp. 287–308

——, 'Theories of the media, Theories of Society', in Michael Gurewitch, Tony Bennett, James Curran, and Janet Woollacott, eds, *Culture, Society and the Media* (London, 1982), pp. 30–55

Best, Geoffrey, 'Militarism and the Victorian Public School', in Brian Simon and Ian Bradley, eds., *The Victorian Public School* (Dublin, 1975), pp. 129–146

[Bethell, L.A.], 'A Footnote, by Pousse Caillox', *Blackwood's Magazine*, 225, 1929, pp. 147–76

Blackbourn, David, 'Politics as Theatre: Metaphors of the Stage in German History 1848–1933', *Transactions of the Royal History Society*, 37, 1987, pp. 149–67

Bodin, L., 'The Mad Mullah of Somaliland', *Soldiers of the Queen, First and Second Expeditions*, 24, 1981, pp. 6–16; *Third and Fourth Expeditions*, 27, 1982, pp. 16–22

Booth, Allyson, 'Figuring the Absent Corpse: Strategies of Representation in World War I', *Mosaic*, 26, 1993, pp. 69–85

Bosworth, R. J. B., 'Italy and the End of the Ottoman Empire', in Marian Kent, ed., *The Great Powers and the End of the Ottoman Empire* (London, 1984), pp. 52–75

Bratton, J. S., 'Of England, Home and Duty: The Image of England in Victorian and Edwardian Juvenile Fiction', in John M. MacKenzie, ed., *Imperialism and Popular Culture*, (Manchester, 1984), pp. 73–93

Brown, David W., 'Social Darwinism, Private Schooling and Sport in Victorian and Edwardian Canada', in J. A. Mangan, ed., *Pleasure, Profit, Proselytism: British Culture and Sport at Home and Abroad 1700–1914* (London, 1988), pp. 215–30

Cannadine, David, 'War and Death, Grief and Mourning in Modern Britain', in Joachim Whaley, ed., *Mirrors of Mortality* (London, 1981), pp. 187–242

'Centenary of the *News of the World*: Sunday Newspaper with the Largest Circulation in the World', *World's Press News*, 30, 1943, pp. 12, 18

Christian, Harry, 'Journalists' Occupational Ideologies and Press Commercialisation', in Harry Christian, ed., *The Sociology of Journalism and the Press* (Keele, 1980), pp. 259–306

Crampton, R. J., 'The Balkans 1909–14', in F. H. Hinsley, *British Foreign Policy Under Sir Edward Grey* (Cambridge, 1977), pp. 256–70

Crook, Paul, 'War as Genetic Disaster? The First World War Debate over the Eugenics of Warfare', *War and Society*, 8, 1990, pp. 47–70

Cunningham, Hugh, 'Language of Patriotism 1750–1914', *History Workshop*, 12, 1981, pp. 8–33

Cunningham, John, 'National Daily Newspapers and their Circulation in the United Kingdom', *Journal of Advertising History*, 4 February 1981

Davis, Tracy C., 'Indecency and Vigilance in the Music Hall', in Richard Foulkes, ed., *British Theatre in the 1890s: Essays on Drama and the Stage* (Cambridge, 1992), pp. 113–31

Dresser, Madge, 'Britannia', in Raphael Samuel, ed., *Patriotism: The Making and Unmaking of British National Identity: Volume III, National Fictions* (London, 1989), pp. 26–49

Edwards, David B., 'Mad Mullahs and Englishmen: Discourse in the Colonial Encounter', *Comparative Study of Society and History*, 31, 1989, pp. 649–70

Ferguson, Marjorie, 'The Woman's Magazine Cover Photograph', in Harry Christian, ed., *The Sociology of Journalism and the Press* (Keele, 1980), pp. 219–38

Fest, Wilfred, 'Jingoism and Xenophobia in Electioneering Strategies of Ruling Elites before 1914', in Paul Kennedy and Anthony Nicholls, eds, *Nationalist and Racialist Movements in Britain and Germany before 1914* (London, 1981), pp. 171–89

Fraser, Derek, 'The Edwardian City', in Donald Read, ed., *Edwardian England* (London, 1972), pp. 56–74

Freiburgh, Aaron L., 'Britain Faces the Burdens of Empire: The Financial Crisis of 1901–05', *War and Society*, 5, 1987, pp. 15–37

French, David, 'Spy Fever in Britain 1900–1915', *The Historical Journal*, 21, 1978, pp. 355–70

Gat, Azar, 'Ardant du Picq's Scientism, Teaching and Influence', *War and Society*, 8, 1990, pp. 1–16

Gooch, John, 'Attitudes to War in Late Victorian and Edwardian England', in John Gooch, ed., *The Prospect of War: Studies in British Defence Policy 1847–1942* (London, 1981), pp. 35–51

Greenwall, Ryno, 'Some Contemporary Illustrated and Satirical Periodicals Which Portray the Anglo-Boer War', *Quarterly Bulletin of the South African Library*, 1983, pp. 101–9

Grenville, J. A. S., 'Foreign Policy and the Coming of War', in Donald Read, ed., *Edwardian England* (New Brunswick, NJ, 1982), pp. 162–81

Hall, Stuart, 'Encoding/Decoding', in Stuart Hall, ed., *Culture, Media and Language: Working Papers in Cultural Studies 1972–79* (Keele, 1980), pp. 128–32

——, 'Recent Developments in Theories of Language and Ideology: A Critical Note', in Stuart Hall,ed., *Culture, Media and Language: Working Papers in Cultural Studies 1972–79* (Keele, 1980), pp. 157–62

Herrman, David G., 'The Paralysis of Italian Strategy in the Italian-Turkish War, 1911–12', *English Historical Review*, 104, 1989, pp. 332–56

Hiley, Nicholas, ' "The British Army Film", "You!" and "For the Empire": Reconstructed Propaganda Films, 1914–1916', *Historical Journal of Film, Radio and Television*, 5, 1985, pp. 165–82

——, 'The Failure of British Counter-Espionage Against Germany 1907–14', *The Historical Journal*, 28, 1985, pp. 835–62

——, 'The Failure of British Espionage Against Germany 1907–1914', *The Historical Journal*, 26, 1983, pp. 867–89

——, 'The New Media and British Propaganda 1914–18', in J.-J. Becker and S. Audoin-Rouzeau, eds, *Les Sociétés Européenes et la Guerre de 1914–18* (Paris 1990), pp. 175–81

Hirschfield, Claire, 'The Legacy of Dissent: Boer War Opposition and the Shaping of British South African Policy 1899–1909', *War and Society*, 6, May 1988, pp. 11–39

Holt, R. J., 'Football and the Urban Way of Life in Nineteenth-Century Britain', in J. A. Mangan, ed., *Pleasure, Profit, Proselytism: British Culture and Sport at Home and Abroad 1700–1914* (London, 1988), pp. 67–85

Howard, Michael, 'The Edwardian Arms Race', in Donald Read, ed., *Edwardian England* (New Brunswick, NJ, 1982), pp. 145–61

——, 'Empire, Race and War in pre-Nineteenth Century Britain', in Michael Howard, ed., *The Lessons of History* (Oxford, 1991), pp. 63–80

——, 'Men Against Fire: Expectations of War in 1914', in Stephen Miller, ed., *Military Strategy and the Origins of the First World War'* (Princeton, NJ, 1985), pp. 41–57

——, 'Reflections of the First World War', in Michael Howard, ed., *Studies in War and Peace* (London, 1970), pp. 99–109

Hughes, Clive, 'The New Armies', in Ian F. W. Beckett and Keith Simpson, eds, *A Nation in Arms: A Social History of the British Army in the First World War* (Manchester, 1985), pp. 98–125

Käppeli, Anne-Marie, 'Feminist Scenes', in Geneviève Fraisse and Michelle Perrot, eds, *A History of Women in the West: Emerging Feminism from Revolution to World War* vol 4 (Cambridge, MA, 1993)

Kennedy, Paul, 'The Pre-War Right in Britain and Germany', in Paul Kennedy and Anthony Nichols, eds, *Nationalist and Racialist Movements in Britain and Germany Before 1914* (London, 1981), pp. 1–20

Leaney, Jennifer, 'Ashes to Ashes: Cremation and the Celebration of Death in Nineteenth Century Britain', in Ralph Houlbrooke, *Death, Ritual and Bereavement* (London, 1989), pp. 118–35

Lee, Alan. J., 'The Radical Press', in A. J. A. Morris, ed., *Edwardian Radicalism: Some Aspects of British Radicalism* (London, 1974), pp. 47–61

Lovelace, Colin, 'British Press Censorship During the First World War', in George Boyce, James Curran and Pauline Wingate, eds, *Newspaper History From the Seventeenth Century to the Present* (London 1978), pp. 307–19

Lowe, C. J., 'Grey and the Tripoli War 1911–12', in F. H. Hinsley, ed., *British Foreign Policy under Sir Edward Grey* (Cambridge, 1977), pp. 315–23

Lowerson, John, 'Brothers of the Angle: Coarse Fishing and English Working-Class Culture 1850–1914', in J. A. Mangan, ed., *Pleasure, Profit, Proselytism: British Culture and Sport at Home and Abroad 1700–1914* (London, 1988), pp. 105–27

McDermott, J, 'The Revolution in British Military Thinking from the Boer War to the Moroccan Crisis', in Paul M. Kennedy, ed., *The War Plans of the Great Powers 1880–1914* (London, 1978), pp. 99–117

McKercher, B. J. C., 'Diplomatic Equipoise: The Lansdowne Foreign Office, the Russo-Japanese War (1904–1905) and the Global Balance of Power', *Canadian Journal of History*, 24, 1989, pp. 299–339

Mack, Wolfgang, 'The Function of "Race" in Imperial Ideologies: The Example of Joseph Chamberlain', in Paul Kennedy and Anthony Nicholls, eds, *Nationalist and Racialist Movements in Britain and Germany Before 1914* (London, 1981), pp. 190–203

Mahajan, Sneh, 'The Defence of India and the End of Isolation: A Study in the Foreign Policy of the Conservative Government 1900–1905', *Journal of Imperial and Commonwealth History*, 10, 1982, pp. 168–93

Mangan, J. A., 'The Grit of Our Forefathers: Invented Traditions, Propaganda and Imperialism', in John M. MacKenzie, ed., *Imperialism and Popular Culture* (Manchester, 1986), pp. 113–39

Marshall, Peter J., ' "Cornwallis Triumphant": War in India and the British Public in the Late Eighteenth Century', in Laurence Freedman, Paul Hayes and Robert O'Neill, eds, *War, Strategy and International Relations: Essays in Honour of Michael Howard* (Oxford, 1992), pp. 57–74

Mathews, Joseph J., 'The Genesis of Newspaper War Correspondence', *Journalism Quarterly*, 29, 1953, pp. 3–17

Mayer, David, 'The World on Fire ... Pyrodramas at Belle Vue Gardens, Manchester, *c*.1850–1950', in John M. MacKenzie, ed., *Popular Imperialism and the Military* (Manchester, 1992), pp. 179–97

Morgan, Kenneth, 'Edwardian Socialism', in Donald Read, ed., *Edwardian England* (New Brunswick, NJ, 1982), pp. 93–111

Morten, Patricia, 'A Military Irony: The Victorian Volunteer Movement', *Journal of the Royal United Service Institute*, 131, 1986, pp. 63–70

Myerley, Scott Hughes, 'The Eye Must Entrap the Mind: Army Spectacle and Paradigm in Nineteenth-Century Britain', *Journal of Social History*, 26, 1992, pp. 105–31

Nevett, Terence 'Advertising', in J. Don Vann and Rosemary T. Van Arsdel, eds, *Victorian Periodicals and Victorian Culture* (Toronto, 1995)

Nicolson, Colin, 'Edwardian England and the Coming of the First World War', in Alan O'Day, ed., *The Edwardian Age: Conflict and Stability 1900–1914* (London 1979), pp. 144–68

Palmer, Michael, 'The British Press and International News, 1851–99: Of Agencies and Newspapers', in George Boyce, James Curran, Pauline Wingate, eds, *Newspaper History From the Seventeenth Century to the Present* (London, 1978), pp. 205–977

Paret, Peter, 'Clausewitz and the Nineteenth Century', in Michael Howard, ed., *The Theory and Practice of War* (London, 1965), pp. 21–41

Paris, Michael, 'The First Air Wars: North Africa and the Balkans 1911–13', *Journal of Contemporary History*, 26, 1991, pp. 97–109

Parmentier, Guillaume, 'The British Press in the Suez Crisis', *The Historical Journal*, 23, 1980, pp. 435–48

Perkin, H. J., 'The Origins of the Popular Press', *History Today*, 7, 1957, pp. 425–35

Porter, Andrew, 'The South African War (1899–1902): Context and Motive Reconsidered', *Journal of African History*, 31, 1990, pp. 43–7

Porter, Bernard, 'Edwardians and their Empire', *Edwardian England*, in Donald Read, ed. (New Brunswick, NJ, 1982), pp. 128–44

Porter, Dilwyn, 'Pearson, Sir (Cyril) Arthur', in D. J. Jeremy, ed., *Dictionary of Business Biography* (London, 1985), vol. 4, pp. 575–8

178   *Bibliography*

Richards, Jeffrey, 'Boys' Own Empire: Feature Films and Imperialism in the 1930s', in John M. McKenzie, ed., *Imperialism and Popular Culture* (Manchester, 1986), pp. 140–64

———, 'The Cinema and Cinema-Going in Birmingham in the 1930s', in John Walton and James Walvin, eds, *Leisure in Britain 1780–1939* (Manchester, 1983), pp. 31–52

Riddell, George, 'The Relations of the Press with the Army in the Field', *Journal of the Royal United Service Institution*, 66, 1921, pp. 385–400

Robbins, K. G., 'Public Opinion, the Press and Pressure Groups', in F. H. Hinsley, ed., *British Foreign Policy under Sir Edward Grey* (Cambridge, 1977), pp. 70–88

Russell, Dave, 'Popular Musical Culture and Popular Politics in the Yorkshire Textile Districts 1880–1914', in John K. Walton and James Walvin, eds, *Leisure in Britain 1780–1939* (Manchester, 1983), pp. 99–116

———, 'We Carved our War to Glory: The British Soldier in Music Hall Song and Sketch, *c.*1880–1914', in John M. MacKenzie, *Popular Imperialism and the Military 1850–1950* (Manchester, 1992), pp. 50–79

Samuel, Raphael, 'Introduction: The Figures of National Myth', in Raphael Samuel, ed., *Patriotism: The Making and Unmaking of British National Identity: Volume III National Fictions* (London, 1989), pp. xi–xxxvi

Schreuder, D. M., 'The Cultural Factor in Victorian Imperialism: A Case-Study of the British "Civilising Mission"', *Journal of Imperial Commonwealth History*, 4, 1976, pp. 283–317

Searle, G. R., 'Critics of Edwardian Society: The Case of the Radical Right', in Alan O'Day, ed., *The Edwardian Age: Conflict and Stability 1900–1914* (London, 1979), pp. 79–96

———, 'The Revolt from the Right in Edwardian Britain', in Paul Kennedy and Anthony Nicholls, eds, *Nationalist and Racialist Movements in Britain and Germany Before 1914* (London, 1981), pp. 21–39

Seaton, A. V., 'Cope's and the Promotion of Tobacco in Victorian Britain', *Journal of Advertising History*, 9, 1986, pp. 5–26

Silberman, Leo, 'The "Mad Mullah": Hero of Somali Nationalism', *History Today*, 10, 1960, pp. 523–34

Simkins, Peter, 'Kitchener and the Expansion of the Army', in Ian F. W. Beckett and John Gooch, ed., *Politicians and Defence: Studies in the Formulation of British Defence Policy 1845–1970* (Manchester, 1981), pp. 87–109

Simpson, Keith, 'An Annotated Bibliography of the British Army 1914–18', in Ian F. W. Beckett and Keith Simpson, eds, *A Nation in Arms: A Social History of the British Army in the First World War* (Manchester, 1985), pp. 238–65

———, 'The Officers', in Ian F. W. Beckett and Keith Simpson, eds, *A Nation in Arms: A Social History of the British Army in the First World War* (Manchester, 1985), pp. 62–97

'Sir Emsley Carr: Fifty Years as Editor', *World's Press News*, 1, 1941, pp. 10–11

Smith, Iain R., 'The Origins of the South African War 1899–1902 in the Context of Recent Historiography of South Africa', unpublished symposium paper, Institute of Commonwealth Studies, May, 1989

Spiers, Edward. M., 'The Regular Army in 1914', in Ian F. W. Beckett and Keith Simpson, eds, *A Nation in Arms: A Social History of the British Army in the First World War*, (Manchester 1985), pp. 36–61

Springhall, John, '"Up Guards and At Them!": British Imperialism and Popular Art 1880–1914', in John M. MacKenzie, ed., *Imperialism and Popular Culture* (Manchester, 1986), pp. 49–72

Stearn, Roger T., 'War and the Media in the Nineteenth Century: Victorian Military Artists and the Image of War, 1870–1914', *Journal of the Royal United Service Institution*, 131, 1986, pp. 55–62

——, 'War Correspondents and Colonial Wars *c*.1870–1950', in John M. MacKenzie, ed., *Popular Imperialism and the Military 1850–1950* (Manchester, 1992), pp. 139–61

Summerfield, Penny, 'Patriotism and Empire: Music Hall Entertainment 1870–1914', in John M. MacKenzie, ed., *Imperialism and Popular Culture* (Manchester, 1986), pp. 17–48

Summers, Anne, 'The Character of Edwardian Nationalism: Three Popular Leagues', in Paul Kennedy and Anthony Nicholls, eds, *National and Racialist Movements in Britain and Germany Before 1914* (London, 1981), pp. 68–87

——, 'Militarism in Britain Before the Great War', *History Workshop*, 2, 1976, pp. 104–23

Surel, Jeannine, 'John Bull', in Raphael Samuel, ed., *Patriotism: The Making and Unmaking of British National Identity: Volume III National Fictions* (London, 1989), pp. 3–25

Towle, Philip, 'The Debate on Wartime Censorship in Britain: 1902–1914', in Brian Bond and Ian Roy, eds, *War and Society* (London, 1977), pp. 103–116

Travers, T. H. E., 'Future Warfare: H. G. Wells and British Military Theory 1895–1916', in Brian Bond and Ian Roy, eds, *War and Society* (London, 1975), pp. 67–84

——, 'The Hidden Army: Structural Problems in the British Officer Corps 1900–1918', *Journal of Contemporary History*, 17, 1982, pp. 523–44

——, 'The Offensive and the Problem of Innovation in British Military Thought, 1870–1915', *Journal of Contemporary History*, 13, 1978, pp. 531–53

——, 'Technology, Tactics and Morale: Jean de Bloch, the Boer War and British Military Theory 1900–1914', *Journal of Modern History*, 51, 1979, pp. 264–86

Vamplew, Wray, 'Sport and Industrialisation: An Economic Interpretation of the Changes in Popular Sport in Nineteenth-Century England', in J. A. Mangan, ed., *Pleasure, Profit, Proselytism: British Culture and Sport at Home and Abroad 1700–1914* (London, 1988), pp. 7–20

Vance, Norman, 'The Idea of Manliness', in Brian Simon and Ian Bradley, eds, *The Victorian Public School* (Dublin, 1975), pp. 115–28

Verbitsky, S. I., 'Russian Notions About Japan', in Ian Nish, ed., *Contemporary European Writings on Japan*, (Ashford, Kent, 1988), pp. 38–44

Wadsworth, Alfred Powell, 'Newspaper Circulations, 1800–1954', *Manchester Statistical Society Transactions*, 1955, pp. 1–40

Waters, Judith and George Ellis, 'The Selling of Gender Identity', in Mary Cross ed., *Advertising and Culture: Theoretical Perspectives* (Westport, CT, 1996)

Wilkinson, Glenn R., '"To The Front": British Newspaper Advertising and the Boer War', in John Gooch ed., *The Boer War: Direction, Experience and Image.* (London, 2000), pp. 203–12

Winter, J. M., 'Army and Society: The Demographic Context', in Ian F. W. Beckett and Keith Simpson, eds, *A Nation in Arms: A Social History of the British Army in the First World War* (Manchester, 1985), pp. 193–209

Woollacott, Janet, 'Messages and Meanings', in Michael Gurewitch, Tony Bennett, James Curran and Janet Woollacott, eds, *Culture, Society and the Media* (London, 1982), pp. 91–111
Younghusband, Francis, 'In the Heart of Asia: A Summary of the Record of the Expedition to the Forbidden City of Lhasa', *Canadian Geographical Journal*, 1, 1930, pp. 52–59

Bibliographies

Foster, Janet and Julian Sheppard, *British Archives: A Guide to Archive Resources in the United Kingdom* (London, 1989)
Linton, David and Ray Boston, eds, *The Newspaper Press in Britain: An Annotated Bibliography* (London, 1987)
Marshall, Julie G., *Britain and Tibet 1765–1947: The Background to the India–China Border Dispute. A Select Annotated Bibliography of Printed Material in European Languages* (Bundoora, 1977)

Theses

Catt, Jon, 'Victorian Newspapers in Lancaster and Morecambe', unpublished MA thesis, Preston Polytechnic, 1983
Hiley, Nicholas, 'The British News Media and Government Control 1914–1916', unpublished PhD thesis, Open University, 1984
Moon, Howard Roy, 'The Invasion of the United Kingdom: Public Controversy and Official Planning 1888–1918', unpublished PhD thesis, University of London, 1968 (2 vols)
Quinney, Nigel P., 'Edwardian Militarism and Working Class Youth', unpublished DPhil. thesis, University of Oxford, 1987
Stearn, Roger Thomas, 'War Images and Image Makers in the Victorian Era: Aspects of the British Visual and Written Portrayal of War and Defence *c*.1866–1906', unpublished PhD thesis, University of London, 1987

Index